Certified Rehabilitation Counselor Examination Preparation

Fong Chan, PhD, CRC, is a professor of rehabilitation psychology and director of clinical training, Department of Rehabilitation Psychology and Special Education, University of Wisconsin-Madison. He is also the codirector of the Rehabilitation Research and Training Center on Effective Vocational Rehabilitation Service Delivery Practices.

Malachy Bishop, PhD, CRC, is a professor of rehabilitation counseling, Department of Special Education and Rehabilitation Counseling, University of Kentucky.

Julie Chronister, PhD, CRC, is an associate professor of rehabilitation counseling, Department of Counseling, San Francisco State University.

Eun-Jeong Lee, PhD, CRC, is an assistant professor of rehabilitation psychology, College of Psychology, Illinois Institute of Technology.

Chung-Yi Chiu, PhD, CRC, is an assistant professor, Department of Rehabilitation Counseling, University of Texas Southwestern Medical Center.

Certified Rehabilitation Counselor Examination Preparation

A Concise Guide to the Rehabilitation Counselor Test

Fong Chan, PhD, CRC
Malachy Bishop, PhD, CRC
Julie Chronister, PhD, CRC
Eun-Jeong Lee, PhD, CRC
Chung-Yi Chiu, PhD, CRC

EDITORS

SPRINGER PUBLISHING COMPANY
NEW YORK

Copyright © 2012 Springer Publishing Company, LLC

Springer Publishing Company, LLC
11 West 42nd Street
New York, NY 10036
www.springerpub.com

Acquisitions Editor: Sheri W. Sussman
Production Editor: Lindsay Claire
Composition: Newgen Imaging

ISBN: 978-0-8261-0841-8
E-book ISBN: 978-0-8261-0842-5

12 13/5 4 3

Library of Congress Cataloging-in-Publication Data

CIP data is available from the Library of Congress.

Special discounts on bulk quantities of our books are available to corporations, professional associations, pharmaceutical companies, health care organizations, and other qualifying groups.

If you are interested in a custom book, including chapters from more than one of our titles, we can provide that service as well.

For details, please contact:
Special Sales Department, Springer Publishing Company, LLC
11 West 42nd Street, 15th Floor, New York, NY 10036–8002s
Phone: 877-687-7476 or 212-431-4370; Fax: 212-941-7842
Email: sales@springerpub.com

Printed in the United States of America by Bradford and Bigelow.

Contents

Contributors

Arlene Bagain, MS, is a graduate of the San Francisco State University's Rehabilitation Counseling program and is a counselor at Pyramids Alternatives, Pacifica California

Jessica Brooks, MS, CRC, is a doctoral student in rehabilitation psychology, Department of Rehabilitation Psychology and Special Education, University of Wisconsin, Madison, Wisconson

Gerald Casenave, PhD, CRC, is an associate professor, Department of Rehabilitation Counseling, University of Texas Southwestern Medical Center, Dallas, Texas

Nicole Ditchman, PhD, CRC, is an assistant professor of rehabilitation psychology, College of Psychology, Illinois Institute of Technology, Chicago, Illinois

Robert Drake, MS, CRC, LPC-S, is an assistant professor, Department of Rehabilitation Counseling, University of Texas Southwestern Medical Center, Dallas, Texas

Christina T. Espinosa, MRC, CRC, is a disability program administrator, Human Development Institute, University of Kentucky, Lexington, Kentucky

Maureen Fitzgerald, MS, CRC, is a vocational rehabilitation counselor, California Department of Rehabilitation, Berkeley, California

Karena Kirkpatrick, MS, is a graduate of the San Francisco State University's Rehabilitation Counseling & Marriage and Family Therapy program and holds a certificate in Counseling Late Deafened and Hard of Hearing individuals, Hearing and Speech Center, San Francisco, California

Veronica Muller, MEd, CRC, is a doctoral student in rehabilitation psychology, Department of Rehabilitation Psychology and Special Education, University of Wisconsin, Madison, Wisconsin

Lindsey Rose, MS, CRC, is an associate faculty, Department of Rehabilitation Counseling, University of Texas Southwestern Medical Center, Dallas, Texas

Kristin Sokol, MS, CRC, LSPC, is a doctoral student in rehabilitation counseling/psychology, College of Psychology, Illinois Institute of Technology, Chicago, Illinois

David Strand, MS, CRC, is a doctoral student in rehabilitation psychology, Department of Rehabilitation Psychology and Special Education, University of Wisconsin, Madison, Wisconsin

Connie Sung, MPhil, OTR, is a doctoral candidate in rehabilitation psychology, Department of Rehabilitation Psychology and Special Education, University of Wisconsin, Madison, Wisconsin

Jeffrey F. Thomas, MS, is a doctoral student in rehabilitation counseling, Department of Rehabilitation Studies, East Carolina University, Greenville, North Carolina

Misty Trujillo, MS, CRC, is a vocational rehabilitation counselor, California Department of Rehabilitation, San Francisco, California

Veronica I. Umeasiegbu, MS, CRC, is a doctoral student in rehabilitation counseling, Department of Special Education and Rehabilitation Counseling, University of Kentucky, Lexington, Kentucky

Brittany Waletich, MRC, CRC, is a doctoral student in rehabilitation counseling, Department of Special Education and Rehabilitation Counseling, University of Kentucky, Lexington, Kentucky

Preface

The purpose of this book is to provide a concise yet comprehensive preparation guide for the Commission on Rehabilitation Counselor Certification's (CRCC) Certified Rehabilitation Counselor (CRC®) examination. Designed and produced by rehabilitation counselor educators and content experts, this text has been carefully designed to provide a complete and up-to-date detailed review of the CRC examination content in a well-organized and user-friendly manner. The content of this book is based on the most recent empirically derived rehabilitation counselor roles and functions studies (Leahy, Chan, & Saunders, 2003), which inform the test specifications for the CRC examination. In addition, this book corresponds to the recently revised Council on Rehabilitation Education (CORE) standards that must be covered by CORE-accredited master's degree programs in rehabilitation counseling. These standards are addressed in the 10 chapters that comprise this volume: (1) "Professional Identity and Ethical Behavior," (2) "Psychosocial Issues and Cultural Diversity," (3) "Human Growth and Development," (4) "Employment and Career Development," (6) "Counseling Approaches and Principles," (6) "Group Work and Family Dynamics," (7) "Assessment," (8) "Research and Program Evaluation," (9) "Medical, Functional, and Environmental Aspects of Disability," and (10) "Rehabilitation Services, Case Management, and Related Services." Each chapter provides a concise overview of the key concepts, practice questions (with annotated answers), and resources to related web-based materials for further study and review. Many chapters contain summary tables of the key concepts.

Considered to be among the fastest growing health professions in the United States (Bureau of Labor Statistics, U.S. Department of Labor, 2011), the rehabilitation counseling profession requires the CRC credential for professional practice. Thus, this book is highly valuable to rehabilitation counseling graduate students, working rehabilitation counselors who are seeking to get the CRC credential, and those in allied rehabilitation professions who are seeking to become a CRC through additional coursework and the CRC examination. In addition, rehabilitation educators who use the CRC examination as an alternative to a comprehensive examination for graduation may find this book useful to offer and/ or require of students. We encourage rehabilitation educators to build a CRC preparation strategy into master's-level rehabilitation programs that begins early in the program and prepares students for taking the CRC examination prior to their graduation. This guide would serve as an important component to this curricular supplement.

In sum, we see this book as a necessary and important tool for adequately preparing for the CRC examination. Existing resources do not sufficiently address the most recent changes in the knowledge and skill domains expected of today's rehabilitation counselors. Specifically, there have been significant changes in the delivery of rehabilitation counseling services due to changes in legislative mandates, changes in health care, changes in those served in rehabilitation (i.e., the increasing multicultural, younger, and older populations that are served), the evidence-based practice movement, the counselor licensure movement, and significant changes in the economic and business environment. Nearly every practice setting where rehabilitation counseling services are provided (public, private for profit, community-based rehabilitation organizations, etc.) has undergone significant changes in the way that services are delivered to persons with disabilities, and the emergence of new knowledge and skill requirements for practitioners who deliver these services. In light of these changes, we believe this contemporary, user-friendly, and expert-written preparation guide responds to these changes and will provide those preparing to take the examination with the most up-to-date content and knowledge domains required on the examination.

Fong Chan
Malachy Bishop
Julie Chronister
Eun-Jeong Lee
Chung-Yi Chiu

Madison, Wisconsin

■ REFERENCES

Bureau of Labor Statistics, U.S. Department of Labor (2011). *Occupational outlook handbook, 2010–11 Edition*. Retrieved March 10, 2011 from http://www.bls.gov/oco/ocos067.htm

Leahy, M. J., Chan, F., & Saunders, J. L. (2003). Job functions and knowledge requirements of certified rehabilitation counselors in the 21st century. *Rehabilitation Counseling Bulletin, 46,* 66–81.

Professional Identity and Ethical Behavior

FONG CHAN, CONNIE SUNG, VERONICA MULLER,
JESSICA BROOKS, AND DAVID STRAND

1

Rehabilitation counselors have long played a central and an instrumental role in helping persons with disabilities achieve their independent living and employment goals (Maki & Tarvydas, 2011; Martin, West-Evans, & Connelly, 2010). Although the rehabilitation counseling profession is one of the few professions that evolved from the state–federal vocational rehabilitation (VR) program, the professional practice of rehabilitation counseling is no longer restricted to state VR agencies. Today, rehabilitation counselors work in diverse settings and are required to meet the complex needs of a range of disability groups with various degrees of severity (Leahy, Chan, & Saunders, 2003). This chapter reviews the history and background regarding rehabilitation and related legislation, professional identity of rehabilitation counseling, and professional ethics for rehabilitation counselors. Specific topics include the following:

- History, legislation, and philosophy of rehabilitation
- Rehabilitation counseling scope of practice and professional credentialing
- Professional ethics, ethical principles, and ethical issues

HISTORY, LEGISLATION, AND PHILOSOPHY OF REHABILITATION

Overview

The focus on the history and background of rehabilitation and its related legislation is to provide an understanding of the evolution of the vocational rehabilitation field and the professional practice of rehabilitation counseling. In this section, we will review key disability-related legislation and how disability legislation shapes the philosophical foundations and current practice of rehabilitation counseling.

LEARNING OBJECTIVE

By the end of this unit you should be able to:

1. Understand rehabilitation and related legislation, their effect on rehabilitation counseling practices, and the inclusion and participation of people with disabilities.

KEY CONCEPTS

Rehabilitation and Related Legislation

The state–federal VR program is the oldest and most successful public program, supporting the employment and independence of individuals with disabilities (Martin et al., 2010). It is also one of the dominant practice settings for VR counselors. The Smith–Fess Act of 1920, also known as the Civilian Vocational Rehabilitation Act, is considered the starting point of the public rehabilitation for people with physical disabilities. State VR services were expanded to include people with mental disabilities in 1943. To be qualified for state

TABLE 1.1 ■ Rehabilitation Legislation

Rehabilitation Legislation	Purpose
The Smith-Hughes Act of 1917	Provided Federal funding to states on a matching basis for vocational education programs
The Soldier's Rehabilitation Act of 1918	Authorized VR services for World War I veterans
The Smith-Fess Act of 1920	Expanded rehabilitation services to civilians
The Social Security Act of 1935	Made the state–federal VR program permanent
The Randolph-Sheppard Act of 1936	Authorized people with blindness to operate vending stands in federal buildings. (This is an example of specific legislation for individuals with blindness)
The Wagner-O'Day Act of 1938	Required the federal government to purchase designated products produced by persons with blindness in workshops
The Barden-LaFollette Act of 1943	Expanded services to include people with mental disabilities. It also established the state–federal program for individual with blindness
The Vocational Rehabilitation Act Amendments of 1954	Provided funding to universities to train master's level rehabilitation counselors resulting in the professionalization of the rehabilitation counseling profession
The Vocational Rehabilitation Act Amendment of 1965	Added extended evaluation in the vocational rehabilitation process
The Rehabilitation Act Amendments of 1973	Mandated services for people with severe disabilities; emphasized consumer involvement by requiring the Individualized Written Rehabilitation Program (IWRP); and guaranteed employment rights of people with disabilities. Section 501 (Affirmative Action in Federal Hiring), 503 (Affirmative Action by Federal Contract Recipient), and 504 (Equal Opportunities)
The Rehabilitation Act Amendments of 1978	Mandated the provision of independent living services
The Rehabilitation Act Amendments of 1984	Mandated the establishment of Client Assistance Programs
The Rehabilitation Act Amendments of 1986	Added the provision of rehabilitation engineering services and established supported employment as an acceptable goal for rehabilitation services
The Rehabilitation Act Amendments of 1992	Advanced the concepts of empowerment, self-determination and informed choice; required state VR agencies to establish "qualified personnel" standards for rehabilitation counselors; and mandated the development of the Comprehensive System of Personnel Development (CSPD) to ensure the quality of personnel who provide VR services and assist individuals with disabilities to achieve employment outcomes through the VR program. Other highlights include: • Presumption of ability • Career-based job placement • Improving services to minority groups • Client involvement • Determining eligibility within 60 days • Order of selection • Federal share 78.7% (peaked at 80%—1968 Rehabilitation Act) • Rehabilitation engineering • Similar benefits (purchasing diagnostic services only when not readily available)

(continued)

TABLE 1.1 ■ Rehabilitation Legislation (*continued*)

Rehabilitation Legislation	Purpose
The Rehabilitation Act Amendments of 1998	Replaced the IWRP with the Individualized Plan for Employment (IPE) to support the exercise of informed choice of the individual in the selection of the IPE's employment outcome, specific services, service providers, and the methods to procure the services; introduced a new category of service, namely, the provision of technical assistance and consultation to individuals to pursue self-employment, telecommuting, or a small business operation; and authorized to provide this service to facilitate the transition of students with disabilities from school to post-school activities, including employment

VR services, people with disabilities must meet two eligibility criteria: (1) the presence of a physical or a mental impairment which for such an individual constitutes or results in a substantial impediment to employment and (2) the individual with disability can benefit in terms of an employment outcome from VR services.

With the passage of the 1973 Rehabilitation Act Amendments emphasizing services to people with severe disabilities, the philosophy of rehabilitation has evolved from an "economic-return" philosophy to a "disability rights" philosophy (Rubin & Roessler, 2008). The goals of VR have been identified as (a) inclusion, (b) opportunity, (c) independence, (d) empowerment, (e) rehabilitation, and (f) quality of life. Table 1.1 provides a description of the purpose and implications of key rehabilitation legislation. Figure 1.1 depicts the evolution of major rehabilitation and related legislation.

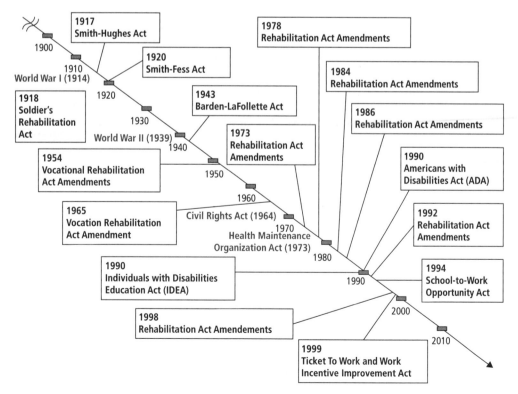

FIGURE 1.1 ■ Timeline of disability-related legislation.

The Americans with Disabilities Act

The Americans with Disabilities Act (ADA) of 1990 is a federal civil rights law designed to prevent discrimination and enable individuals with disabilities to participate fully in all aspects of society. The ADA guarantees equal opportunity for individuals with disabilities in employment (Title I), public services (Title II), public accommodations (Title III), telecommunications (Title IV), and other miscellaneous provisions (Title V). The employment provisions of Title I of the ADA are particularly relevant to rehabilitation counselors as the goal of VR is employment. An individual with a disability under the ADA is a person with a physical or mental impairment that substantially limits a major life activity (e.g., cognitive, social, emotional, and physical). The impairment must be severe, not temporary, and must have a permanent or long-term impact on the individual. A person may also be protected by ADA if he or she has a record of impairment or is regarded by others as a person with impairment. The "regarded as" standard (the third prong) applies to a person who is excluded from any basic life activity (e.g., employment), or is otherwise discriminated against, because of a covered entity's (e.g., an employer) negative attitudes toward that person regarded as having an impairment.

The ADA Amendments Act (ADAAA) of 2008 overturns the controversial Supreme Court decisions in *Sutton v. United Airlines* and *Toyota v. Williams*. The Supreme Court stated that courts should interpret the definition of "disability" strictly in order to create a demanding standard for qualifying as disabled, denying individuals with epilepsy, diabetes, cancer, HIV, and mental illness protection from disability discrimination, the very people whom Congress intended to protect. The ADAAA asserts that the definition of disability is intended to be a less-demanding standard than the standard applied by the court. Specifically, the ADAAA clarifies and expands the meaning and application of the definition of disability in the following ways:

- It provides that the definition of disability shall be construed in favor of *broad coverage* of individuals under this Act, to the maximum extent permitted by the terms of this Act.
- It prohibits consideration of *mitigating* measures such as medication, assistive technology, accommodations, or modifications when determining whether an impairment substantially limits a major life activity.
- It removes from the "regarded as" prong of the disability definition (the third prong of the definition), the requirement that an individual demonstrates that the impairment that he or she has, or is perceived to have, limits a major life activity in a way that is *perceived to be substantial*.

While the ADAAA is important, it addresses mostly Title I (employment provisions) of the Act which suggests that the remaining four titles (mostly public access provisions) were working rather well (McMahon, 2010). Table 1.2 provides a description of key concepts in ADA.

TABLE 1.2 ■ **Key Concepts in ADA**

Key Concept	Definition
Major life activities	An impairment must substantially limit one or more major life activities to be a disability covered by the ADA. These are activities that an average person can perform with little or no difficulty, for example, walking, speaking, breathing, performing manual tasks, seeing, hearing, learning caring for oneself, and working. These are only examples. Other activities such as sitting, standing, lifting, or reading are also major life activities.

(continued)

TABLE 1.2 ■ Key Concepts in ADA (continued)

Key Concept	Definition
Substantially limiting	An impairment is only a "disability" under the ADA if it substantially limits one or more major life activities. An individual must be unable to perform, or be significantly limited in the ability to perform, an activity compared with an average person in the general population. The regulations provide three factors to consider in determining whether a person's impairment substantially limits a major life activity: • its nature and severity; • how long it will last or is expected to last; • its permanent or long-term impact, or expected impact.
Qualified individual with a disability	A person with a disability who satisfies the requisite skill, experience, education and other job-related requirements of the employment position such individual holds or desires, and who, with or without reasonable accommodation, can perform the essential functions of such position.
Essential function	1. The position exists to perform the function. 2. There are a limited number of other employees available to perform the function, or among whom the function can be distributed. 3. A function is highly specialized, and the person in the position is hired for special expertise or ability to perform it.
Reasonable accommodation	Reasonable accommodation is a modification or adjustment to a job, the work environment, or the way things usually are done that enables a qualified individual with a disability to benefit from an equal employment opportunity. The ADA requires reasonable accommodation in three aspects of employment: (1) to ensure equal opportunity in the application process; (2) to enable a qualified individual with a disability to perform the essential functions of a job; and (3) to enable an employee with a disability to enjoy equal benefits and privileges of employment.
Undue hardship	An undue hardship is an action that requires "significant difficulty or expense" in relation to the size of the employer, the resources available, and the nature of the operation. The concept of undue hardship includes any action that is (a) unduly costly; (b) extensive; (c) substantial; (d) disruptive; or (e) that would fundamentally alter the nature or operation of the business.

Philosophy of Rehabilitation

As mentioned, the philosophy of rehabilitation has evolved from "economic return" philosophy to "disability rights" philosophy with the passage of the Rehabilitation Act of 1973, which mandated consumer involvement in the rehabilitation planning process (Rubin & Roessler, 2008). Not surprisingly, the statutory requirements for an Individualized Plan for Employment (IPE) were the result of efforts by advocacy groups such as the American Coalition of Citizens with Disabilities (Corthell & Boskirk, 1988). Further regulations to enhance consumer participation in the IPE were promulgated by the Rehabilitation Act Amendments of 1992 (Chan, Shaw, McMahon, Koch, & Strauser, 1997). Today, there is a strong consensus among rehabilitation professionals that the goals of rehabilitation can be better achieved when there is maximum consumer involvement in the development, implementation, and use of rehabilitation services (McAlees & Menz, 1992). Some of the key concepts underlying the disability rights philosophy are advocacy, informed choice, and consumer empowerment.

Advocacy

Community participation and inclusion of people with disabilities are the ultimate goal of vocational rehabilitation. Specifically, the philosophical foundation of rehabilitation counseling includes the belief in advocacy and the rights of people with disabilities for opportunity, independence, empowerment, rehabilitation, and quality of life. Self-advocacy means advocating for disability rights by people with disabilities themselves. The self-advocacy movement was started by and for people with developmental disabilities because they wanted to be their own advocates rather than having others, such as professionals, parents and other family members, and advocates with or without other disabilities, speak about their needs and desires and to affect social change. As a part of the broader disability rights/independent living movement, the self-advocacy movement is first and foremost a civil rights movement.

Empowerment

Empowerment, self-determination, and informed choice promulgated by the Rehabilitation Act Amendments of 1992 are central to the philosophy of contemporary rehabilitation practices. It is generally agreed that the goals of rehabilitation can be better achieved when there is maximum consumer involvement in the development, implementation, and use of VR services. West and Parent (1992) defined empowerment as the transfer of power and control over decisions, choices, and values from external entities to the consumers of disability services.

Informed Choice and Self-Determination

Informed choice in rehabilitation counseling refers to the process by which consumers make insightful decisions about personal goals and necessary services. Self-determination refers to directing one's own course of action, which requires active personal agency in implementing informed choices. Kosciulek and Wheaton (2003) indicated that informed choice and self-determination, along with an effective counselor–consumer working alliance, are the necessary components of increased consumer empowerment.

REHABILITATION COUNSELORS SCOPE OF PRACTICE AND PROFESSIONAL CREDENTIALING

Overview

The focus on rehabilitation counseling as a profession is to provide insight about the development and current state of this multifaceted career. It defines the key notions of the title to form a professional identity to distinguish itself from other disciplines and the functions and roles of rehabilitation counseling professionals in diverse settings with various populations. The understanding of professional identity is essential in aiding with the provision of services to people with disabilities. In this section, the understanding of professional identity, functions, and roles are discussed to help practitioners develop awareness about the impact of the rehabilitation practice and process on people with disabilities.

■ LEARNING OBJECTIVES

By the end of this unit you should be able to:

1. Understand the professional identity of rehabilitation counselors.
2. Understand the rehabilitation counselor roles and functions in professional practice.
3. Understand current issues faced by rehabilitation counselors.

■ KEY CONCEPTS

The Rehabilitation Counseling Profession

Rehabilitation counselors play a central role in the VR process. Rehabilitation counseling has been described as a process in which the counselor works collaboratively with the client to understand existing problems, barriers, and potentials to facilitate the client's effective use of personal and environmental resources for career, personal, social, and community adjustment following disability. In carrying out this multifaceted process, rehabilitation counselors must be prepared to assist individuals in adapting to the environment, to assist environments in accommodating the needs of the individuals, and to work toward the full participation of individuals in all aspects of society, with a particular focus on independent living and work (Parker & Szymanski, 1998).

The professionalization of rehabilitation counseling has been shaped significantly by graduate training programs that have, for many years, been grounded in providing students with the knowledge and skills necessary for working with persons with physical and mental disabilities within the state–federal VR program. The professional practice of rehabilitation counseling, however, is no longer restricted to the state VR agency setting. Today, rehabilitation counselors work in various settings, including private practice, private nonprofit rehabilitation facilities/organizations, private-for-profit rehabilitation firms, insurance companies, medical centers or general hospitals, and businesses/corporations, and are required to meet the diverse needs of a wider and more complex spectrum of disability groups with various degrees of severity (Chan, Leahy, Saunders, Tarvydas, Ferrin, & Lee, 2003).

CRCC and CORE

The Commission on Rehabilitation Counselor Certification (CRCC) was officially incorporated in 1974 to conduct certification activities on a nationwide basis for rehabilitation counselors. Its creation was directed to assure that VR services are to be provided in a manner that meets the national standards of quality, and that protects the best interest of the client. The typical pathway to certification is a master's degree in rehabilitation counseling from a Council for Rehabilitation Education (CORE) accredited rehabilitation counselor education (RCE) program. CORE was incorporated in 1972 for the purpose of promoting the effective delivery of rehabilitation services to individuals with disabilities by promoting and fostering continuing review and improvement of RCE programs.

Roles and Functions

In their seminal roles and functions study, Muthard and Salamone (1969) found that state VR counselors divide their time equally among three areas including (a) counseling and guidance; (b) clerical work, planning, recording, and placement; and (c) professional growth, public relations, reporting, resource development, travel, and supervisory administrative duties. Leahy et al. (2003) identified seven major job functions that are essential to the professional practice of rehabilitation counseling in today's practice environment including (1) vocational counseling and consultation, (2) counseling interventions, (3) community-based rehabilitation service activities, (4) case management, (5) research application, (6) assessment, and (7) professional advocacy. Leahy et al. further identified six knowledge and skill domains reported by certified rehabilitation counselors (CRCs) as important for contemporary practice including (a) career counseling, assessment, and consultation; (b) counseling theories, techniques, and applications; (c) rehabilitation services and resources; (d) case and caseload management; (e) health care and disability systems; and (f) medical, functional, and environmental implications of disability.

Current Issues

Determining the roles and functions of rehabilitation counselors has been subjected to considerable debate. Patterson (1968) proposed that the practice of rehabilitation counseling is primarily a subspecialty within the broader field of counseling and involves two fundamental roles. Specifically, Patterson posited that state VR agencies should use graduate-level-trained rehabilitation counselors to function as either psychological counselors or rehabilitation coordinators, with the former role to involve working with clients who need personal adjustment counseling and the latter role to involve providing case management and vocational adjustment counseling. While Patterson advocated a "two-hats theory," Whitehouse (1975) advocated the "big-hat theory," proposing that rehabilitation counseling involves a number of roles and functions that justify a separate and distinct practice area that should not be subsumed under the greater rubric of counseling. Specifically, Whitehouse suggested that rehabilitation counselors should be trained to work with the whole person and should have skills that encompass many roles including those of a therapist, guidance counselor, case manager, case coordinator, psychometrician, vocational evaluator, educator, community and consumer advocate, and placement counselor. This "big-hat" definition of rehabilitation counseling became the primary model used in the development of rehabilitation education and training curricula and certification since the 1970s. Although this approach facilitated the development of a separate professional status for rehabilitation counseling, it also weakened the relationship of rehabilitation counseling to the broader field of counseling.

Today, the external pressure of the counselor licensure movement has re-ignited the debate about the wisdom of maintaining a separate professional status for rehabilitation counseling or aligning rehabilitation counseling firmly as a specialty of counseling. Leahy (2002) is a major proponent for the adoption of the 60-hour credit requirement as the educational standard for master's level rehabilitation counseling program. He views generic licensure as a threat to the survival of rehabilitation counseling. With the American Counseling Association and the American Association of State Counselor Licensure Boards working closely to develop portability standards, Leahy contends that it will ultimately drive the standardization of educational requirements and give even more momentum to the 60-hour requirement. The current 48-credit educational requirement for rehabilitation counselors may place the rehabilitation counseling profession in a vulnerable position, and in fact threatens its professional viability. Conversely, Patterson and Parker (2003) expressed concern about aligning CORE standards with state licensure requirements suggesting that this alignment weakens the identity of rehabilitation counseling and will be detrimental to the preparation of students for employment in state VR agencies and community-based rehabilitation programs. Havranek and Brodwin (1994) proposed a model that suggests streamlining current core rehabilitation and counseling specialty courses and providing students the opportunity to take 12 addition elective credits to develop informal specializations such as clinical counseling, community-based rehabilitation, assistive technology, or disability management. This option allows students the ability to pursue jobs in an array of settings such as in mental health agencies, nonprofit rehabilitation agencies, or private rehabilitation, and it affords the choice to pursue licensure.

PROFESSIONAL ETHICS, ETHICAL PRINCIPLES, AND ISSUES

Overview

The principle of ethics and conduct in rehabilitation counseling denotes well-founded standards or fundamental assumptions concerning the rights of people with disabilities and recommends what practitioners ought to do, ordinarily in terms of obligations, rights, fairness, specific virtues, or benefits pertaining to this target population. Ethical codes adopted by the rehabilitation counseling profession regulate the professional responsibility of its members and aid in the management of challenging issues. In this section, key concepts will be introduced, salient ethic codes presented, and ethical principles affecting client rights described.

■ LEARNING OBJECTIVES

By the end of this unit you should be able to:

1. Understand ethical principles governing rehabilitation counselors.
2. Understand rehabilitation counseling code of ethics.
3. Understand the applicability of ethical behavior.

■ KEY CONCEPTS

Professional Ethics

Ethics and ethical behavior encompassing legal, value, and moral issues are inherently complex (Patterson, 1998). Rehabilitation counselors must be able to use their rehabilitation knowledge and skills in an ethical manner, recognize ethical dilemmas fundamental to the profession, and apply ethical decision-making skills to solve ethical dilemmas. Ethics is defined as a set of moral principles or values and the principles of conduct governing an individual or group. Ethical behavior is therefore essential to the professional practice of rehabilitation counseling. To recognize ethical dilemmas, a rehabilitation counselor must first have a working knowledge of the codes of ethics. The most recent Code of Professional Ethics for Rehabilitation Counselor (CRCC, 2011) was adopted in June 2009 and was effective as of January 1, 2010, for CRCs. The new Code clearly delineated that the primary obligation of rehabilitation counselors is to their clients. The basic objectives of the Code are to (1) promote public welfare by specifying ethical behavior expected of rehabilitation counselors; (2) establish principles that define ethical behavior and best practices of rehabilitation counselors; (3) serve as an ethical guide designed to assist rehabilitation counselors in constructing a professional course of action that best serves those utilizing rehabilitation services; and (4) serve as the basis for the processing of alleged code violations by CRCs. The Code explicitly stated that rehabilitation counselors are committed to facilitating the personal, social, and economic independence of individuals with disabilities. In fulfilling this commitment, rehabilitation counselors recognize diversity and embrace a cultural approach in support of the worth, dignity, potential, and uniqueness of individuals with disabilities within their social and cultural context. The CRC Code of Professional Ethics includes the following 12 enforceable standards:

1. Counseling Relationship
2. Confidentiality, Privileged Communication, and Privacy
3. Advocacy and Accessibility
4. Professional Responsibility
5. Relationships with Other Professionals
6. Forensic and Indirect Services
7. Evaluation, Assessment, and Interpretation
8. Teaching, Supervision, and Training
9. Research and Publication
10. Technology and Distance Counseling
11. Business Practices
12. Resolving Ethical Issues

Ethical Principles

The fundamental spirit of caring and respect with which the Code is written is based on six principles of ethical behaviors:

- *Autonomy:* To respect the rights of clients to be self-governing within their social and cultural framework
- *Beneficence:* To do good to others and to promote the well-being of clients
- *Fidelity:* To be faithful, to keep promises, and to honor the trust placed in rehabilitation counselors
- *Justice:* To be fair in the treatment of all clients and to provide appropriate services to all
- *Nonmaleficence:* To do no harm to others
- *Veracity:* To be honest

These ethical principles can be tremendously helpful for rehabilitation counselors in the ethical decision-making process. However, these principles can also conflict with one another. For example, rehabilitation counselors may be faced with an ethical dilemma when they encourage consumers to make career choices (autonomy) and consumers select occupation preferences that are beyond their abilities; this may result in disappointment and poor employment outcomes (nonmaleficence). Patterson (1998) suggested that when principles are in conflict, rehabilitation counselors should use ethical theory for guidance. There are three types of ethical theories: (a) normative ethical theories, (b) meta-ethical theories, and (c) good reason theories. When ethical principles are in conflict, rehabilitation counselors should use the good reason approach and ask themselves the following two questions: (1) Would they want this for themselves or their loved ones in the same situations?; and (2) Would this action produce the least amount of avoidable harm? However, rehabilitation counselors' ethical behaviors are primarily governed by normative ethical theories that have a focus on establishing general principles for determining right or wrong. CRCC determines the seriousness of unethical behavior based on the potential harm (teleological principles) and to what extent the behavior is deliberate and persistent. Unethical behavior can be influenced by multiple factors and a function of one's developmental stages of ethical reasoning.

1. *Punishment orientation*: Following unbendingly social standards related to punishment
2. *Institutional orientation*: Focusing on expectations of an institution or other higher authorities
3. *Societal orientation*: Maintaining societal standards, getting approval of others, and avoiding difficulties
4. *Individual orientation*: Promoting individual welfare without undermining laws and welfare of the society
5. *Principle or conscience orientation*: Demonstrating concern for the client based on internal standards without regard for legal and social consequences

Client Rights

Professional Disclosure Statement

According to the CRC Code, rehabilitation counselors have an obligation to review with clients orally, in writing, and in a manner that best accommodates any of their limitations, their rights, and responsibilities of both rehabilitation counselors and clients. Disclosure at the outset of the counseling relationship should minimally include (1) the qualifications, credentials, and relevant experience of the rehabilitation counselor; (2) purposes, goals, techniques, limitations, the nature of potential risks, and benefits of services; (3) frequency and length of services; (4) confidentiality and limitations regarding confidentiality (including how a supervisor and/or treatment-team professional is involved); (5) contingencies for continuation of services upon the incapacitation or death of the rehabilitation counselor; (6) fees and billing arrangements; (7) record preservation and release policies; (8) risks associated with electronic communication; and (9) legal issues affecting services.

Informed Consent

Rehabilitation counselors must recognize that clients have the freedom to choose whether to enter into or remain in a rehabilitation counseling relationship. Rehabilitation counselors should respect the rights of clients to participate in ongoing rehabilitation counseling planning and to make decisions to refuse any services or modality changes, while also ensuring that clients are advised of the consequences of such refusal.

Cultural Sensitivity

Rehabilitation counselors must communicate information in ways that are both developmentally and culturally appropriate. Rehabilitation counselors should provide accommodation services (e.g., arranging for a qualified interpreter or translator) when necessary to ensure comprehension by clients.

Ethical Issues in Rehabilitation Counseling

The CRC Code identified several ethical issues germane to rehabilitation counseling practices. According to the CRC Code, rehabilitation counselors must respect privacy rights of clients and should not solicit private information from clients that is not beneficial to the counseling process. The concepts of privacy, confidentiality, and privileged communication are defined below:

■ *Privacy*: The right of the individual to choose for himself or herself the time and the circumstances under which, and the extent to which, his or her beliefs, behaviors, and opinions are to be shared or withheld from others. (The right to privacy belongs to clients, is for protecting the clients [not counselors], and only clients can waive that right.)
■ *Confidentiality*: The ethical responsibility of the rehabilitation counselor to safeguard clients from unauthorized disclosures of information given in the therapeutic relationship.
■ *Privileged communication*: The legal right that exists by statute and protects the client from having his or her confidences revealed publicly from the witness stand during legal proceedings without her or his permission.

Limits of Confidentiality

According to the CRC Code, rehabilitation counselors must inform their clients of the limitations of confidentiality, including the qualification that they will not share confidential information without consent from clients or without sound legal or ethical justification. For example, in the workers' compensation system, the client is presumed to have given up a large measure of his or her right to privacy by accepting the benefits offered. Client records are routinely exchanged among claim adjustors, rehabilitation professionals, and attorneys. The CRC Code requires that clients should be informed of the limits of confidentiality at the onset of the counseling relationship. As another example, suspicion of child abuse and neglect abrogates nearly all privileges that might otherwise exist. The *Tarasoff v. Regents of the University of California* case has established that the counselor has the "duty to protect or duty to warn." The duty is a mandate for the counselor to take some actions to prevent foreseeable harm to a third party (an "identifiable victim") by the client. Thus, it may require the counselor to warn the intended victim, to notify the police, or to take whatever steps are reasonably necessary under the circumstances. Similarly, when clients disclose that they have a disease commonly known to be both communicable and life threatening (e.g., HIV/AIDS), rehabilitation counselors may be justified in disclosing information to identifiable third parties, if they are known to be at demonstrable and high risk of contracting the disease.

Dual Relationships

The CRC Code explicitly prohibits sexual or romantic rehabilitation, counselor–client interactions or relationships with current clients, their romantic partners, or their immediate family members. Rehabilitation counselors cannot have sexual or romantic relationships with former clients for a period of 5 years following the last professional contact. Rehabilitation counselors cannot engage in sexual or romantic relationships with clients with significant cognitive impairments regardless of the length of time elapsed since termination of the client relationships.

ACKNOWLEDGMENT

The contents of this chapter were developed with support through the Rehabilitation Research and Training Center on Effective Vocational Rehabilitation Service Delivery Practices established at both the University of Wisconsin-Madison and the University of Wisconsin-Stout under a grant from the Department of Education, National Institute on Disability and Rehabilitation Research (NIDRR) grant number PR# H133B100034. However, the content does not necessarily represent the policy of the U.S. Department of Education, and endorsement by the federal government should not be assumed.

▩ INTERNET RESOURCES

CRCC Code of Ethics
http://www.crccertification.com/pages/crc_ccrc_code_of_ethics/10.php

Kenneth Pope's Therapy, Ethics, Malpractice, Forensics, Critical Thinking
http://kspope.com/index.php

▩ MULTIPLE CHOICE QUESTIONS

1. The Rehabilitation Act Amendments of 1984:
   A. Mandated that all public transit buses equipped with lifts
   B. Extended services to children 12 years of age or older
   C. Required each state rehabilitation agency to have its own written code of ethics
   D. Required each state rehabilitation agency to have a Client Assistance Program

2. State rehabilitation agencies were mandated to increase the utilization of rehabilitation engineering by persons with disabilities by the
   A. Rehabilitation Act of 1973
   B. Rehabilitation Engineering Act of 1990
   C. Rehabilitation Act Amendments of 1986
   D. Rehabilitation Act Amendments of 1992

3. The Rehabilitation Act of 1973 mandated:
   A. Program evaluation for state–federal rehabilitation agencies
   B. A reduction in the federal–state funding split from 80–20 to 70–30
   C. Rehabilitation services for the culturally deprived
   D. More emphasis on behavioral disorders (alcoholics, drug abusers, etc.)

4. The primary function of the Smith-Fess Act of 1920 was to:
   A. Create the Veteran's Administration
   B. Create the Federal Workmen's Compensation Board
   C. Establish the Federal Board of Education
   D. Launch the civilian vocational rehabilitation program in the United States
   E. None of the above

5. An impairment is only a "disability" under the ADA if it substantially limits one or more major life activities. The concept of substantially limiting is based on:
   A. Severity
   B. Duration
   C. Impact
   D. All the above

6. The "two-hats theory" and "big-hat theory" debate regarding the roles and functions of rehabilitation counselors have been re-ignited in the form of 48- versus 60-credit debate. The most important concern about the "two hats theory" and the 60-credit approach is:
   A. It will weaken the identity of rehabilitation counseling
   B. It will be detrimental to the preparation of students for employment in state VR agencies and community-based rehabilitation programs
   C. A and B
   D. None of the above

7. Which of the following is not a criterion of undue hardship under the ADA?
   A. Unduly costly
   B. Extensive
   C. Substantial
   D. Lack of knowledge

8. CRC Code mandates that rehabilitation counselors cannot have sexual or romantic relationship with former client for a period of ___ years following the last professional contact.
   A. 3
   B. 4
   C. 5
   D. 7

9. The ethical responsibility of the rehabilitation counselor to safeguard clients from unauthorized disclosures of information given in the therapeutic relationship is:
   A. Privacy
   B. Confidentiality
   C. Privileged communication
   D. Limits of confidentiality

10. The ADA Amendments Act clarifies and expands the meaning and application of the definition of disability by:
    A. Providing a broad coverage of individuals under this act
    B. Prohibiting consideration of mitigating measures when determining whether an impairment substantially limits a major life activity
    C. Removing from the "regarded as" prong of the disability definition (the third prong of the definition) the requirement that an individual demonstrates that the impairment that he or she has, or is perceived to have, limits a major life activity in a way that is perceived to be substantial
    D. All the above

ANSWER KEY

1. D; 2. D; 3. A; 4. D; 5. D; 6. C; 7. D; 8. C; 9. B; 10. D

■ ADVANCED MULTIPLE CHOICE QUESTIONS

1. The professionals who have the primary responsibility for providing vocational rehabilitation services and assistance to enable people with disabilities meet their needs for equal employment opportunities and quality of life satisfaction are:
   A. Job placement specialists
   B. Employee assistance counselors
   C. Rehabilitation counselors
   D. Rehabilitation psychologists

2. The first piece of rehabilitation legislation enacted supporting of the practice of vocational rehabilitation was:
   A. The Soldiers Rehabilitation Act of 1918
   B. The Smith-Fess Act of 1920
   C. The Social Security Act of 1935
   D. The States Rights Rehabilitation Act of 1902

3. Nondiscrimination in employment practices is mandated by which Title of the ADA?
   A. Title I
   B. Title II
   C. Title III
   D. Title IV

4. Under the Rehabilitation Act Amendments of 1992, rehabilitation counselors must determine whether an individual is eligible for VR services within a reasonable period of time, not to exceed _____ days:
   A. 120
   B. 90
   C. 60
   D. 30

5. The Barden-LaFollette Act of 1943
   A. made culturally deprived persons eligible for state VR services
   B. created a market for products made by blind people
   C. extended civilian vocational rehabilitation services to veterans with disabilities
   D. made persons with mental illness and persons with mental retardation eligible for state VR services

6. The Rehabilitation Act of 1973 mandated which of the following as a high priority state–federal program rehabilitation service?
   A. Behavioral disorders
   B. All industrially injured workers
   C. Socially disadvantaged
   D. Persons with severe disabilities

7. Several sections of the Rehabilitation Act of 1973 under Title V prohibit employment discrimination against people with disabilities. Which section requires affirmative action and prohibits discrimination in employment by federal agencies of the executive branch of government?
   A. Section 501
   B. Section 502
   C. Section 503
   D. Section 504

8. Which of the following is NOT an ethical principle that the CRC Code of Professional Ethics is based on?
   A. Nonmaleficence (i.e., inflict no harm)
   B. Autonomy
   C. Justice (i.e., fairness)
   D. Dignity

9. Which of the following is an occasion when the rehabilitation counselor should breach confidentiality?
   A. When the client's spouse wants to know the psychosocial adjustment of the client
   B. When it is clear that a third party (an "identifiable victim") will be severely injured by the client
   C. When confidential information is requested by the employer of the client
   D. None of the above

10. The thrust of the Randolph-Sheppard Act of 1936 was to:
    A. Make it mandatory for the federal government to purchase designated products from workshops for individuals with blindness
    B. Create federal employment opportunities for individuals with deafness
    C. Enable individuals with blindness to operate vending machines on federal property
    D. None of the above

ANSWER KEY AND EXPLANATION OF ANSWERS

1-C: The rehabilitation counselor plays the most central role in the vocational rehabilitation process assisting people with disabilities to obtain and retain employment.

2-A: The Soldier's Rehabilitation Act of 1918 enacted the first VR program for veterans with disabilities. The Smith-Fess Act of 1920, also known as the Civilian Vocational Rehabilitation Act, is considered the starting point of the public rehabilitation for people with physical disabilities.

3-A: The Americans with Disabilities Act guarantees equal opportunity for individuals with disabilities in five areas: employment (Title I), public services (Title II), public accommodations (Title III), telecommunications (Title IV), and other miscellaneous provisions (Title V). Title I is related to employment and the other titles are concerned with public access issues.

4-C: Under the Rehabilitation Act Amendments of 1992, rehabilitation counselors must determine eligibility within 60 days and clients must stay on a job for 90 days to be considered as successful closure.

5-D: The Barden-LaFollette Act of 1943 expanded VR services for persons with physical disabilities to persons with mental illness and mental retardation.

6-D: Prior to the Rehabilitation Act of 1973, the emphasis of VR services was to serve people with mild and moderate disabilities (economic return philosophy). The Rehabilitation Act of 1973 mandated services to people with severe disabilities (disability rights philosophy). The Rehabilitation Act also emphasized accountability (e.g., program evaluation) and empowerment and partnership between the counselor and his or her client through the development of the Individualized Written Rehabilitation Program (currently the Individualized Plan for Employment).

7-A: Section 501 prohibits discrimination in employment by federal agencies of the executive branch of government. Specifically, Section 501 requires affirmative action and prohibits discrimination in employment by federal agencies of the executive branch of government. Section 503 requires affirmative action and prohibits employment discrimination by federal government contractors and subcontractors with contracts of more than U.S. $10,000. This section would include employers with such contracts such as colleges and universities, training programs, and private defense and research companies. Section 504 requires that qualified individuals with disabilities shall not be excluded from, denied access to or be subjected to discrimination under any program or activity that either receives federal financial assistance or is conducted by any executive agency or the U.S. Postal Service.

8-D: The CRC Code is written based on six ethical principles (autonomy, beneficence, fidelity, justice, nonmaleficence, and veracity). In the literature, the most critical principles for resolving ethical dilemmas are autonomy, nonmaleficence and beneficence, fidelity, and justice.

9-B: Limits of confidentiality include child abuse and imminent danger to a third party ("identifiable victim") among others. In workers' compensation rehabilitation, client records are routinely exchanged among claim adjustors, rehabilitation professionals, and attorneys. The rehabilitation client must be informed of the limits of confidentiality within the context of insurance rehabilitation at the onset of the rehabilitation counseling relationship.

10-C: This is an example of specific legislation for individuals with blindness.

▨ REFERENCES

Chan, F., Leahy, M., Saunders, J., Tarvydas, V., Ferrin, M., & Lee, G. (2003). Training needs of rehabilitation counselors for contemporary practices. *Rehabilitation Counseling Bulletin, 46*, 82–91.

Chan, F., Shaw, L., McMahon, B.T., Koch, L., & Strauser, D. (1997). A model for enhancing consumer-counselor working relationships in rehabilitation. *Rehabilitation Counseling Bulletin, 41*, 122–137.

Commission on Rehabilitation Counselor Certification. (2011). *Code of professional ethics for rehabilitation counselors*. Rolling Meadows, IL: Author.

Corthell, D., & Boskirk, C. V. (1988). *Client involvement: Partnerships in the vocational rehabilitation process*. Menomonie, WI: Stout Vocational Rehabilitation Institute, Research and Training Center.

Havranek, J. E., & Brodwin, M. G. (1994). Rehabilitation counselor curricula: Time for a change. *Rehabilitation Education, 8*, 369–379.

Kosciulek, J. F., & Wheaton, J. E. (2003). Rehabilitation counseling with individuals with disabilities: An empowerment framework. *Rehabilitation Education, 17*, 207–214.

Leahy, M. J. (2002). Professionalism in rehabilitation counseling: A retrospective review. *Journal of Rehabilitation Administration, 26*, 99–109.

Leahy, M. J., Chan, F., & Saunders, J. L. (2003). Job functions and knowledge requirements of certified rehabilitation counselors in the 21st century. *Rehabilitation Counseling Bulletin, 46*, 66–81.

Maki, D., & Tarvydas, V. (2011). Professional practice of rehabilitation counseling. New York, NY: Springer Publishing Company.

Martin, R., West-Evans, K., & Connelly, J. (2010). Vocational rehabilitation: celebrating 90 years of careers and independence. *American Rehabilitation, Special Edition/Summer*, 15–18.

McAlees, D., & Menz, F. (1992). Consumerism and vocational evaluation. *Rehabilitation Education, 6*, 213–220.

McMahon, B. T. (2010). The ADA Amendments Act of 2008: Pocket guide for rehabilitation professionals. *The Rehabilitation Counseling Professional, 18*, 11–18.

Muthard, J. E., & Salamone, P. R. (1969). The roles and functions of the rehabilitation counselor. *Rehabilitation Counseling Bulletin, 13*, 81–168.

Parker, R. M., & Szymanski, E. M. (1998). *Rehabilitation counseling: Basics and beyond* (3rd ed.). Austin, TX: Pro-Ed.

Patterson, C. H. (1968). Rehabilitation counseling: A profession or a trade? *Personnel and Guidance Journal, 46*, 567–571.

Patterson, J. (1998). Ethics and ethical decision making in rehabilitation counseling. In R. Parker & E. Szymanski (Eds.), *Rehabilitation counseling: Basics and beyond* (pp. 181–207). Austin, TX: Pro-Ed.

Patterson, J., & Parker, R. M. (2003). Rehabilitation counselor education at the crossroads: Private practice or human service? *Rehabilitation Education, 17*, 9–18.

Rubin, S. E., & Roessler, R. T. (2008). *Foundations of the vocational rehabilitation process* (6th ed.). Austin, TX: Pro-Ed.

West, M., & Parent, W. (1992). Consumer choice and empowerment in supported employment services: Issues and strategies. *Journal of the Association for Persons with Severe Handicaps, 17*, 47–52.

Whitehouse, F. A. (1975). Rehabilitation clinician. *Journal of Rehabilitation, 41*, 24–26.

Psychosocial Issues and Cultural Diversity

2

JULIE CHRONISTER, KARENA KIRKPATRICK,
AND JEFFREY F. THOMAS

Psychosocial issues and cultural diversity factors play a critical role in a client's response to disability and rehabilitation success. The disability experience reflects an interaction between societal factors, such as environmental forces (e.g., attitudes, economic, access, and healthcare), psychosocial issues (e.g., identity, coping, adjustment, and social support), and diversity factors (e.g., culture, disability, gender, sexual orientation, and age). To facilitate a holistic, biopsychosocial approach with clients, rehabilitation counselors must have working knowledge of the psychosocial and diversity factors that may interact to influence adjustment and rehabilitation success. Therefore, in this chapter, we will review the following topics:

- Sociological dynamics related to self-advocacy, environmental influences, and attitude formation
- Psychological dynamics related to self-identity, growth, and adjustment
- Implications of diversity including cultural, disability, gender, sexual orientation, and aging

SOCIOLOGICAL DYNAMICS RELATED TO SELF-ADVOCACY, ENVIRONMENTAL INFLUENCES, AND ATTITUDE FORMATION

Overview

The focus of this section is to review the social factors that contribute to the response to disability, such as the major models of disability and the World Health Organization International Classification of Functioning; economic and environmental influences, such as social support, transportation, social security disability insurance, architectural barriers; availability and accessibility of job opportunities, and other forms of institutional support; and the role of attitudes and related concepts (stereotype, prejudice, discrimination, and stigma) as invisible barriers that contribute to the response to disability process.

■ LEARNING OBJECTIVES

By the end of this unit you should be able to:

1. Understand the social, economic, and other environmental factors affecting individuals with disabilities and presenting barriers to rehabilitation.
2. Understand attitude formation and strategies to reduce attitudinal barriers affecting people with disabilities.

■ KEY CONCEPTS

Social Factors

The ways in which society and rehabilitation practitioners define "disability" influences the nature of service provision, societal attitudes, and a person's experience living with a disability. Definitions of disability help to identify the location of the problem and who is held responsible for the solution (Smart, 2009). According to Smart (2009):

> Models of disability are abstractions or theories and do not exist in reality. However, they are not harmless abstractions. Models guide legislation and determine the service settings for PWDs [persons with disabilities] and where PWDs live. Models guide the training of professionals who serve PWDs, and models have a significant impact on the popular media. Most of all, models determine the daily, lived experience of having a disability. (p. 59)

Four of the most frequently discussed models of disability include the (a) biomedical model; (b) environmental model; (c) functional model; and (d) sociopolitical model. The biomedical model has the longest history. This model defines disability as a pathology located within the individual and is a deviation from the norm. Treatment is therefore focused solely on "fixing" the individual. The environmental model suggests that the individual's environment may cause, define, or exaggerate the disability. For example, if a person with paraplegia does not have a wheelchair then the impairment is worse. The functional model posits that the functions of the individual influence the definition of the disability. For example, an individual who is physically active would be much more affected by mobility impairments. Finally, the sociopolitical model, also known as the Minority Group Model or the Independent Living Model, proposes that disability is not a personal attribute, but caused by society, and thus society should bear the responsibility for dealing with disability (Smart, 2009).

Self-advocacy is a critical component of the sociopolitical model of disability. Self-advocacy is rooted in the American ideals of autonomy and self-determination, and it is based on Americans with disabilities engaging in social and political collective action to shape their social role and legal treatment (Scotch, 2009). In contrast to consequences of the medical model such as dependency, marginality, and social exclusion, self-advocacy refers to people with disabilities taking control of their own lives, speaking up for themselves, being in control of their own resources, and having the right to make life decisions without undue influence or control from others. The existence of self-advocacy organizations has thus been instrumental in the pursuit of rights for persons with disabilities and promoted independent lives in which disability is a positive connection rather than simply a stigmatized status (Scotch, 2009).

The World Health Organization International Classification of Functioning (WHO ICF, 2001) is a contemporary, biopsychosocial approach to defining disability that considers the biomedical, environmental, functional, and social models in its explanation of disability. The WHO ICF model has also adopted the use of person's first and positive language. This model conceptualizes disability to include five major areas: (a) body functions and structures, (b) activities, (c) participation, (d) personal, and (e) environmental factors (Chan, Gelman, Ditchman, Kim, & Chiu, 2009) and proposes that disability is an interaction between all these factors and cannot be defined in isolation from an individual's context.

Economic Influences

Disability is expensive for both the individual and for society. A large majority of PWDs live at or below the poverty level (Smart, 2009). On a national level, the annual economic losses related to disability for persons with moderate disabilities are $54.1 billion and $122.6 billion for persons with severe disabilities (Chirikos, 1989). Although most PWDs report that they want to work (Louis Harris Associate Inc. Polls, 1986, 1994), and despite protections afforded by the ADA, PWDs have greater difficulty finding or maintaining work, and unemployment and underemployment rates of persons with disabilities are high (Smart, 2009). This is due in part to prejudice and discrimination, worksite inaccessibility, and to financial disincentives built into many government programs (e.g., Supplemental Security Income [SSI] and Social Security Disability Insurance [SSDI]). Financial disincentives occur when individuals are faced with the loss of benefits, including their health insurance, if they accept a job. For many PWDs, accepting a job may cause financial hardship because of low pay in conjunction with the need to pay for disability-related expenses (Berkowitz, 1987; Berry, 1995; Chubon, 1994; DeJong & Batavia, 1990; McCarthy, 1982).

Environmental Influences

Other environmental factors that may present barriers to a client's rehabilitation include limited social support systems, restricted mobility and transportation, architectural barriers, frequency and duration of hospitalizations, unavailable institutional support (medical services, educational programs and technological supports, political, and religious groups), living conditions, availability of job opportunities, and inaccessibility of worksites (Livneh, 2001). In regard to social support, social relationships and support are critical to the health and well-being of persons with disabilities. Studies suggest that persons with disabilities have smaller social support systems than the general population (Chronister & Johnson, 2009). In addition, studies indicate that higher levels of support are linked to more positive rehabilitation outcomes (Chronister, Chou, Frain, & Cardoso, 2008).

Attitude Formation

Attitudes are defined as the observable consequences of customs, practices, ideologies, values, norms, factual beliefs, and religious beliefs (Chan, Livneh, Pruett, Wang & Zheng, 2009; Chan, Gelman, et al., 2009). More specifically, an attitude is "an evaluative statement (favorable or unfavorable) related to a person, object or event" (Chan, Livneh, et al., 2009, p. 335). Attitudes are typically comprised of *affect* (feelings), *cognitions* (beliefs), and *behaviors* (Chan et al., 2009). Additional concepts connected to attitude include *stereotypes, prejudice, discrimination,* and *stigma.* Allport (1968) defined stereotype as "an exaggerated belief associated with a category" (p. 19). An example of a stereotype is, "Asians are good at math." Prejudice is a negative generalization toward a group of people and the assumption that an individual belonging to that group has the characteristics based on the generalization. For example, "all PWDs are intellectually inferior." Discrimination is the action carried out based on prejudice. For example, an employer who does not hire a PWD because he believes PWDs are "unsafe." Finally, stigma is a term that encompasses the problems associated with stereotyping, prejudice, and discrimination; it is the chain of events resulting from negative attitudes and beliefs, resulting in discrimination. Persons with disabilities who are stigmatized often cannot access work, housing, and other community resources because of stigmatizing attitudes that have led to discriminatory behavior (Chan et al., 2009).

Sources of Attitudes Toward Disability

Negative attitudes toward PWDs are well documented in the literature (Brodwin & Orange, 2002; Wang, Thomas, Chan, & Cheing, 2003). Negative attitudes are considered invisible barriers from the environment that impact opportunities, access, help-seeking behaviors, and overall rehabilitation success (Chan et al., 2009; Chubon, 1982). The formation of negative attitudes toward PWDs is connected to a broad range of personal, interpersonal, and environmental factors. Livneh (1982, 1988) identified several major attitudinal sources including (a) sociocultural conditions in which people are persuaded by societal and cultural norms, standards, and expectations (e.g., standards of beauty and body image); (b) childhood influences, such as parents' preoccupation with health and normalcy of child's growth and development that can lead to fear and anxiety of illness and disability; (c) psychodynamic mechanisms that occur in persons without disabilities to preserve the value of societal value of a full functioning, "normal" body by negatively responding to PWDs who are not mourning the loss or suffering; (d) punishment for sin, or the view that disability is a punishment for an evil act; (e) anxiety provoking unstructured situations refers to when a lack of exposure to PWDs makes those without disabilities uncomfortable; (f) aesthetic aversion, which involves feelings of repulsion and discomfort experienced by persons without disabilities; and (g) threats to body image integrity, which occurs when persons without disabilities experience an unconscious threat to their body image that is elicited by the interaction with PWDs.

There are also several disability-related factors that influence negative attitudes including (a) functionality versus organicity, (b) severity, (c) visibility and cosmetic involvement, (d) contagiousness, and (e) predictability. Specifically, those with more functional limitations, higher severity of disability, and those with highly visible disabilities are likely to experience more negative attitudes (Livneh, 1988). Cook (1998) indicated that the general public exhibits a "hierarchy of preferences" for specific groups of PWDs. For example, people hold more favorable attitudes toward persons with physical disabilities than individuals with mental disabilities and persons tend to have more positive attitudes toward persons with intellectual disabilities than those with psychiatric disabilities (Rubin & Roessler, 1983).

Rehabilitation counselors are the gatekeepers of information and services provided to PWDs (Wong, Chan, Cardoso, Lam, & Miller, 2004), and they may unknowingly restrict service options, reduce the quality of service delivery, and impede rehabilitation success (Paris, 1993) by maintaining conscious or subconscious stereotypic views of PWDs. Marshak and Seligman (1993) identified five conscious and subconscious reactions to disability by rehabilitation counselors that may impact the counseling process. These are: (a) Inaccurate perceptions; client characteristics are obscured by the disability leading to underestimation of abilities, stereotypical impressions, and paternalistic treatment approaches. Accordingly, the intervention to reduce the negative attitudes is to have knowledge of the disability and confront stereotypes. (b) Fatalistic or passive therapeutic stances. Responses to client problems occur as if the problems cannot be significantly alleviated, resulting in a failure to draw on therapeutic skill. (c) Exaggeration of psychopathology. A client's psychological adjustment is underestimated and adaptive strategies may be erroneously seen as maladaptive behavior. Intrapsychic causes for problems are often the focus versus environmental factors that contribute to client problems. (d) Psychological distance occurs in the counseling relationship because of characteristics associated with the disability that prevents effective treatment. (e) An exclusive focus on the client's disability occurs and the disability becomes the reason for all the presenting issues, even those unrelated to the disability.

Attitude-Change Strategies

Attitudes toward PWDs are known to be complex, stable, and resistant to change (Cook, 1998). Typical interventions used to change negative attitudes in rehabilitation include classroom lectures, disability simulations, and contact with PWDs (Smart, 2001). Donaldson (1980) and Chan et al. (2009) provided a more exhaustive list of change strategies including (a) contact or personal experience; (b) information and education or factual exchange; (c) social influence and persuasion; (d) disability simulation; (e) protest; (f) affirmative action or legislative and political efforts; and (g) impression management.

PSYCHOLOGICAL DYNAMICS, SUCH AS SELF-IDENTITY, GROWTH, AND ADJUSTMENT

Overview

The focus of this section is to review strategies that promote coping and adjustment to disability including basic definitions of adjustment, adaptation, acceptance, and coping, as well as to review Wright's (1983) "coping versus succumbing" model. In addition, this section reviews stereotypic views toward individuals with disability including views such as the safety threat, spread, moral accountability, and the fear of acquiring disability and the negative impact of these views on persons with disabilities. This section reviews stage models of adjustment and how developmental stages may be impacted by disability.

▦ LEARNING OBJECTIVES

By the end of this unit you should be able to:

1. Identify strategies for self-awareness and self-development that will promote coping and adjustment to disability.
2. Identify and demonstrate an understanding of stereotypic views toward individuals with a disability and the negative effects of these views on successful completion of the rehabilitation outcomes.
3. Explain adjustment stages and developmental issues that influence adjustment to disability.

▦ KEY CONCEPTS

Strategies That Promote Coping and Adjustment to Disability

There are several terms used to describe the adjustment-to-disability process. Specifically, adjustment, adaptation, and acceptance of disability are commonly used to describe the process and outcome of coping with a disability (Lindeman, 1981; Linkowski & Dunn, 1974; Livneh, 1986a, 1986b; Moos, 1984). Adaptation has been defined as the dynamic process that a PWD experiences to achieve the final state of optimal person–environment congruence known as adjustment (Smedema, Bakken-Gillen, & Dalton, 2009). The term acceptance was coined by Wright (1960, 1983) who defined disability acceptance as an outcome in which the disability is incorporated as a part of the individual's self-concept and is accepted as nondevaluing (Smedema et al., 2009). Today, response to disability (Livneh & Antonak, 1997) is considered a more accurate way of describing the adjustment process, because it communicates more fully that response to disability is a subjective experience that is not necessarily negative and is a dynamic process not a one-time event (Smart, 2009; Wortman & Silver, 1989).

Strategies used to cope with the stressors associated with a disability can be divided into three psychological categories: cognitive, behavioral, and affective (Smart, 2009). Cognitive response refers to how an individual chooses to think or view the disability. Behavioral response refers to actions taken to manage the disability including treatment compliance, seeking out social support, returning to work, and using self-advocacy skills to manage societal stigma and prejudice. Affective response refers to how the individual feels about the disability and how he or she manages the emotions associated with the disability (Smart, 2009). Strategies that fall into these categories are often conceptualized as coping skills that generally refer to cognitions, emotions, or behaviors that mediate between the stressors associated with the disability (i.e., nature, type, duration, prognosis, perception, and severity) and response to disability. Coping therefore implies that the PWD is drawing on some personal or environmental resource to reduce the negative impact of a stressor (Chronister, Johnson, & Lin, 2009) and may include both helpful and nonhelpful strategies. For example, a positive coping strategy within the context of disability may include having a realistic view of the disability and an awareness of limitations but not exaggerating them (Yoshida, 1993). Conversely, a negative coping strategy may involve using substances or blaming oneself or others for the disability. The coping strategies used are critical to positive and negative responses to disability. For example, positive, healthy coping strategies such as seeking out social support or redefining life goals may improve body image and quality of life and decrease social isolation and feelings of helplessness.

Wright (1983) developed a cognitive restructuring framework known as the "coping versus succumbing" model. In this model, a person who is *succumbing* to a disability emphasizes the negative effects of the disability and neglects the challenge for change and meaningful adaptation. Conversely, people who focus on their individual assets and are oriented toward what they can do may be described as *coping* (Smedema et al., 2009). Wright (1983) proposed four major value changes, or cognitions, that reflect acceptance: (a) *enlargement of the scope of values*, which subscribes to values that are not in conflict with the disability; (b) *subordination of the physique,* which occurs when the individual does not think of his or her body as a symbol of worth, desirability, or competency; (c) *containment of disability effects*, which occurs when the individual does not deny the disability but contains or limits the effects, realizing that there are other activities that he or she can do; and (d) *transformation from comparative status to asset values*, which occurs when the individual does not compare himself or herself to others who do not have disabilities, and focuses attention on his or her assets.

Stereotypic Views Toward Individuals With Disabilities

Sources of prejudice and discrimination against PWDs stem from stereotypic views, or exaggerated beliefs associated with a category that functions to justify conduct in relation to a particular category (Allport, 1968). These stereotypic views are invisible barriers in the environment that play a significant role in response to disability process (Chan et al., 2009). Common stereotypic views toward PWDs stem from: (a) the safety threat, where PWDs are perceived to be a threat to the physical safety of persons without disabilities; (b) the *ambiguity of disability*, which results in the tendency to ascribe negative aspects or greater limitations to the disability; (c) the *salience of the disability*, which considers the disability to be the most important or the only aspect of the individual; (d) *spread or overgeneralization*, which involves discounting and underrating all the abilities of the PWD and focusing on the disability as the sole aspect of the person's identity; (e) *moral accountability for the cause and management of the disability*, which involves placing blame on the PWD for the cause and how they deal with his or her condition; (f) *inferred emotional consequences of the disability*, which assumes that all PWDs are experiencing negative emotions because of their disability; and (g) the *fear of acquiring a disability*, which involves an unfounded fear by others that if they interact with a PWD they will "catch" the disability. These stereotypic views toward PWDs have a negative impact on achieving rehabilitation success, and for some, these views become internalized whereby the PWD believes these negative views about themselves and other PWDs.

Adjustment Stages

The adjustment-to-disability process has been conceptualized to include a sequence of stages, similar to those experienced during grief (Smedema et al., 2009). Stage models typically describe the process of adjustment as a linear series of psychological stages through which one has to progress before finally reaching the final stage of adjustment. Many stage models have been proposed to describe stages of adjustment (e.g., Dunn, 1975; Fink, 1967; Meyer, 1971; Roessler & Bolton, 1978; Shontz, 1965; Whitehouse, 1962). The most common concepts in stage models include: (a) shock, (b) denial, (c) anger, (d) depression, and (e) adaptation. Livneh (1986) concluded that the numerous models may be described in these five broad categories: (a) initial impact, which includes shock and anxiety; (b) defense mobilization, which include bargaining and denial; (c) initial realization, which includes mourning, depression, and internalized anger; (d) retaliation, which includes externalized anger or aggression; and (e) reintegration or reorganization, which includes acknowledgement, acceptance, and final adjustment.

The stage models provide a structure for understanding and predicting the course and outcome of an individual's response process (Smart, 2009). For example, rehabilitation counselors may draw on this model to better understand and respond to verbal attacks, low motivation, or withdrawal—understanding that these responses may reflect a process being used to move toward positive coping and integration. Nonetheless, the applicability of the stage theory to PWDs has been criticized for the following three reasons: (a) "stages" are not universally experienced; (b) a state of final adjustment (e.g., resolution, acceptance, and assimilation) is not always achieved; and (c) psychological recovery does not follow an orderly sequence of reaction phases (Livneh, 1986). Finally, the existence of a universal, progressive, phase-like, orderly sequence of predetermined psychosocial reactions to disability has not been adequately supported by empirical research (Livneh & Antonak, 1997).

Developmental Issues

Developmental stages such as those identified by Erikson (1968) may be impacted by disability either in childhood or during adulthood depending on whether the disability occurred at birth (congenital) or was acquired later in life. For example, for an infant with a congenital disability, the primary task of establishing trust in the world through the relationship with mother or primary caregiver may be compromised if the infant is hospitalized for long periods and is cared for by various health professionals (Smart, 2009). For a preschool child, the developmental tasks of mastering his or her environment, gaining independence from a primary caregiver, and learning to communicate may be compromised by disability. For example, children with cognitive or intellectual disabilities are often unable to master some of these tasks, and children with hearing impairments may not learn to communicate. Overprotection by family members may also limit the child's independence (Smart, 2009).

For school-aged children, the developmental milestones of achieving industry, such as doing homework and developing friendships, may be impacted because disability may interrupt school attendance and restrict participation in peer activities and relationships. Cognitive and intellectual impairments may influence the development of a competent, able student's self-concept, resulting in an unpleasant and frustrating school experience. During adolescence, emotionally separating from family, developing a work and adult identity, and developing romantic relationships and a sexual identity may be impacted because adolescents with disabilities need to also integrate their disability into these identities and much of this process involves feedback from others, which may be negative. In addition, a disability may impact the opportunity to participate in important milestones such as driving, which may in turn, impact the separation process and social relationships (Smart, 2009). During early adulthood, establishing a family and beginning a career are important tasks that may be impacted by disability. Specifically, PWDs may have fewer opportunities for career development because of limited exposure and they also experience attitudinal and physical barriers to employment. Establishing a family may also be hindered by the negative societal attitudes that PWDs are asexual. Sexuality and establishing relationships are especially important during this stage and for many PWDs, their perception of themselves as sexual beings is severely compromised (Smart, 2009; Wilson, 1990).

Middle adulthood is typically a time of individual and career achievement. Personal satisfaction and feelings of mastery are at their greatest during this stage and preparation for retirement may begin. Individuals who experience disability during this stage may experience a loss of identity, loss of status, and loss of economic security (Smart, 2009). Finally, for those who are age 65 years and older, the impact of disability on independence and functioning can range from a normal expectation to substantial lifestyle changes. Although functional loss and disability may be a normal part of aging for some, social isolation, dependence, restricted activities and participation, and the loss of loved ones surrounding the individual can impact quality of life. In addition, older adults must face societal ageism that values youth, productivity, independence, achievement, and competition, and the view that older adults are "burdens" because they no longer contribute to the economy (Smart, 2009; Zola, 1988).

IMPLICATIONS OF CULTURAL AND INDIVIDUAL DIVERSITY INCLUDING CULTURAL, DISABILITY, GENDER, SEXUAL ORIENTATION, AND AGING ISSUES

Overview

The focus of this section is to review the role of culture, worldview, and other diversity issues in the response to disability process. This section will provide information about specific cultural influences to consider (e.g., age, religion, ethnicity, sexual orientation, gender) in the rehabilitation process. This section will review important disability-related factors such as type and time of onset, course of disability, functions impaired, and degree of stigma experienced as well as the aging process and response to disability, and strategies to consider when working with older adults.

▩ LEARNING OBJECTIVES

By the end of this unit you should be able to:

1. Provide rehabilitation counseling services in a manner that reflects an understanding of psychosocial influences, cultural beliefs, and values and diversity issues that may affect the rehabilitation process.
2. Identify the influences of cultural, gender, sexual orientation, aging, and disability differences and integrate this knowledge into practice.
3. Articulate an understanding of the role of ethnic/racial and other diversity characteristics, such as spirituality and religion and socioeconomic status in groups, family, and society.

▩ KEY CONCEPTS

Culture, Worldview, and Diversity Issues

Culture involves the beliefs, customs, practices, social behaviors, and set of attitudes of a particular nation or group of people (National Center for Cultural Competence [NCCC], 2011). Worldview is the framework of ideas and beliefs through which an individual interprets the world and interacts with it based on their philosophy, values, emotions, and ethics (Ivey & Ivey, 2007). A person's cultural background and worldview are critical factors to consider in the response to disability process. Culture and worldview inform how disability is defined and experienced, and contribute to how PWDs seek and access rehabilitation services and develop salient goals. For example, in contrast to the medical approach to explain disability, many cultures perceive the origin of disability from a metaphysical–spiritual realm. For other cultures, disability is a condition that should not be altered as it is considered to be predetermined by fate and not amenable to adaptive device (Sotnick & Jezewski, 2005). The Deaf culture rejects the notion of group members having a disability as opposed to a different communication modality in a hearing world.

Rehabilitation counselors need to incorporate culture and worldview into rehabilitation planning. Rehabilitation counseling involves working with individuals from diverse (the ethnic, socioeconomic, and gender variety in a group, society, or institution) cultural groups. Specifically, population estimates from the last decade suggest a dramatic change in the racial/ethnic diversity of the U.S. population (U.S. Census Bureau, 2005), with White Americans considered a distinct minority as of 2010 (D'Andrea & Daniels, 1991; Rosenthal, Wilson, Ferrin, & Frain, 2005). In addition, there are a disproportionate number of persons from culturally diverse backgrounds in the United States with disabilities (Cartwright, 2001), and these individuals are often at risk for experiencing multiple negative experiences or "double" discrimination and stigmatization (Brodwin, 1995), which arguably influences response to disability (Chronister & Johnson, 2009). For example, an African American gay man with bipolar disorder is likely to experience multiple forms of discrimination, and

TABLE 2.1 ■ ADDRESSING Model (Cultural Influences)

Cultural Influence	Minority Group
Age and generational influences	Children, adolescents, and elders
Developmental disabilities	Persons with developmental disabilities
Disabilities acquired later in life	Persons with disabilities acquired later in life
Religion and spiritual orientation	Religious minority cultures
Ethnic and racial identity	Ethnic and racial minority cultures
Socioeconomic status	Persons of lower status based on class, education, occupation, income, or rural habitat
Sexual orientation	Persons who were identified as lesbian, gay, bisexual, queer, questioning, or asexual
Indigenous heritage	Indigenous, aboriginal, and native persons
National origin	Refugees, immigrants, and international students
Gender	Women, intersex, and transgender people

Adapted from Hays (2008).

PWDs who have other minority statuses often have greater systemic issues such as access to mental health care. Finally, studies show that PWDs from culturally diverse racial and ethnic groups are accepted less often, have fewer case closures, and receive less training and less case expenditures in the public vocational rehabilitation system than those from the majority culture (Atkins & Wright, 1980; Wilson, Harley, & Alston, 2001).

The discipline of rehabilitation is shaped by Western cultural values such as independence, work, achievement, and self-sufficiency (Sotnick & Jezewski, 2005). Rehabilitation counselors need to consider whether these values are consistent with those from different, nonmajority cultures and incorporate these values and beliefs into rehabilitation planning. Hays's (2008) ADDRESSING model provides a framework for rehabilitation counselors to understand and recognize various cultural influences and their corresponding cultural minority groups (see Table 2.1 for the ADDRESSING model). In addition to this framework, Arredondo and Toporek (2004) identified language, physicality, geographic location, relationship status, work experience, hobbies, and recreational interests as important cultural factors to consider in client conceptualization.

Influences of Gender, Disability, Sexual Orientation, and Aging

Gender

Gender roles and stereotypes are important variables for rehabilitation counselors to consider in response to disability process. Vocational rehabilitation programs were initially developed to serve returning World War I veterans, and thus, services were originally designed for men (Patterson, DeLaGarza, & Schaller, 2005). When working with women, rehabilitation counselors should be conscientious of vocational aspirations by understanding their knowledge of occupations, work values, and career goals (prior to assessment). Restrictions often result from (a) the nature and type of disability; (b) socialization that may restrict range of career to traditional jobs held by women; and (c) limited opportunities of mentors or role models (Patterson et al., 2005). In addition, rehabilitation counselors should also be cognizant of the following psychosocial implications when working with women clients: (a) women may consider themselves incapable of succeeding in male-dominated occupations; (b) women may question their ability to successfully balance family, home, and career; (c) women may experience double discrimination (being a woman and seen as fragile with a disability may heighten stereotypes); (d) women may experience loss as an assault to themselves that leads to greater loss of identity; (e) women may experience higher rates of depression and grief, which is further compounded with the presence of disability; and (f) women usually have more favorable attitudes toward PWDs than their counterparts (Chan, Livneh, et al., 2009).

Rehabilitation counselors should also be aware of the following psychosocial implications when working with male clients: (a) society values and rewards, physical capacity, and the loss of functioning can be significantly challenging for men; (b) men often define themselves through their vocation or career; thus, men no longer able to participate or perform in their chosen career may experience a loss of identity; (c) men equate their masculinity with the ability to have intercourse; thus, men who are unable to get an erection due to a disability may feel emasculated; (d) men often cope with sadness and grief through distraction such as playing sports or through physical fitness activity; those unable to use these coping methods because of the disability may be at greater risk for depression due to this additional loss; (e) in most cultures, men are the providers for their families; those unable to work because of a disability may feel as though they are disappointing or failing their family (Patterson et al., 2005).

Patterson et al. (2005) suggested that men and women respond differently to various disabilities. For example, in the area of spinal cord injury, men experience greater difficulties around sexual functioning than women, resulting in feelings of loss of "manhood" or "masculinity." In regard to HIV/AIDS, women are more socially isolated than men because of cultural backgrounds commonly associated with women with HIV/AIDS, and because rates of transmission of the disease are less and different in mode. In addition, women with HIV/AIDS experience issues related to pregnancy including the potential transmission from mother to child. With respect to myocardial infarction, men return to work sooner than women and typically participate in physical activity to cope with the stressors related to the condition. Rehabilitation programs are commonly geared toward this type of coping style, which is advantageous for men, yet not for women (Patterson et al., 2005).

Patterson et al. (2005) suggested that rehabilitation counselors should not assume that gender stereotyping occurs only in cross-gender counseling situations (i.e., men counseling women or vice versa). Specifically, gender stereotypes, values, and attitudes are not based solely on the rehabilitation counselor's gender. For example, both men and women rehabilitation counselors are at risk for possessing stereotypic values and beliefs about women. Sociocultural context informs different expectations of men and women and their opportunities and rewards (i.e., men are expected to hide their feelings). Men and women with disabilities, as well as rehabilitation counselors, are equally prone to possessing gender-based expectations for the type of rehabilitation services sought after and provided.

Patterson et al. (2005) asserted that rehabilitation counselors need to take the following self-evaluation steps to prevent gender stereotyping: (a) evaluate attitudes (i.e., awareness, feelings, and actions) and gender stereotypes possessed; and (b) examine behavior through self-examination questions, such as, "Is it as important for a woman to have a career as it is for a man?" "What are my feelings about men or women having nontraditional jobs (i.e., woman machine operator; man registered nurse)?" "What are my feelings regarding nontraditional family unit gender norms (i.e., stay-at-home dad with the mom as the family provider)?"

Disability

Disability varies significantly across and within conditions. According to Smart (2009), there are 10 disability factors that influence response to disability including: time of onset (congenital, acquired), type of onset (insidious versus acute), course of disability (direction, pace of movement, and degree of predictability), functions impaired (meaning of functioning, degree of intrusiveness, residual functioning, and assistive technology), severity of the disability (number of disabilities experienced and areas of functioning affected, treatment necessary, and degree of stigma directed at the individual), visibility of the disability, degree (if any) of disfigurement, and prognosis (what is expected for the future).

In addition, rehabilitation counselors should be aware of the sociocultural factors related to being a PWD and how these may influence response to disability. For example, clients may have histories of stigmatization, prejudice, and discrimination (perhaps less so than prior to the passage of the ADA [1990] and IDEA). In addition, PWDs may have internalized stigma based on years of being stereotyped as incapable and deficient. Finally, despite protections afforded by the ADA, PWDs continue to have greater difficulty in finding or maintaining work, with nearly one quarter of PWDs living in poverty.

Sexual Orientation/Identity

Sexual orientation must be considered in rehabilitation planning. Persons who identify as/with sexual orientations, such as lesbian, gay, bisexual, transgender, queer, questioning, intersex, and asexual (LGBTQQIA) are vulnerable to stereotypes, bigotry, abuse, bullying, and violence (Ortiz, 2009). Studies report the following negative consequences associated with those identifying as/with LGBTQQIA: (a) higher rates of mood, anxiety, and substance abuse disorders; (b) societal oppression and greater risk for internalized homophobia, biphobia, and transphobia; (c) adolescent suicide rates that are two to three times higher in sexual minority populations (Russell & Joyner, 2001); and (d) low self-esteem and poor self-identity development among adolescents (Miville, Romero, & Corpus, 2009).

Miville et al. (2009) suggested that to increase the effectiveness of rehabilitation services for those identifying as LGBTQQIA, rehabilitation counselors should be aware of the following: (a) heterosexism and its role in societal expectations of gender-appropriate norms; (b) their own heterosexist attitude, whether they are heterosexual; (c) APA guidelines for psychotherapy with LGB clients; and (d) multiple identity factors and developmental tasks, ethnic, and cultural aspects; socioeconomic status; gender role differences; and generational differences. LGBTQQIA individuals with disabilities are subject to a complex array of prejudices by the mainstream population including facing double prejudices for equal rights, experiencing higher rates of marginalization and discrimination, confusion in navigating identity development, and being seen as asexual and enduring a myriad of messages that they are not suitable sexual partners (Miville et al., 2009; National Disability Authority, 2005; Ortiz, 2009). Pachankis and Godfried (as cited by Miville et al., 2009) posit that a comprehensive understanding of the following is needed to navigate working with the LGBTQQIA population: (a) sexual orientation/identity development models (e.g., Cass, 1979); (b) the coming out processes; (c) same-sex relationships; (d) what it means to be seropositive (HIV+); (e) parenting and familial concerns; (f) unique experiences of LGBTQQIA ethnic minorities; and (g) religious and/or aging issues. Rehabilitation counselors are advised to be knowledgeable of LGBTQQIA-affirmative therapists in their areas so that they can make appropriate counseling referrals for clients.

Aging

With average life expectancy increasing, so is the aging population. According to the U.S. Census Bureau (2010a, 2010b), one in five Americans will be of age 65 years or older by 2050. In the United States, 78 million "baby boomers" began turning 65 this year—around two thirds of them have at least one chronic disease—and 20% have five or more (American Medical Association [AMA], 2010). Indeed, the chance of disability increases with age, and today's workforce is working later in life due to increased costs of living. Thus, rehabilitation counselors can expect to work with an increased number of older adults.

Aging well requires effective interaction, adaptation, accommodation, and adjustment to one's environment to navigate age-related changes successfully (Teri, McCurry, & Logsdon, 1997). Moreover, variability in health issues exists due to genetics, environment, past illnesses and injuries, socioeconomic status (SES), and behavioral problems. Older adults face multiple life transitions in later years of life, including changes in health, roles, work, housing, social support, transportation, monetary and economic position, utility, and loss of spouse, friends, and other supports. The most common stressors for older adults are health-related issues due to chronic illness, diminished functioning (e.g., having to use a hearing aid), and role strains (e.g., living with a child that is substance dependent). Loss of independence issues such as the loss of ability to drive, taking up residence in an assisted living community or skilled nursing facility, as well as having to depend on others in general for help in matters they once enjoyed handling themselves are additional stressors. Older adults also experience high rates of psychological problems. Specifically, there are high rates of depression and depressive symptom among older adults; older White men are at greatest risk for suicide (e.g., loss of spouse); dementia increases with age; and 80% of mental health issues are associated with chronic illness or disabilities, of which older adults experience at a high rate.

Societal Response to Aging

Western society values youthfulness and society perpetuates ageism and stereotypes of older adults as senile, sick, frail, asexual, and a burden on their families as well as financially burdening the United States due to entitlements (e.g., Social Security, Medicare). Ageism is often combined with other prejudices and biases, such as gender, race, sexual orientation, SES, and disability. Rehabilitation counselors are cautioned not to be prejudicial by setting inappropriate rehabilitation goals based on an older adult's age as opposed to their interests and abilities, and to examine their own fears, stereotypes, and biases about aging and the older adult population.

Strategies for Working With Older Adults

The normal aging process typically involves loss of physical and cognitive functioning that impacts memory, fluid intelligence, mobility, and cardiovascular, respiratory, digestion, excretory and central nervous systems, as well as reaction time. However, there is great variability in how the aging process impacts older adults. Thus, rehabilitation counselors can work with older adults to limit, minimize, and reverse the effects of aging through lifestyle changes. Coping strategies are important factors to consider when working with older adults. For example, clients should be encouraged to stay active by participating in family and other social gatherings, church and other secular functions, maintain good nutrition, get exercise and physical activity, engage in cognitive activities, and follow wellness and prevention health measures.

In addition, many older adults do not completely understand the impact that age-related changes have on prescribed medications. Clients should be encouraged to maintain a list of all medications taken, dosage, and side effects, and review it with their physician at every visit. In addition, rehabilitation counselors need to look out for any signs and symptoms of older adult abuse, as they are mandated reporters. Importantly, older adults are not asexual; despite a decline in sexual functioning, sexual satisfaction remains rather stable. Therefore, rehabilitation counselors should discuss preventing sexually transmitted diseases with older clients (e.g., transmission of HIV). Rehabilitation counselors must also be prepared to have discussions about mortality. Conversations can be difficult for both clients and rehabilitation counselors; some clients fear dying and may be hesitant to discuss this topic, and rehabilitation counselors may experience countertransference issues or be reluctant to have these conversations based on their own fear of dying.

End-of-Life Care

When dealing with end-of-life care for terminally ill clients, the CRCC (2010) Code of Ethics declares that rehabilitation counselors take measures that enable clients to (a) obtain high-quality, end-of-life care for their physical, emotional, social, and spiritual needs; (b) exercise the highest degree of self-determination as possible; (c) be given every opportunity possible to engage in informed decision making regarding their end-of-life care; and (d) receive complete and adequate assessment regarding their ability to make competent, rational decisions on their own behalf from mental health professionals who are experienced in end-of-life care practice. Rehabilitation counselors may choose to work with terminally ill clients who wish to explore their end-of-life options or not. However, appropriate referrals must be made if they choose not to address such concerns. In addition, rehabilitation counselors who provide services to terminally ill individuals who are considering hastening their own deaths have the option to break or not break confidentiality on this matter, depending on the applicable laws and the specific circumstances of the situation. Rehabilitation counselors must however seek consultation or supervision from appropriate professional and legal parties prior to making these decisions.

■ MULTIPLE CHOICE QUESTIONS

1. Which of these refers to the framework of ideas and beliefs through which an individual interprets the world and interacts with it based on their philosophy, values, emotions, and ethics?
   A. Culture
   B. Belief system
   C. Worldview
   D. Perceptual understanding

2. The "L" and the "T" in LGBTQQIA refer to:
   A. Loss and time
   B. Lesbian and transgender
   C. Label and testing
   D. None of the above

3. The most common stressors for older adults are health-related issues due to:
   A. Chronic illness
   B. Diminished functioning
   C. Loss of ability to drive
   D. A and B

4. Which disability model states that disability is not a personal attribute but caused by society?
   A. Social model
   B. Biomedical model
   C. Functional model
   D. Environmental model

5. This World Health Organization International Classification of Functioning conceptualizes disability to include all the following major domains EXCEPT:
   A. Body function and structure
   B. Activity and participation
   C. Person and environment
   D. Psychosocial adjustment

6. Which of these is a financial disincentive for going to work that is available for many persons with disabilities through government programs?
   A. Tax breaks for employers to hire PWD
   B. SSI/SSDI
   C. Food stamps
   D. Social security

7. This is the action carried out based on prejudice.
   A. Discrimination
   B. Stigma
   C. Attitudes
   D. Stereotypes

8. Which of these are invisible barriers from the environment that impact opportunities, access, help-seeking behaviors, and overall rehabilitation success for persons with disabilities?
   A. Lack of family support
   B. Negative attitudes
   C. Service delivery inequities
   D. None of the above

9. Examples of interventions for changing negative attitudes include:
   A. Contact of personal experience
   B. Disability simulation
   C. Classroom lectures
   D. All the above

10. Individuals who experience disability at this developmental stage may experience loss of identity, loss of status, and loss of economic security.
    A. Early adulthood
    B. Adolescence
    C. Preschool age
    D. Middle adulthood

◼ ANSWER KEY

1. C; **2.** B; **3.** D; **4.** A; **5.** D; **6.** B; **7.** A; **8.** B; **9.** D; **10.** D

◼ ADVANCED MULTIPLE CHOICE QUESTIONS

1. This model of disability defines disability as a pathology that lies within the individual.
   A. Social model
   B. Functional model
   C. Biomedical model
   D. Environmental model

2. This refers to persons with disabilities taking control of their own lives, speaking up for themselves, being in control of their own resources, and having the right to make life decisions without undue influence from others.
   A. Independence
   B. Rehabilitation success
   C. Self-sufficiency
   D. Self-advocacy

3. Social support, architectural barriers, available health care and other institutional resources, and accessibility to workplace are considered what factors that contribute to response to disability?
   A. Personal
   B. Environmental
   C. Psychological
   D. All the above

4. This is an evaluative statement (favorable or unfavorable) related to a person, object, or event.
   A. Stigma
   B. Prejudice
   C. Discrimination
   D. Attitude

5. This term refers to the dynamic process that a persons with a disability experiences to achieve the final state of optimal person-environment congruence.
   A. Adaptation
   B. Adjustment
   C. Acceptance
   D. Quality of life

6. This refers to the cognitive, emotional, and/or behavioral responses that persons with disabilities use to mediate the stressors associated a disability.
   A. Self-efficacy
   B. Value shift
   C. Coping
   D. Stress management

7. The "coping versus succumbing" model includes all the following value changes associated with acceptance of disability EXCEPT:
   A. Enlargement of the scope of values
   B. Subordination of the physique
   C. Containment of disability effects
   D. Adherence to treatment

8. When disability is perceived to be the sole aspect of an individual with a disability's identity and all other aspects of the person are discounted or underrated, this is called:
   A. Ambiguity of disability
   B. Spread
   C. Safety threat
   D. Invisible barrier

9. Which of the following represents the typical order of the "stage" process of adjustment to disability?
   A. Denial, shock, anger, depression, and adaptation
   B. Shock, denial, anger, depression, and adaptation
   C. Depression, shock, denial, anger, and adaptation
   D. Anger, shock, depression, denial, and adaptation

10. This involves the beliefs, customs, practices, social behaviors, and set of attitudes of a particular nation or group of people.
    A. Worldview
    B. Ethnicity
    C. Race
    D. Culture

■ ANSWER KEY AND EXPLANATION OF ANSWERS

1-C: The biomedical model is based on the notion that health conditions/disabilities are explained and defined as a biological abnormality that lies within the individual versus a condition/disability that is explained by functional, environmental, or social factors.

2-D: Self-advocacy refers to persons with disabilities and chronic illness having control over their own life and life choices, making decisions for themselves regarding their life and treatment options, and choosing what is best for them with respect to rehabilitation services and goals. In addition, self-advocacy refers to standing up for one's rights and speaking up for themselves without undue influence from others.

3-B: Social support, architectural barriers, available health care and other institutional resources, and accessibility to workplace are all environmental factors that contribute to response to disability versus personal factors, such as age, severity of disability, gender, SES, or psychological factors such as emotional functioning, coping styles, and stage of adjustment.

4-D: "Attitude" refers to an evaluative statement (favorable or unfavorable) related to a person, object, or event versus stigma that refers to problems of knowledge, attitude, and behavior that is a behavioral chain that results in discrimination. Prejudice is an aversive or hostile attitude toward a person who belongs to a group simply because he belongs to that group and is therefore presumed to have the objectionable qualities ascribed to in that group. Discrimination is the negative action that a person carries out, based on prejudice.

5-A: Adaptation is the dynamic process that a persons with a disability experiences to achieve the final state of optimal person–environment congruence, whereas adjustment is the final stage of congruence. Acceptance describes an outcome in which the disability or chronic illness is incorporated as a part of the individual's self-concept, and it is accepted as nondevaluing. The latter is based on Wright's model of disability acceptance.

6-C: Coping involves the cognitive, emotional, and/or behavioral responses that persons with disabilities use to mediate the stressors associated a disability, whereas self-efficacy refers to the belief that an individual can achieve a specific goal within a specific situation; value shift refers to Wright's coping versus succumbing model in which an individual shifts their values from values related to who their were prior to disability onset to more positive and accepting values related to who they are today; and stress management refers to general techniques used to decrease the negative impact of stress.

7-D: The "coping versus succumbing" model includes four major changes in a person's value system that are indicative of acceptance including enlargement of the scope of values, subordination of the physique, containment of disability effects, and transformation from comparative to asset values. Adherence to treatment is not part of Wright's theory of acceptance of disability. Adherence to treatment is conceptualized more often as an outcome reflecting positive response to disability or a personal factor contributing to response to disability.

8-B: Spread refers to when disability is perceived to be the sole aspect of an individual with a disability's identity and all other aspects of the person are discounted or underrated. The ambiguity of disability refers to the tendency to ascribe negative aspects or greater limitations to the disability. The safety threat refers to the perception that persons with disabilities or chronic illness are perceived to be a threat to the physical safety of those without disabilities or chronic illness, and invisible barriers refers to societal attitudes and related prejudicial beliefs and stereotypes that cause barriers to access for persons with disabilities and chronic illness.

9-B: The stage of loss model typically is conceptualized to follow this order of sequence: shock, denial, anger, depression, and adaptation; although, we know today that most individuals do not follow this linear process but move in a more circular fashion and may not even experience certain stages.

10-D: Culture involves the beliefs, customs, practices, social behaviors and set of attitudes of a particular nation or group of people. Worldview includes the beliefs about religion, humanity, nature, and one's existence and relates to one's philosophical ideas of being. Race has to do with the biological components of being human, and ethnicity refers to groups of people who are united socially, politically, and geographically and possess a common pattern of values, beliefs, and behaviors as well as language.

■ REFERENCES

Allport, G. W. (1968). The historical background of modern social psychology. In G. Lindzey, & E. Aronson (Eds.), *Handbook of social psychology* (Vol. 1, pp. 1–80). Reading, MA: Addison-Wesley.

American Medical Association (AMA). (2010). Retrieved from http://www.ama-assn.org

Americans with Disability Act. (1990). 42 U.S.C. II 12101 *et seq*. Retrieved from www.usdoj.gov/crt/ada/adahomal.htm

Arredondo, P., & Toporek, R. L. (2004). Multicultural Counseling Competencies = Ethical practice. *Journal of Mental Health Counseling, 26*(1), 44–55.

Atkins, B. J., & Wright, G. N. (1980). Vocational rehabilitation of Blacks. *Journal of Rehabilitation, 46*, 42–26.

Berkowitz, E. D. (1987). *Disabled policy: America's programs for the handicapped*. London, England: Cambridge University.

Berry, J. O. (1995). Employing people with disabilities: Impact on attitude and situation. *Rehabilitation Psychology, 40*, 211–222.

Brodwin, M. G. (1995). Barriers to multicultural understanding: Improving university rehabilitation counselor education programs. *Rehabilitation and Diversity: New Challenges, New Opportunities, 39–45*.

Brodwin, M. G., & Orange, L. M. (2002). Attitudes toward disability. In J. D. Andrew, & C. W. Faubion (Eds.), *Rehabilitation services: An introduction for the human services professional* (pp. 145–173). Osage Beach, MO: Aspen Professional Services.

Cartwright, B. Y. (2001). Multicultural counseling training: A survey of CORE-accredited programs. *Rehabilitation Education, 15*, 233–242.

Cass, V. C. (1979). Homosexual identity formation: A theoretical model. *Journal of Homosexuality, 4*, 219–235.

Chan, F., Gelman, J. S., Ditchman, N. M., Kim, J. H., & Chiu, C. Y. (2009). The World Health Organization ICF model as a conceptual framework of disability. In F. Chan, E. Cardoso, & J. Chronister (Eds.), *Psychosocial interventions for people with chronic illness and disability: A handbook for evidence-based rehabilitation health professionals*. New York, NY: Springer Publishing.

Chan, F., Livneh, H., Pruett, S., Wang, C.-C., & Zheng, L. X. (2009). Societal attitudes towards disability: Concepts, measurements, and interventions. In F. Chan, E. Da Silva Cardoso, & J. A. Chronister (Eds.), *Understanding psychosocial adjustment to chronic illness and disability: A handbook for evidence-based practitioners in rehabilitation* (pp. 333–367). New York, NY: Springer Publishing.

Chirikos, T. N. (1989). *Nothing about us without us. Disability oppression and empowerment*. Berkeley, CA: University of California.

Chronister, J., Chou, C. C., Frain, M., & Cardoso, E. (2008). The relationship between social support and rehabilitation related outcomes: A meta-analysis. *Journal of Rehabilitation, 74*, 16–32.

Chronister, J. & Johnson, E. (2009). Multiculturalism and adjustment to disability. In F. Chan, E. Da Silva Cardoso, & J. A. Chronister (Eds.), *Understanding psychosocial adjustment to chronic illness and disability: A handbook for evidence-based practitioners in rehabilitation* (pp. 479–528). New York, NY: Springer Publishing.

Chronister, J., Johnson, E., & Lin, C. P. (2009). In F. Chan, E. Da Silva Cardoso, & J. A. Chronister (Eds.), *Understanding psychosocial adjustment to chronic illness and disability: A handbook for evidence-based practitioners in rehabilitation* (pp. 111–148). New York, NY: Springer Publishing.

Chubon, R. A. (1982). An analysis of research dealing with the attitudes of professionals toward disability. *Journal of Rehabilitation, 48*, 25–30.

Chubon, R. A. (1994). *Social and psychological foundations of rehabilitation*. Springfield, IL: Charles C. Thomas.

Commission on Rehabilitation Counselor Certification (CRCC). (2010). Code of Professional Ethics for Rehabilitation Counselors. Retrieved from https://www.crccertification.com/filebin/pdf/CRCC_COE_1-1-10_Rev12-09.pdf

Cook, D. (1998). Psychosocial impact of disability. In R. M. Parker, & E. M. Szymanski (Eds.), *Rehabilitation counseling: Basics and beyond* (3rd ed., pp. 303–326). Austin TX: Pro-Ed.

D'Andrea, M., & Daniels, J. (1991). Exploring the different levels of multicultural counseling training in counselor education. *Journal of Counseling & Development, 70*, 78–85.

DeJong, G., & Batavia, A. I. (1990). The Americans with Disabilities Act and the current state of U.S. disability policy. *Journal of Disability Policy Studies, 1*, 65–75.

Donaldson, J. (1980). Changing attitudes toward handicapped persons: A review and analysis of the research. *Exceptional Children, 46*, 504–514.

Dunn, M. E. (1975). Psychological intervention in a spinal cord injury center: An introduction. *Rehabilitation Psychology, 22*(4), 165–178.

Erikson, E. H. (1968). *Identity and crisis*. New York, NY: Norton.

Fink, S. (1967). Crisis and motivation: A theoretical model. *Archives of Physical medicine and Rehabilitation, 48*, 592–597.

Hays, P. A. (2008). *Addressing cultural complexities in practice: Assessment, diagnosis and therapy* (2nd ed.). United States of America: American Psychological Association.

Ivey, A. E., & Ivey, M. B. (2007). *Intentional interviewing and counseling: Facilitating client development in a multicultural society* (6th ed.). Belmont, CA: Thompson Brooks/Cole.

Lindeman, J. E. (1981). *Psychological and behavioral aspects of physical disability: A manual for health practitioners.* New York, NY: Plenum Press.

Linkowski, D. C., & Dunn, M. A. (1974). Self-concept and acceptance of disability. *Rehabilitation Counseling Bulletin, 17*, 28–32.

Livneh, H. (1982). On the origins of negative attitudes toward people with disabilities. *Rehabilitation Literature, 43*, 338–347.

Livneh, H. (1986). A unified approach to existing models of adaptation to disability: Part I-A model adaptation. *Journal of Applied Rehabilitation Counseling, 17*, 5–16.

Livneh, H. (1988). A dimensional perspective on the origin of the negative attitudes toward people with disabilities. In H. E. Yuker (Ed.), *Attitudes toward people with disabilities* (pp. 35–46). New York, NY: Springer Publishing.

Livneh, H. (2001). Psychosocial adaptation to chronic illness and disability: A conceptual framework. *Rehabilitation Counseling Bulletin, 44*(3), 151–160.

Livneh, H., & Antonak, R. F. (1997). *Psychosocial adaptation to chronic illness and disability.* Gaithersburg, MD: Aspen.

Louis Harris Associate Inc. Polls. (1986). *The ICD survey of disabled Americans: Bringing disabled Americans into the mainstream.* New York, NY: Author.

Louis Harris Associate Inc. Polls. (1994). *N.O.D.L. Harris survey of disabled Americans.* Washington, D.C.: National Organization of Disability.

Marshak, L. E., & Seligman, M. (1993). *Counseling persons with physical disabilities: Theoretical and clinical perspectives.* Austin, TX: Pro-Ed.

McCarthy, H. (1982). Partnership as a method of enhancing attitudes and behaviors toward employment of disabled individuals. *Rehabilitation Counseling Bulletin, 26*, 119–132.

Meyer, G. G. (1971). The psychodynamics of acute blindness. *Ophthalmology Digest,* October, 31–37.

Miville, M. L., Romero, L., & Corpus, M. J. (2009). Incorporating affirming, feminist and relational perspectives: The case of Juan. In M. E. Gallardo, & B. W. McNeil (Eds.), *Intersections of multiple identities: A casebook of evidence-based practices with diverse populations* (pp. 175–201). New York, NY: Routledge.

Moos, R. H. (Ed.). (1984). *Coping with physical illness. Volume 2: New perspectives.* New York, NY: Plenum Press.

National Center for Cultural Competence. (2011). Retrieved from http://nccc.georgetown.edu/AZresources.html

National Disability Authority. (2005). *How far towards equality? Measuring how equally people with disabilities are included in Irish society.* Dublin: NDA.

Ortiz, F. (2009). Spirituality and psychotherapy: A gay Latino client. In M. E. Gallardo, & B. W. McNeil (Eds.), *Intersections of multiple identities: A casebook of evidence-based practices with diverse populations* (pp. 137–173). New York, NY: Routledge.

Paris, M. J. (1993). Attitudes of medical students and health care professionals towards people with disabilities. *Archives of Physical Medicine and Rehabilitation, 74*, 818–825.

Patterson, J. B., DeLaGarza, D., & Schaller, J. (2005). Rehabilitation counseling practice: Considerations and interventions. In R. M. Parker, E. M. Szymanski, & J. B. Patterson (Eds.), *Rehabilitation counseling, basics and beyond* (4th ed., pp. 155–186). Austin, TX: Pro-Ed.

Roessler, R., & Bolton, B. (1978). *Psychosocial adjustment to disability.* Baltimore, MD: University Park Press.

Rosenthal, D. A., Wilson, K. B., Ferrin, J. M., & Frain, M. (2005). Acceptable rates of African Americans versus White consumers of vocational rehabilitation services: A meta-analysis. *Journal of Rehabilitation, 71*, 36–44.

Rubin, S. E., & Roessler, R. T. (1983). *Foundations of the vocational rehabilitation process* (2nd ed.). Baltimore, MD: University Park Press.

Russell, S. T. & Joyner, K. (2001). Adolescent sexual orientation and suicide risk: Evidence from a national study. *American Journal of Public Health, 91*(8), 1276–1281.

Scotch R. K. (2009). Nothing about us without us: Disability rights in America. *OAH Magazine of History,* 17–22.

Shontz, F. C. (1965). Reaction to crisis. *Volta Review, 67,* 364–370.

Smart, J. F. (2001). *Disability, society, and the individual.* Austin, TX: Pro-Ed.

Smart, J. F. (2009). *Disability, society, and the individual* (2nd ed.). Austin. TX: Pro-Ed.

Smedema, S. M., Bakken-Gillen, S. K., & Dalton, J. (2009). Psychosocial adaptation to chronic illness and disability: Models and measurement. In F. Chan, E. Da Silva Cardoso, & J. A. Chronister (Eds.), *Understanding psychosocial adjustment to chronic illness and disability: A handbook for evidence-based practitioners in rehabilitation* (pp. 51–73). New York, NY: Springer Publishing.

Sotnick, P., & Jezewski, M.A. (2005). Culture and the disability services. In J. H. Stone (Ed.), *Culture and disability: Providing culturally competent services* (pp. 15–36). Thousand Oaks, CA: Sage Publications.

Teri, L., McCurry, S., & Logsdon, R. (1997). Memory, thinking and aging: What we know about what we know. *Western Journal of Medicine, 167*(4), 269–275. Retrieved from http://www.ncbi. nlm.nih.gov/pmc/articles/PMC1304543/pdf/westjmed00338-0077.pdf

U.S. Census Bureau. (2005*). National population by race United States: 2005.* Retrieved from http://2005.census.gov/2005census/data

U.S. Census Bureau. (2010a). *National population by race United States: 2010.* Retrieved from http://2010.census.gov/2010census/data

U.S. Census Bureau. (2010b). *The next four decades: The older population in the United States: 2010–2050: Population estimates and projections.* Retrieved from http://www.census.gov/ prod/2010pubs/p25–1138.pdf

Wang, M. H., Thomas, K., Chan, F., & Cheing, G. (2003). A conjoint analysis of factors influencing American and Taiwanese college students' preference for people with disabilities. *Rehabilitation Psychology, 48,* 195–201.

Whitehouse, F. A. (1962). Cardiovascular disability. In J. F. Garrett & E. S. Levin (Eds.), *Psychological practices with the physically disabled* (Chap. 3, pp. 85–124). New York, NY: Columbia University Press.

Wilson, D. J. (1990). *Living with polio: The epidemic and its survivors.* Chicago, IL: University of Chicago.

Wilson, K. B., Harley, D. A., & Alston, R. J. (2001). Race as a correlate of vocational rehabilitation acceptance. Revisited. *Journal of Rehabilitation, 67,* 35–41.

Wong, D. W., Chan, F., Cardoso, E., Lam, C. S., & Miller, S. (2004). Rehabilitation counseling students' attitudes toward people with disabilities in three social contexts: A conjoint analysis. *Rehabilitation Counseling Bulletin, 47,* 194–204.

World Health Organization. (2001). *International classification of functioning, disability, and health: ICF.* Geneva: World Health Organization. Retrieved from http://www.who.int/ classification/icf

Wortman, C. B., & Silver, R. C. (1989). The myths of coping with loss. *Journal of Consulting and Clinical Psychology, 57,* 349–357.

Wright, B. A. (1960). *Physical disability: A physical approach.* New York, NY: Harper and Row.

Wright, B. A. (1983). *Physical disability: A physical approach* (2nd ed.) New York, NY: Harper and Row.

Yoshida, K. K. (1993). Reshaping of self: A pendular reconstruction of self and identity among adults with traumatic spinal cord injury. *Sociology of Health and Illness, 15,* 217–245.

Zola, I. (1988). Policies and programs concerning aging and disability: Toward a unifying agenda. In S. Sullivan, & M. Lewin (Eds.), *The economics and ethics of long-term care and disability* (pp. 90–130). Washington, DC: American Enterprise Institute for Public Policy Research.

Human Growth and Development

3

MALACHY BISHOP AND BRITTANY WALETICH

Rehabilitation counseling practice has expanded beyond its traditional focus on the employment-related issues faced by working-age adults with disabilities. Reflecting the demographic and sociological shifts in the U.S. population, rehabilitation counselors are now working with both younger and older clients in traditional (e.g., state–federal vocational rehabilitation) and nontraditional service settings. As a result, effective and comprehensive rehabilitation counseling across the life span will increasingly require an understanding of theories, processes, and issues associated with human growth and development. In this chapter, we will review the following topics:

- Rehabilitation counseling across the life span: older Americans
- Debates and important issues in early developmental processes
- Individual and family response to disability
- Theories of personality development
- Human sexuality and disability
- Learning styles and strategies

REHABILITATION COUNSELING ACROSS THE LIFE SPAN: OLDER AMERICANS

Overview

In this section, we discuss rehabilitation counseling issues associated with aging and older Americans. We discuss employment trends and changing health circumstances.

■ LEARNING OBJECTIVES

By the end of this unit you should be able to:

1. Describe the current status and trends in employment among older Americans.
2. Identify key rehabilitation counseling issues associated with disability or chronic illness among older Americans.

■ KEY CONCEPTS

Older Americans and Employment

Older workers are the fastest growing sector of the U.S. labor market and are predicted to become and remain a greater proportion of vocational rehabilitation caseloads (Barros-Bailey et al., 2007). The baby-boom generation (defined as Americans who were born between 1945 and 1964; a period during which high birth rates were seen, relative to the years prior or after) is approaching the ages typically associated with retirement. By 2020, the percentage of the U.S. population 65 years of age and older is projected to reach over 16.4%, or 53 million, and by 2030, it is estimated that over 70 million individuals (about 1 person in 5) will be in this age group (Swett & Bishop, 2003). This population shift will have an important impact on U.S. employment demographics. For example, between 2000 and 2018, the number of workers in the age group of 55 to 64 will have roughly doubled (from 14.4 to around 28.8 million), and there will be about 11.1 million workers over age 65—almost three times as many as in 2000 (U.S. Census Bureau, 2011).

Older Americans, Health, and Disability

As people age, the probability of acquiring a disability or chronic illness increases dramatically (Barros-Bailey et al., 2007). According to 2005 U.S. Census data, among Americans between the ages 65 and 69 the incidence of disability is 37.4%; between 70 and 74 the incidence is 43.8%; between 75 and 80, the incidence is 55.9%; and among people 80 years and older the incidence of disability is 71% (Brault, 2008). By 2030, 20% of the population will be people age 65 and older with chronic conditions (U.S. Census Bureau, 2000).

A particularly important component of the rehabilitation counselor's ability to most effectively serve older individuals is to understand the significant impact of mental health on employment-related and general functioning (Swett & Bishop, 2003). Due to the prevalence of mental health disorders among older Americans and the potential impact of these disorders on function and rehabilitation, it is vital that rehabilitation counselors are prepared to recognize and deal with mental health problems. Mental illness, and particularly depression, is a significant problem for adults age 65 years and older. Prevalence rates of mental illness among older adults range from 12.3% for individuals living in the community to 70% for residents of nursing homes and are around 50% for individuals in acute care hospitals (Swett & Bishop, 2003).

Chronic medical disorders commonly co-occur with psychiatric disorders such as depression and anxiety and are an established risk factor (Borson et al., 2001). Often, the effects of mental illness and medical disorders on functioning are additive (Reynolds, Alexopoulos, Katz, & Lebowitz, 2001). This comorbidity of medical problems with mental health issues in the elderly population can be attributed to a number of precipitating factors, including multiple personal losses, chronic insomnia, risk factors of heart disease and stroke, neurodegenerative diseases, progressive reduction in the number of social supports, and limited access to adequate treatment (Reynolds et al., 2001). Unfortunately, older adults are significantly underserved in the mental health service arena. Although people over the age of 65 comprise approximately 12.8% of the population (Administration on Aging, 2000), older adults are only using about 2% of private mental health services, between 4% and 7% of community mental health services, and approximately 9% of inpatient psychiatric services (Robb, Chen, & Haley, 2002).

In summary, recent and expected sociodemographic changes have led to increased awareness among rehabilitation counselors of the employment and disability issues of older Americans with disabilities. Trends toward increased labor force participation and increased disability among older Americans will translate into opportunities for rehabilitation counselors to increasingly serve older consumers. Based on their comprehensive training in case management, disability, and employment issues, rehabilitation counselors have a combination of knowledge and skills that enable them to effectively address the needs of older adults (Bishop, Boland, & Sheppard-Jones, 2008; Swett & Bishop, 2003).

DEBATES AND IMPORTANT ISSUES IN EARLY DEVELOPMENTAL PROCESSES

Overview

Rehabilitation counselors are increasingly recognizing opportunities for working with younger clients in a range of professional settings, but primarily in the context of transition from school to work or postsecondary education. Effective and comprehensive rehabilitation counseling across the life span will increasingly mean that rehabilitation counselors have an understanding of a number of processes and issues associated with human growth and development. In this section we review some of the key theories, debates, and ideas associated with personal and physical development.

◼ LEARNING OBJECTIVES

By the end of this unit you should be able to:

1. Describe the nature versus nurture debate in human development.
2. Discuss the differences between continuous or discontinuous theoretical perspectives on human growth and development.
3. Identify issues and processes in genetic testing and prenatal diagnostic tests.

◼ KEY CONCEPTS

The Nature Versus Nurture Debate in Human Development

The nature versus nurture debate concerns the question of the degree to which innate characteristics and environmental factors influence development. The nativist perspective suggests that hereditary, genetic, or biological factors are the primary influence on development (Table 3.1). One implication of this perspective is that modifying the environment will have little effect on development. Evidence supporting the nativist perspective includes evidence from twin studies (monozygote identical twins and dizygote fraternal twins) that there is a genetic component to the development of specific speech and language disorders, autism spectrum disorders, and personality attributes such as happiness, loneliness, timidness, aggression, and hostility.

The nurturist perspective suggests that the environment shapes behavior and can modify genetic inclinations. Evidence for this perspective suggests that an enriched environment, a supportive or adaptive environment, and early and appropriate interventions can promote language and cognitive development, and that a stimulus-deprived environment has negative consequences for social and cognitive development.

The combined perspective suggests that both nature and nurture have relative influence on human development. The interactional model suggests that genotype (genetic inheritance) defines a range of capacity, or sets absolute limits on phenotype (the observed characteristics). In other words, the genotype defines maximum limits, which, without a supportive and positive environment, cannot be achieved. A fast-growing understanding of human biology has generally confirmed the idea that development and behavior result from the combined effects of environment and biology.

Continuous and Discontinuous Development

Depending on the theoretical orientation, human development has been conceived in terms of continuous or discontinuous patterns. Theories proposing developmental continuity suggest

TABLE 3.1 ◼ **Key Concepts in Developmental Ideas and Debates**

Key Concept	Summary
Nativist perspective	Hereditary, genetic, or biological factors are the primary influence on development
Nurturist perspective	The environment shapes behavior, and can modify genetic inclinations
Combined perspective	Both nature and nurture have relative influence on human development
Continuity	Development occurs as a process of smooth, gradual, and incremental change
Discontinuity	Development is a series of steps with clear-cut, qualitatively different changes occurring from one phase to the next

that development occurs as a process of smooth, gradual, and incremental change. Theories proposing discontinuity describe development as a series of steps with clear-cut, qualitatively different changes occurring from one phase to the next. Recent studies have shown that development demonstrates some stage-like properties and some consistency across domains.

Issues and Processes in Genetic Testing and Prenatal Diagnostic Tests

Genetics is fast becoming a topic of critical interest and concern among disability advocates and professionals, as increasingly complex ethical questions emerge from our growing understanding and capacities in genetics. Along with the increasing capacity for early detection of genetic conditions come difficult questions for parents and society. Rehabilitation counselors should be prepared with knowledge of genetic counseling and prenatal testing.

Genetic counselors assist in determining the likelihood of genetic/biological conditions, and in making decisions about genetic testing, or decisions based on the results of completed genetic testing. Genetic counselors obtain information about a couple's genetic background and history, including family diseases, genetic conditions and disorders, and evaluate laboratory tests. They counsel people about genetic conditions, the probability of transmitting a genetic condition, and promote informed decision making.

People seek genetic counseling at different times and for different reasons. Before or during pregnancy, couples or individuals might see a genetic counselor to learn about factors that might increase the chance for having a child with a genetic condition. Families might seek genetic counseling after a child is born with a genetic disease, condition, or disorder to help better understand the condition and associated developmental issues. Adults may visit a genetic counselor to discuss the probability of developing a hereditary condition that occurs later in life, particularly if they have a parent or older relative with a genetically determined or influenced condition.

INDIVIDUAL AND FAMILY ADAPTATION TO CHRONIC ILLNESS AND DISABILITY

Overview

Psychosocial adaptation to chronic illness and disability (CID) is one of the most important and extensively researched topics in rehabilitation counseling (Parker, Schaller, & Hansmann, 2003). Understanding how people adapt to the changes associated with the onset of CID helps clinicians to effectively help persons to cope with these changes and maintain their quality of life (QOL). Rehabilitation researchers have applied a wide variety of theoretical frameworks to the understanding of the psychosocial adaptation process over the past several decades.

Psychological and psychosocial distress are commonly associated with CID onset and are associated with such factors as the crisis nature of CID onset; chronicity, or the idea of permanence; the uncertain prognosis frequently associated with CID; the sometimes prolonged course of treatments; interference (sometimes increasing) with one's ability to perform life roles and activities; and the impact on family, friends, and one's social network.

LEARNING OBJECTIVES

By the end of this unit you should be able to:

1. Describe key findings in the research on psychosocial adaptation to chronic illness and disability.
2. Describe models of adjustment to disability used in rehabilitation counseling research and practice.
3. Describe important elements of the family's response to chronic illness or disability, and related research.

▓ KEY CONCEPTS

Assessment of Psychosocial Adaptation and Research Findings

Psychosocial adaptation has been defined in rehabilitation counseling in a wide variety of ways, including functional and psychosocial outcomes. Some of these include one's capacity to manage pain and symptoms and master skills associated with functional changes; participation in health care regimens; presence, absence, or levels of significant psychological clinical disorders such as depression, anxiety, or adjustment disorder; one's sense of mastery; self-esteem; functional status and role-related behavior in work, school, or social domains; social participation; well-being, QOL, and satisfaction in domains of life; and various coping frameworks.

Research on adjustment and adaptation to disability has revealed that: (1) there is no personality type associated with a specific disability, (2) there is no simple or direct relationship between adjustment and the severity of the disability, and (3) adjustment to disability is an individual reaction and similar people with similar disabilities react differently. Among the factors identified in the psychosocial adaptation and coping research as being associated with more positive psychosocial outcomes are the ability to develop resources (internal and external) to cope with change, social support, and finding positive consequences or meaning in the CID. Coping styles and strategies and personal characteristics associated with more positive psychosocial outcomes include higher levels of optimism, an active and problem-focused coping style (person's attention focused on what can be done to change the situation; manage the source of the problem; active planning, information seeking, seeking social support, and expressing feelings), information seeking, and having an internal locus of control.

Research also supports the idea that people often experience high levels of psychological distress initially with CID, but that for most people, this appears to be a temporary state that diminishes over time.

Models of Adjustment to Disability

Wright's Somatopsychological Approach and Acceptance of Disability

Beatrice Wright and other researchers in the somatopsychological tradition proposed a number of perspectives on adaptation to CID that continue to influence the field of rehabilitation counseling. These include the importance of recognizing the influence of the environment in understanding the individual's response (Barker, Wright, & Gonick, 1946; Wright, 1960, 1983); the distinction between the insider (individual experiencing the CID) and outsider (e.g., professionals, family members, persons in social network, society perspectives); and the transformation of values following the onset of CID (Dembo, Leviton, & Wright, 1956; Wright, 1960, 1983). The transformation of values framework describes the following changes associated with acceptance of disability: (1) enlarging the scope of values—the person realizes values other than those affected by disability; (2) containing disability effects—limiting the impact of the condition; (3) subordinating physique—seeing body image as other than a symbol of worth, desirability, and reconceptualizing physical attributes; (4) transforming comparative status values into asset values—focusing on one's assets versus comparing oneself to others.

Stage/Phase Models

In stage or phase models, the process of adjustment is seen as a gradual, developmental process of assimilation of the changes in body, self-concept, and person–environment interaction. It is proposed that the individual passes through a series of stages or phases of response, typically including reactions such as shock, denial, depression, and eventually acceptance and adjustment. Criticisms of the various stage or phase models that have been proposed include (1) that the proposed reactions to CID are not universally experienced; (2) that a state of final adjustment is not in reality experienced but that in reality the process of adjustment is cyclical or recurring; and (3) the fact that the concept of unavoidable stages may lead professionals to withhold or delay interventions while waiting for the client to experience some stage or level of adjustment. Many clinicians and researchers do, however, support the existence of observable phases of reaction, though they may not be temporally ordered and discrete (one following the other in established and well-defined order).

Ecological Models

Ecological models of adaptation suggest that adjustment depends on the balance between the person's available personal, social, and environmental resources and the demands on resources in the person's environment. The process of adjustment is seen as being mediated by characteristics inherent in (1) the event or transition, (2) the environment, and (3) the person. Such models suggest that in considering the personal impact of CID, professionals must consider characteristics of the individual, including his or her personal, economic, psychological, and social resources; the sociocultural and physical environment; and the condition or disability.

Individual variables to be considered include the person's gender, age, ethnicity, assets and resources, and education. Also considered are personality variables, level of family and social support, and coping style. For example, the individual could be emotion-focused (focus is on alleviating emotional distress, changing the meaning of the problem); avoidant (disengagement, denying, engaging in wishful thinking); or active and problem focused.

Environmental variables to be considered include one's family response and relationships within the family, family support, social support, community and financial resources, availability of assistive technology and resources for modification, and the physical environment in which the individual lives and works.

Variables associated with the disability or illness include time and type of onset, course and prognosis, level of controllability or predictability, treatability, visibility, perceived cause and stigma associated with the condition, severity, functions impaired, pain, lethality, and prognosis (Livneh & Antonak, 1997; Smart, 2009).

Quality-of-Life Models

Finally, several researchers have proposed QOL-based models of adaptation to disability (e.g., Bishop, 2005; Devins et al., 1983; Livneh, 2001; Schwartz & Sprangers, 2000). Generally, these models suggest that adaptation can be assessed and understood in terms of the effect of CID on and the attempt to restore QOL. Livneh (2001) proposed that successful adaptation is reflected in the ability to effectively reestablish and manage both the external environment and one's internal experiences and as a result to attain improved QOL.

Family Response to Disability and the Rehabilitation Counseling Process

The rehabilitation counseling client is generally a member of a family and social system that may both affect and be affected by the rehabilitation counseling process. It is an ethical responsibility for rehabilitation counselors to enlist the support of family members as a positive resource in the rehabilitation counseling process, if appropriate, and with consent from the client. Researchers have demonstrated the influence of a client's family, for example, on the individual's feelings of independence and competence, on changing self-defeating beliefs, improving adjustment to work, complying with medical rehabilitation regimens, and facilitating the adjustment. Clients with disabilities who have family support (financial, emotional, and decision-making support) are more likely to be successful in achieving their rehabilitation goals. Family dynamics and family members may also have an unproductive or unhelpful influence on a client, resisting rehabilitation efforts and hindering positive change and adaptation. Rehabilitation professionals also know that families can have a powerful influence in the lives and development of children with disabilities (Lustig, 2002). An understanding of family processes can increase the effectiveness of rehabilitation counseling professionals (Lustig, 2002).

To assess the client's family situation, in addition to demographic information, the counselor might also discuss family communication patterns, the division of labor within the family, family health or illness, the impact of CID on the family and the family's reaction to the disability, and the family's reaction to the rehabilitation counseling process (Power & Dell Orto, 1980). In addition, the family's resiliency, coping processes, and adaptation can be assessed using a wide variety of inventories designed for the purpose (Frain et al., 2007).

Research on the predictors of psychosocial outcome of CID has recognized the interacting influence of the family on the individual's recovery and the effects of the illness or disability on the family (Degeneffe & Lynch, 2006). With the onset of CID, family members may experience a range of adverse physical and psychosocial effects, including depression, anxiety, stress associated with changes in family roles and social support, substance use, communication difficulties, and health problems (Frain et al., 2007). For families of a child with a disability, adjustment involves coping with the educational implications of the disability, dealing with the reactions of peer groups, accessing community resources, adjusting emotionally to the chronicity of the CID, adjusting family roles, dealing with the financial implications and caregiving requirements, planning for future vocational development, and arranging for socialization opportunities in the community (Frain et al, 2007; Lustig, 2002).

A variety of coping techniques have been found to be effective in handling the stresses associated with family adjustment to disability. Cognitive beliefs that positively affect family adjustment include a shared commitment and purpose, positive reframing of life and events, and social comparisons that enhance self-esteem (Lustig, 2002). Receiving assistance from friends, extended family, support groups, and professionals have also been found to promote effective coping. Other factors predicting positive coping include the capacity to balance various roles (e.g., spouse, employee, parent), religious beliefs, and the ability to get periods of rest and breaks from their caregiving responsibilities (Lustig, 2002).

THEORIES OF PERSONALITY DEVELOPMENT

Overview

Many theories of development have been proposed over the course of the past century to explain and describe the development of personality, behavior, motivation, and environment. Some of these theories have been based on the concept of critical physical, social, or emotional developmental tasks or stages throughout the life span; others on the impact of environmental influences; others on specific learning and cognitive processes (Vander Zanden, Crandell, & Crandell, 2007). In this section, we review the key concepts of several major theories of personality development.

▪ LEARNING OBJECTIVES

By the end of this unit, you should be able to:

1. Describe key aspects of psychoanalytic theories of personality development.
2. Describe key aspects of the personality development theories of Erikson, Piaget, and Vygotsky.
3. Describe key aspects of cognitive learning theory.

▪ KEY CONCEPTS

Psychoanalytic Theories

Throughout the late 19th and early 20th centuries, Sigmund Freud and other psychoanalytically oriented theorists were responsible for introducing a number of ideas that changed the way children and childhood was viewed. Key ideas introduced by Freud include: (1) the idea that personality develops progressively as the individual passes through various stages, during which he or she is faced with specific developmental tasks that must be mastered, or conflicts that must be resolved, before advancing to the next stage and (2) the importance of the first 6 years of life as a critical social developmental period and as an important precursor to later personality.

Psychosexual Stages of Development

Freud's theory of development is described in terms of the psychosexual stages. These stages are each dominated by the development of sensitivity in a particular erogenous or pleasure-giving zone of the body. Each stage presents a unique conflict that must be resolved before passing on to the next stage. Unsuccessful resolution of the conflict leads to fixation—the tendency to stay at a particular stage. The stages and key elements are portrayed in Table 3.2.

Criticisms of Freud's Psychosexual Stages

Many criticisms have been aimed at Freud's concept of development through the psychosexual stages. Among the many general criticisms are that few of Freud's proposals about developmental processes can be tested using the scientific method, and that the theory reflects the social structures and biases of the era in which Freud lived, and are no longer relevant. In addition, aspects of the theory have been criticized for being sexist.

Erik Erikson: Psychosocial Stages of Development

Erik Erikson (1902–1994) proposed eight stages of psychosocial development, each of which confronts the individual with a major conflict that must be successfully resolved if healthy development is to occur. Unlike Freud, Erikson emphasizes social processes rather than sexual (as defined by Freud) processes in the developmental stages, and he described processes of personality development throughout a person's life span. Table 3.3 identifies Erikson's psychosocial stages and key developmental issues associated with each stage.

Jean Piaget: Cognitive Stages in Development

Jean Piaget (1896–1980) proposed sequential periods of cognitive development in an individual's ability to think about and understand one's self and one's environment. His work raised awareness of the idea that children think differently from adults. Piaget proposed that children progress through distinct but interrelated stages of cognitive development.

TABLE 3.2 ■ Psychosexual Stages of Development: Stages and Key Elements

Stage	Age	Key Element
1. Oral stage	birth to 2	*Focus* The mouth and digestive tract. Interaction with the world is through activities associated with the mouth and digestive tract (eating, nursing, pleasure associated with oral stimulation, satisfaction)
		Conflict or challenge Issues in this stage involve the need to rely upon and trust caregivers to provide nurturance and satisfaction, and moving toward weaning, independence
		Resolution Develop trust that the world will fulfill needs and that one can achieve satisfaction
		Fixation If an infant gets too much or too little satisfaction during this stage, he or she may become fixated, with either oral receptive (dependent, gullible [e.g., willing to swallow anything, overly concerned with obtaining goods, information, or knowledge]) or oral aggressive (conversationally aggressive, sarcastic, biting, possessive of others) tendencies and characteristics of personality
2. Anal stage	2 to 3	*Focus* Satisfaction and tension release through bowel movements and control
		Conflict or challenge Self-control over bowels & toilet training; conflicts with parents over control and power, played out in toilet training. The reactions and responses of parents at this stage affect one's personal view (e.g., if parent/caregiver is supportive and encouraging, the child is likely to experience self-esteem)
		Fixation Anal retentive—stingy, saving, orderly; anal expulsive—messy, sloppy, prone to tantrums, and outbursts
3. Phallic stage	4 to 5	*Focus* Satisfaction through genital stimulation; awareness develops at this stage of the presence or absence of a penis
		Conflict or challenge Sexuality and relationships with same sex and opposite sex parent. This stage introduces the Oedipal complex (boy wants to possess mother and father is seen as rival); and Electra complex (girl wants to possess father and mother is seen as rival); the concepts of castration anxiety and penis envy are associated with this stage. Formation of introjected superego also occurs at this stage; the superego is formed out of father's/mother's interpretation of society's rules.
		Resolution Identification with same sex parent
4. Latency stage	6 to 12	*Focus* This stage is associated with a decrease, or repression of, sexual interest and energies are redirected to more personally and culturally acceptable objects
		Conflict or challenge Development of social skills, communication skills, and self-confidence
5. Genital stage	12 to maturity	*Focus* Genitals, sexuality
		Conflict or challenge Sexual energy is increasingly invested in mature sexual relationships, friendship, leisure, career development and psychological balance

Although recent empirical evidence suggests that Piaget underestimated the cognitive abilities of infants and young children, his theory and his emphasis on the active nature of the child had a significant impact on human developmental theory and research. Below we list the key terms and concepts associated with Piaget's theory and in Table 3.4 identify Piaget's stages of cognitive development and associated developmental characteristics.

Table 3.3 ■ Erikson's Psychosocial Stages and Key Developmental Issues

Stage/Age	Issue
1. Birth to 1	Trust vs. mistrust
2. 2 to 3 years	Autonomy vs. shame and doubt
3. 4 to 5 years	Initiative vs. guilt
4. 6 to 11 years	Industry vs. inferiority
5. Adolescence	Identity vs. role confusion
6. Young adulthood	Intimacy vs. isolation
7. Middle age	Generativity vs. stagnation
8. Later life	Integrity vs. despair

Table 3.4 ■ Piaget's Stages of Cognitive Development

Stage and Age Period	Characteristics of Developmental Stage
1. Sensorimotor— birth to 2	Characterized by: – Increasing awareness of sensory–motor integration – Object permanence—the understanding that objects that are not within the visual field do not cease to exist – Cause and effect understanding
2. Preoperational— 2 to 7 years	Characterized by: – Capacity to use symbols to portray external world internally (especially language) – Egocentrism—child's own point of view is only point of view
3. Concrete operations— 7 to 11 years	Characterized by: – Mastery of logical operations, math, hierarchical structures, quantity, and shape – Rule–based operation in environment
4. Formal operations— 11 and older	Characterized by: – Capacity for abstract thinking – Capacity for understanding scientific principles

Terms Associated With Piaget's Theory

1. *Schema:* a cognitive structure, or set of related ideas or concepts, that people use to function in and respond to situations in their environment. In Piaget's theory, cognitive development is a stage-based process of adaptation, involving alternating processes of assimilation and accommodation of schemata.
2. *Assimilation:* refers to the process of taking in new knowledge and information and interpreting it so as to fit in the existing schema or view of the world. People generally stretch a schema as far as possible to fit new observations before accepting that the existing schema requires modification.
3. *Disequilibrium:* the result of awareness that current observations cannot be made to fit within the existing schema.
4. *Accommodation:* the development or evolving of new schemata to fit existing and new information and resulting in a new understanding of the world.

Cognitive Learning Theory and Information Processing

Albert Bandura's cognitive learning theory places heavy reliance on information processing and how children and adults operate mentally in their social experiences and how these mental operations in turn influence their behavior. Cognitive learning is also referred to as observational learning, social learning, and modeling.

Lev Vygotsky's Sociocultural Social Development Theory

Vygotsky's theory emphasizes the influence of social interaction and culture in development. He suggested that development occurs in and depends upon social interaction and that culture is assimilated by interactions with other people. The potential for individual cognitive development depends on the "zone of proximal development," which represents the difference between where the child is currently functioning and his or her potential development, achieved through the guidance of adults or capable peers. Language, communication, and the development of internal speech also play a key role in development.

DISABILITY AND SEXUALITY

Overview

Sexuality is one of the most significant psychosocial factors in an individual's life, and sexual adjustment may be an important aspect of the rehabilitation counseling and psychosocial adaptation process. Historically, and in the rehabilitation counseling profession, the sexuality of individuals with disabilities has been disregarded and overlooked for a number of reasons. This section reviews fundamental aspects of sexuality and disability, and explores the role of rehabilitation counselors and sexuality in the rehabilitation counseling process.

▥ LEARNING OBJECTIVES

By the end of this unit you should be able to:

1. Describe the historical issues and current models of sexuality and disability.
2. Describe the importance of sexuality to rehabilitation counseling consumers.
3. Discuss the rehabilitation counselor's roles related to sexuality and disability.

▥ KEY CONCEPTS

Sexuality has been recognized as one of the most significant psychosocial factors in an individual's life. Sexual adjustment has been recognized as one of the key components of overall rehabilitation success (Kazukauskas & Lam, 2010). Sexuality is important to the rehabilitation process because of its close relationship to self-esteem, body image, and an individual's overall well-being (Juergens, Smedema, & Berven, 2009).

Historical and Current Perspectives on Disability and Sexuality

Throughout history, the sexuality of individuals with disabilities has been disregarded and stigmatized by society (Esmail, Darry, Walter, & Knupp, 2010). Reasons for this failure to recognize individuals with disabilities as having sexual needs stemmed from lack of public education and limited exposure to topics related to sexuality and disability (Esmail et al., 2010). Prior to the 1970s, there was limited research conducted on sexuality and disability. Research that was conducted during this era was derived from the medical model, which was also the key model for research related to disability studies (Esmail et al., 2010).

TABLE 3.5 ■ Key Concepts in Disability and Sexuality

Key Concept	Summary
Sexuality	A collection of characteristics that identify and communicate the sexual nature of an individual (Dombrowski, Petrick, & Strauss, 2000)
Social model of disability	Disability is the result of a social structure that excludes certain people from accessing employment, social resources and positive identities. Disability is not an individual possessive trait, but rather an external socially mediated phenomenon (Esmail et al., 2010)

Traditional models of sexual response focus on a linear staged sequence of physiological functioning. Masters and Johnson's (1966) model is a widely accepted model of sexual functioning. In this model, "normal" sexual response moved through four stages: excitement, plateau, orgasm, and resolution. The *Diagnostic and Statistical Manual of Mental Disorders (DSM)* uses this model as a basis for diagnosis for sexual dysfunction. Use of these types of physiological models of sexual response can be problematic for addressing the sexual health and sexuality issues of individuals with disability because among persons with a disability, the healthy functional sexual response may be more varied, though this does not make the sexual functioning any less satisfying (Di Giulio, 2003).

Over the past 20 years, the social model (see Table 3.5) has become the predominant model used for both sexuality and disability studies (Esmail et al., 2010; Sakellariou, 2006). Current research is looking at public response to individuals with disabilities and society's inability to remove barriers from society and the environment. Due to the increased shift toward the social model, sexual development is now recognized as a multidimensional process that is greatly influenced by society. Societal barriers are one of the key issues individuals with disabilities face in regard to sexuality. In the United States, a new view of sexuality is developing. Sexuality is now being recognized as more than just physical performance and also relies on emotional closeness and pleasure (Esmail et al., 2010).

Sexuality in Rehabilitation Counseling

Sexuality has been noted to be one of the most significant psychosocial factors in a person's life; this is true for individuals with and without disabilities (Kazukauskas & Lam, 2010). Sexual adjustment is predictive of overall disability adjustment, QOL, body image, and self-esteem (Juergens et al., 2009; Kazukauskas & Lam, 2010). Sexual adjustment has been shown to be an important part of the overall rehabilitation process. The presence of a disability has been found to affect an individual's ability to find a partner and personal confidence levels in the area of sexuality (Esmail et al., 2010). Taleporos, Dip, and McCabe (2002) found that sexual esteem and sexual satisfaction were strong predictors of self-esteem in individuals with physical disabilities. Individuals with physical disabilities in this study were found to have a smaller likelihood of feeling depressed if they felt good about their bodies and were satisfied sexually (Taleporos et al., 2002).

Rehabilitation Counselors Roles in Sexuality and Disability

Sexuality is a topic that is commonly left out of the rehabilitation process (Kazukauskas & Lam, 2010). Reasons for this omission range from limited staff knowledge and training to negative attitudes about disability and sexuality, and discomfort in discussing sexuality issues with consumers (Kazukauskas & Lam, 2010). Certified rehabilitation counselors (CRCs) can play a key role in helping consumers acquire knowledge about sexuality issues and disability. As part of the holistic rehabilitation counseling process, sexuality is an issue that consumers may feel comfortable discussing with CRCs (Kazukauskas &

Lam, 2010). Topics that CRCs should be prepared to discuss include the areas of fertility, sexual expression, prevention of unwanted pregnancy, prevention of sexual abuse, establishing sexual relationship with a partner, dating issues, and sexual orientation issues (Juergens et al., 2009). Juergens et al. suggest conducting a detailed interview when a consumer approaches the counselor about sexuality, or it is found appropriate to discuss issues of sexuality. A CRC who is comfortable with issues regarding sexuality should conduct the detailed interview. Information that can be gathered during the interview process includes sexual expectations, the consumer's sexual knowledge, and more specific questions related to the consumer's disability and sexuality concerns (Juergens et al.). Consumers should receive information about the sexual response cycle and sexual anatomy, information on how the individual's specific disability may affect sexual functioning, and education to the individual, his or her partner or family on how various treatments and medications may affect sexuality. Along with the information to be provided to consumers, CRCs should also encourage new sexual expectations and help the consumer to explore different means of sexual connections. CRCs should also have resources available to consumers so that referrals can be made to other trained professionals in the area of sexuality (Juergens et al., 2009).

LEARNING STYLES

Overview

In this section, learning styles are identified as an important aspect of human development and rehabilitation counseling. Learning styles are defined using several examples, and the role of rehabilitation counselors in assisting consumers with different learning styles is discussed.

▓ LEARNING OBJECTIVES

By the end of this unit you should be able to:

1. Define learning styles.
2. Discuss what rehabilitation counselors can do to assist consumers with different learning styles.

▓ KEY CONCEPTS

Differences in Learning Styles

Learning styles refer to the idea that individuals learn in different ways. Individuals have different ways of instruction and studying that is more effective for them (Pashler, McDaniel, Rohrer, & Bjork, 2008). Learning styles are described as an aspect of individual's personality, because of this learning styles are not expected to change in the short term (Serife, 2008). The idea of learning styles has been gaining increased influence over the years in the United States. Educators and psychologists have embraced the idea of learning styles, and educational psychologists and teachers are being taught that students have different learning styles that should be accommodated through instruction (Pashler et al., 2008).

Learning Style Models

Several models of learning style have been developed, including the models by Kolb (1984), Honey and Mumford (1982), Entwistle (1981), Pask (1976), and Felder and Silverman

(1988), among others. Each model describes different aspects of how people prefer to learn. As an example of learning styles, Felder and Silverman describe learning styles in terms of four dimensions, combining major learning style models (Liu & Graf, 2009). In broad strokes, the styles include (Felder & Silverman, 1988):

1. *Active/reflective learners.* Active learners retain and understand information best through activity, such as discussing, or applying, or explaining the information. Reflective learners prefer to think through the material and tend to prefer working alone.
2. *Sensing/intuitive learners.* Sensing learners prefer learning facts, whereas intuitive learners prefer discovering possibilities and relationships.
3. *Visual/verbal learners.* Visual learners remember best what they see. Verbal learners remember words best, both written and spoken.
4. *Sequential/global learners.* Sequential learners gain understanding in logical, linear steps. Global learners absorb material in terms of the big picture.

Dunn and Dunn (as cited in Heiman, 2006; Honigsfeld & Dunn, 2006) describe five factors that influence an individual's learning style. These include environmental situation, personal–emotional characteristics, sociological preferences for learning, physiological characteristics, and global aspects. Along with these five factors, individuals have strategies that they seem to prefer in order to best learn academic materials. Strategies of learning include visual learning, tactual learning, auditory learning, and kinesthetic learning (Honigsfeld & Dunn, 2006).

Assisting Consumers With Different Learning Styles

Learning style theorists recommend that students explore their own individual learning styles. By exploring learning styles, students will be better able to deal with academic goals they are striving to meet, as well as better able to handle stress that entering the academic world can impose upon them (Heiman, 2006). It should be noted, however, that recently researchers have suggested the concept of using learning styles as a means of delivering educational material is associated with a number of limitations (e.g., Riener & Willingham, 2010; Scott, 2010).

▓ INTERNET RESOURCES

Rehabilitation Counseling Across the Life Span: Older Americans

Administration on Aging
www.aoa.gov/

Center for Healthy Aging
http://healthyagingprograms.org/

Early Developmental Processes

Child Development (Centers for Disease Control and Prevention)
http://www.cdc.gov/ncbddd/child/

Genetic Counseling information from the Human Genome Project
http://www.ornl.gov/sci/techresources/Human_Genome/medicine/genecounseling.shtml

Genetic Counseling information from MedLinePlus (NIH)
http://www.nlm.nih.gov/medlineplus/geneticcounseling.html

Infant and Newborn Development information from MedLinePlus (NIH)
http://www.nlm.nih.gov/medlineplus/infantandnewborndevelopment.html

National Society of Genetic Counseling
http://www.nsgc.org/

Individual and Family Response to Disability

Coping with Chronic Illness information from MedLinePlus (NIH)
http://www.nlm.nih.gov/medlineplus/copingwithchronicillness.html

Chronic Illness (Professional journal on Chronic Illness and related content)
http://chi.sagepub.com/

Theories of Personality Development

American Counseling Association
http://www.counseling.org

American Psychoanalytic Association
http://apsa.org/

American Psychological Association
www.apa.org

Theories of Personality-Study Guide
http://psychology.about.com/od/psychologystudyguides/a/personalitysg_3.htm

Human Sexuality and Disability

Sexuality and Disability information from WebMD
http://emedicine.medscape.com/article/319119-overview

Sexuality and Disability (Professional journal)
http://www.springer.com/psychology/community+psychology/journal/11195

Sexuality and Intellectual Disability information from the American Association of Intellectual and Developmental Disabilities
http://www.aamr.org/content_198.cfm

MULTIPLE CHOICE QUESTIONS

1. The baby-boomer generation is defined as Americans who were born
   A. prior to 1940
   B. between 1950 and 1970
   C. between 1945 and 1964
   D. since 1980

2. Sexuality is important to the rehabilitation process because of its relationship with:
   A. Self-esteem
   B. Body image
   C. Well being
   D. All of the above

3. Prior to the 1970s, research conducted on sexuality and disability was based on the:
   A. Social model
   B. Medical model
   C. Holistic model
   D. Rehabilitation model

4. It is projected that in 2018, workers in the 55–64 age group
   A. will make up the largest number of workers in the U.S. workforce
   B. will make up the smallest number of workers in the U.S. workforce
   C. will have experienced the greatest and steadiest percentage increase of any age group
   D. will outnumber workers aged 25–34

5. Over the past 20 years, the _____ has become the predominant model used for sexuality and disability studies.
   A. Psychological model
   B. Medical model
   C. Social model
   D. Biological model

6. The transformation of values framework associated with acceptance of disability describes all but which one of the following value changes:
   A. Enlarging the scope of values
   B. Containing disability costs
   C. Subordination of physique
   D. Transforming comparative status values into asset values

7. Strategies of learning include all but which of the following?
   A. Visual learning
   B. Somatosensory learning
   C. Auditory learning
   D. Kinesthetic learning

8. Reason(s) sexuality is left out of the rehabilitation process include:
   A. Limited staff knowledge
   B. Comfort with sexuality issues
   C. Increased training for staff
   D. Positive attitudes about sexuality and disability.

9. Learning styles are a part of a person's _____.
   A. Biology
   B. Character
   C. Ego
   D. Personality

10. An infant learns that when a ball that she has been playing with is placed under a blanket, the ball still exists even though she cannot see it. According to Piaget, this occurs during which stage of cognitive development?
    A. Sensorimotor
    B. Concrete operations
    C. Formal operations
    D. Preoperational

▨ ANSWER KEY

1. C; **2.** D; **3.** B; **4.** C; **5.** C; **6.** B; **7.** B; **8.** A; **9.** D; **10.** A

▨ ADVANCED MULTIPLE CHOICE QUESTIONS

1. The co-occurrence of mental health issues with medical problems among the elderly is best described as follows:
   A. Such comorbidity is rarely seen.
   B. Unlike in younger Americans, a higher risk for medical issues has been associated with a decreased risk for mental health diagnoses.
   C. Limited access to mental health care for older Americans makes it unclear whether such comorbidity exists.
   D. A variety of factors associated with medical problems seem to increase the risk for mental health issues.

2. Several limitations have been associated with the stage/phase model approach to understanding adjustment to disability, including all but which one of the following?
   A. While waiting for the client to complete the grieving process, the counselor working from this approach might feel it is acceptable to withhold or delay treatment or implementing rehabilitation interventions.
   B. The proposed reactions to CID are not universally experienced.
   C. Counselors might decide that different counseling approaches (e.g., Gestalt, person-centered, REBT) are more appropriate at different stages.
   D. A state of final adjustment is not experienced.

3. The prevalence of mental illness among older adults
  A. will reach 20% among the population of people aged 65 and older
  B. varies considerably depending on one's form of residence
  C. is currently roughly equal to that seen in the general population
  D. is considerably lower than that seen in the general population

4. Research among twins suggests that compared with other contributing factors, the most important predictor of an individual's level of happiness appears to be genetics. This could be interpreted as support for:
  A. The nativist perspective
  B. Adaptive environmental techniques
  C. The nurturist perspective
  D. The combined perspective

5. Both Freud's and Piaget's theories of development would both be best described as
  A. proposing developmental continuity
  B. proposing developmental discontinuity
  C. somatopsychological approaches to development
  D. none of these

6. Research on adaptation to disability has consistently shown that
  A. certain personality types are frequently associated with specific disabilities
  B. severity of the disability is directly related to the expected level of adjustment
  C. people who share common personality types, demographic backgrounds, and are of the same age show remarkably similar reactions to and patterns of adjustment
  D. positive psychosocial outcomes are strongly associated with level of social support

7. Ecological models of adaptation
  A. are associated with 19th-century society and no longer considered relevant
  B. are based on the idea that the earth and its environment are primarily responsible for individual response to disability
  C. are based on the idea that personal, social, and environmental resources and demands interact to influence individual adjustment
  D. suggest that three factors, including the individual's coping style, social support, and acceptance are primarily responsible for individual response to disability on resources in the person's environment

8. Which statement is most accurate concerning families and the rehabilitation counseling process?
  A. Rehabilitation counselors have an ethical responsibility to enlist the support of family, regardless of the client's willingness to include the family member, provided that the involvement of the family member will, in the counselor's opinion, be a positive resource.
  B. Research has demonstrated that the influence of a client's family on the rehabilitation process is almost consistently negative.
  C. Clients with disabilities who have family support are more likely to be successful in achieving their rehabilitation goals.
  D. In order to avoid engaging in dual relationships, rehabilitation counselors are advised to avoid including family members in the rehabilitation counseling process.

9. Which of the following is not among the many criticisms that have been aimed at Freud's theory of development through the psychosexual stages?
  A. Few of Freud's developmental processes can be tested using the scientific method.
  B. The psychosexual stages are based on the social norms, structures, and biases of the era in which Freud developed his theory.
  C. Freud badly misjudged the importance of the first 6 years of life as a critical social developmental period and precursor to later personality.
  D. Aspects of the theory have been criticized for being sexist.

10. According to Piaget's theory, cognitive development involves alternating processes of ___ and ___. The first refers to the process of taking in and interpreting new knowledge to fit in the existing schema or view of world. The second occurs only after a period during which the old schema are seen to be insufficient, and results in the development of a new schema.

A. Disequilibrium and accommodation
B. Accommodation and assimilation
C. Assimilation and disequilibrium
D. Assimilation and accommodation

ANSWER KEY AND EXPLANATION OF ANSWERS

1-D: Comorbidity, or the co-occurrence of mental health issues with medical problems among the elderly has been associated with a variety of factors, including the experience of multiple personal losses, chronic insomnia, neurodegenerative disease, reduced social support, and limited access to treatment.

2-C: Criticisms of the various stage or phase models include that the proposed reactions to CID are not universally experienced; that a state of final adjustment is not experienced but that in reality the process of adjustment is cyclical or recurring; and that the concept of unavoidable stages may lead professionals to withhold or delay interventions while waiting for the client to experience some stage or level of adjustment (such as grieving over losses). Researchers have suggested that different counseling approaches may be more effective during different stages.

3-B: The prevalence of mental illness among older adults varies considerably depending on one's form of residence, with the highest rates found among residents of nursing homes, followed by individuals in acute care hospitals, and the lowest rates are seen among individuals living in the community.

4-A: The nativist perspective suggests that hereditary, genetic, or biological factors are the primary influence on development. Thus, research supporting the importance of these factors would support the nativist, rather than the nurturist perspective on development, although both appear to have influence on human development.

5-B: Unlike theories proposing developmental continuity and a process of smooth, gradual, development, and incremental change, stage theories, such as those proposed by Freud, Erickson, and Piaget are discontinuous, in that they describe development as a series of steps with clear-cut and qualitatively different changes occurring from one phase to the next.

6-D: Social support has consistently been associated with more positive psychosocial outcomes but research on adjustment to disability has consistently shown that there is no personality type associated with a specific disability, no simple or direct relationship between adjustment and the severity of the disability, and that adjustment is a highly individual process so that even similar people with similar disabilities experience different reactions and outcomes.

7-C: Ecological models suggest that adjustment is mediated by characteristics inherent in (1) the condition or disability, (2) the sociocultural and physical environment, and (3) the person, including his or her personal, economic, psychological, and social resources.

8-C: Clients with disabilities who have family support (financial, emotional, and decision-making support) are more likely to be successful in achieving their rehabilitation goals. Rehabilitation counselors have an ethical responsibility to enlist the support of family members as a positive resource in the rehabilitation counseling process, only if appropriate and with the client's consent. Researchers have demonstrated the influence of a client's family on the individual's feelings of independence and competence, on changing self-defeating beliefs, improving adjustment to work, complying with medical rehabilitation regimens, and facilitating the adjustment.

9-C: Although there are many criticisms and limitations associated with Freud's concept of development through the psychosexual stages, including the inability to evaluate many of the proposals empirically, the theory's association with the Western social structures and biases of the late 19th and early 20th centuries, and the apparent sexism, the importance of the early years of life as a critical social developmental period is consistent with current perspectives and knowledge about development.

10-D: In Piaget's theory, cognitive development is a stage-based process of adaptation, involving alternating processes of assimilation and accommodation of schemata. Assimilation refers to the process of taking in new knowledge and information and interpreting it so as to fit in the existing schema or view of world. Disequilibrium occurs when current observations cannot be made to fit within the existing schema. Accommodation is the development or evolving of new schemata to fit new information and results in a new understanding of the world.

◼ REFERENCES

American Board of Genetic Testing. (2010). Retrieved 20 December, 2010, from www.abgc.net/Resources_Links/Consumer_Information.asp

Barker, R. G., Wright, B. A., & Gonick, M. R. (1946). *Adjustment to physical handicap and illness: A survey of the social psychology of physique and disability.* New York, NY: Social Science Research Council.

Barros-Bailey, M., Fischer, J., & Saunders, J. L. (2007). Age, work, and disability: Rehabilitation at the end of the worklife. *Journal of Applied Rehabilitation Counseling, 38*(1), 20–31.

Bishop, M. (2005). Quality of life and psychosocial adaptation to chronic illness and acquired disability: A conceptual and theoretical synthesis. *Journal of Rehabilitation, 71*(2), 5–13.

Bishop, M., Boland, E. A., & Sheppard-Jones, K. (2008). Human growth and development: Educational and professional challenges and opportunities. *Rehabilitation Education, 22*(4), 267–276.

Borson, S., Bartels, S.J., Colenda, C. C., Gottlieb, G. L., & Meyers, B. (2001). Geriatric mental health services research: Strategic plan for an aging population. Report of the health services work group of the American Association for Geriatric Psychiatry. *The American Journal of Geriatric Psychiatry 9,* 191–204.

Brault, M. (2008). *Americans with disabilities: 2005.* Current Population Reports, P70–117. Washington, DC: U.S. Census Bureau.

Degeneffe, C. E., & Lynch, R. T. (2006). Correlates of depression in adult siblings of persons with traumatic brain injury. *Rehabilitation Counseling Bulletin, 49,* 130–142.

Dembo, T., Leviton, G. L., & Wright, B. A. (1956). Adjustment to misfortune: A problem of social-psychological rehabilitation. *Artificial Limbs, 3,* 4–62.

Devins, G. M., Blinik, Y. M., Hutchinson, T. A., Hollomby, D. J., Barre, P. E., & Guttmann, R. D. (1983). The emotional impact of end-stage renal disease: Importance of patients' perceptions of intrusiveness and control. *International Journal of Psychiatry in Medicine, 13*(4), 327–343.

Di Giulio, G. (2003). Sexuality and people living with physical or developmental disabilities: A review of key issues. *Canadian Journal of Human Sexuality, 12*(1), 53–68.

Dombrowski, L. K., Petrick, J. D., & Strauss, D. (2000). Rehabilitation treatment of sexuality issues due to acquired brain injury. *Rehabilitation Psychology, 45*(3), 299–309.

Entwistle, N. J. (1981). *Styles of learning and teaching.* Hoboken, NJ: Wiley.

Esmail, S., Darry, K., Walter, A., & Knupp, H. (2010). Attitudes and perceptions towards disability and sexuality. *Disability & Rehabilitation, 32*(14), 1148–1155.

Felder, R. M., & Silverman, L. K. (1988). Learning and teaching styles in engineering education. *Engineering Education, 78*(7), 674–681.

Frain, M. P., Lee, G. K., Berven, N. L., Tansey, T., Tschopp, M. K., & Chronister, J. (2007). Use of the resiliency model of family stress, adjustment and adaptation by rehabilitation counselors. *Journal of Rehabilitation, 73*(3), 18–25.

Heiman, T. (2006). Assessing learning styles among students with and without learning disabilities at a distance-learning university. *Learning Disability Quarterly, 29*(1), 55–63.

Honey, P., & Mumford, A. (1982). *The manual of learning styles.* Maidenhead, London: Peter Honey.

Honigsfeld, A., & Dunn, R. (2006). Learning-style characteristics of adult learners. *Delta Kappa Gamma Bulletin, 72*(2), 14–31.

Juergens, M. H., Smedema, S. M., & Berven, N. L. (2009). Willingness of graduate students in rehabilitation counseling to discuss sexuality with clients. *Rehabilitation Counseling Bulletin, 53*(1), 34–43.

Kazukauskas, K. A., & Lam, C. S. (2010). Disability and sexuality: Knowledge, attitudes, and level of comfort among certified rehabilitation counselors. *Rehabilitation Counseling Bulletin, 54*(1), 15–25.

Kolb, D. A. (1984). *Experiential learning: Experience as the source of learning and development.* Englewood Cliffs, NJ: Prentice-Hall.

Liu, T., & Graf, S. (2009). Coping with mismatched courses: Students' behaviour and performance in courses mismatched to their learning styles. *Educational Technology Research & Development, 57*(6). 739–752.

Livneh, H. (2001). Psychosocial adaptation to chronic illness and disability: A conceptual framework. *Rehabilitation Counseling Bulletin, 44*(3), 151–160.

Livneh, H., & Antonak, R. F. (1997). *Psychosocial adaptation to chronic illness and disability.* Gaithersburg, MD: Aspen.

Lustig, D. C. (2002). Family coping in families with a child with a disability. *Education and Training in Mental Retardation and Developmental Disabilities, 37*(1), 14–22.

Masters, W. H., & Johnson, V. E. (1966). *Human sexual response.* Boston, MA: Little, Brown.

Parker, R. M., Schaller, J., & Hansmann, S. (2003). Catastrophe, chaos, and complexity models and psychosocial adjustment to disability. *Rehabilitation Counseling Bulletin, 46,* 234–241.

Pashler, H., McDaniel, M., Rohrer, D., & Bjork, R. (2008). Learning styles: Concepts and evidence. *Psychological Science in the Public Interest (Wiley-Blackwell), 9*(3), 105–119.

Pask, G. (1976). Styles and strategies of learning. *The British Journal of Educational Psychology, 46,* 128–148.

Power, P., & Dell Orto, A. (1980). *Role of the family in the rehabilitation of the physically disabled.* Baltimore, MD: University Park Press.

Reynolds, C. F., Alexopoulos, G. S., Katz, I. R. & Lebowitz, B. D. (2001). Chronic depression in the elderly. *Drugs and Aging, 18,* 507–514.

Riener, C., & Willingham, D. (2010). The myth of learning styles. *Change, 42*(5), 32–35.

Robb, C., Chen, H., & Haley, W. E. (2002). Ageism in mental health and health care: A critical review. *Journal of Clinical Geropsychology, 8,* 1–12.

Sakellariou, D. (2006). If not the disability, then what? barriers to reclaiming sexuality following spinal cord injury. *Sexuality & Disability, 24*(2), 101–111.

Schwartz, C. E., & Sprangers, M. A. G. (2000). *Adaptation to changing health: Response shift in quality of life research.* Washington, DC: American Psychological Association.

Scott, C. (2010). The enduring appeal of learning styles. *Australian Journal of Education, 54*(1), 5–17.

Serife, A. K. (2008). A conceptual analysis on the approaches to learning. *Educational Sciences: Theory and Practice, 8*(3), 707–720.

Smart, J. (2009). *Disability, society, and the individual* (2nd ed.). Austin, TX: Pro-Ed.

Swett, E. A., & Bishop, M. (2003). Mental health and the aging population: Implications for rehabilitation counselors. *Journal of Rehabilitation- Special Issue on Mental Health and Aging, 69,* 13–18.

Taleporos, G., Dip, G., & McCabe, M. P. (2002). The impact of sexual esteem, body esteem, and sexual satisfaction on psychological well-being in people with physical disability. *Sexuality & Disability, 20*(3), 177–183.

U.S. Bureau of the Census. (2000). *Projections of the total resident population by 5-Year age groups and sex with special age categories: Middle series, 1999 to 2000.* Washington, DC: Author.

U.S. Census Bureau. (2011). *Statistical Abstract of the United States: 2011: Labor Force, Employment, & Earnings.* Washington, DC: U.S. Government Printing Office. Retrieved January 30, 2011, from www.census.gov/compendia/statab/cats/labor_force_employment_earnings/labor_force_status.html

Vander Zanden, J. W., Crandell, T. L., & Crandell, C. H. (2007). *Human development* (8th ed.). New York, NY: McGraw Hill.

Wright, B. A. (1960). *Physical disability: A psychological approach.* New York, NY: Harper & Row.

Wright, B. A. (1983). *Physical disability: A psychosocial approach.* New York, NY: Harper & Row.

Employment and Career Development

4

CONNIE SUNG, JESSICA BROOKS, VERONICA MULLER, FONG CHAN, AND DAVID STRAND

Work is fundamental to the well-being of people with or without disabilities (Chan et al., 1997; Dutta, Gervey, Chan, Chou, & Ditchman, 2008). Compared to persons who are employed, those who are unemployed tend to experience higher prevalence of depression and anxiety disorders, use alcohol more frequently, and report lower scores on self-esteem and quality-of-life measures (Dutta et al., 2008). Recognizing its importance, rehabilitation counselors have consistently advocated for work as a fundamental human right of people with disabilities (Chan et al., 1997). Therefore, job placement of people with disabilities at the highest level possible has been central to the professional practice of rehabilitation counseling (Chan et al., 1997).

Quality job placements result only from quality vocational assessment, counseling, and planning services in the early rehabilitation phases. To facilitate vocational decision making, a rehabilitation client must be exposed systematically to the world of work; develop insights for skills, abilities, interests and physical functioning; and be sensitive to labor market constraints (Chan et al., 1997). This, in turn, requires the skilled rehabilitation counselor to become knowledgeable about: (a) career development theories, (b) community resources, (c) medical and psychosocial aspects of disability, (d) vocational implications of different disabling conditions, (e) work demands and requirements of different occupations, (f) job trends and training opportunities in the local and national economy, (g) availability of job accommodation methods and assistive devices for people with disabilities, and (h) job placement techniques. This chapter will review occupational information and job analysis, career development theories, and job placement models and techniques.

In this chapter, we review the components of employment and career development in rehabilitation, occupational information systems, theories related to career development, job analysis and job placement strategies, and supported employment. Specific topics include the following:

- Labor market information for career exploration
- Occupational information systems for vocational planning
- Job analysis
- Career development and specific focus theories
- Career counseling
- Vocational consultation and job placement
- Job placement assistance and supported employment

LABOR MARKET AND OCCUPATIONAL INFORMATION FOR VOCATIONAL PLANNING AND CAREER DECISION MAKING

Overview

Accurate labor market information is one of the essential ingredients of career decision making. Rehabilitation counselors play an influential role in helping people gather, analyze, and use this information. This section will provide the current employment situation and discuss the importance of using labor market and occupational information systems for vocational planning and career decision making.

◼ LEARNING OBJECTIVES

By the end of this unit you should be able to:

1. Understand the current employment situation of people with disabilities.
2. Understand the role of labor market and occupational information systems.

◼ KEY CONCEPTS

Labor Market Information

The employment rate for individuals with disabilities continues to be unacceptably low. A recent U.S. Bureau of Labor Statistics (BLS) Employment Situation report estimated the employment rate of individuals with disabilities to be 18.0% compared to 63.9% for people without disabilities (BLS, U.S. Department of Labor, 2010). For workers with disabilities, the unemployment rate of 16.4% is significantly higher than the 9.5% rate for workers without disabilities (BLS, U.S. Department of Labor, 2010). The recent recession has a disproportionate impact on workers with disabilities, with the number of employed workers with disabilities declining at a rate more than three times that of workers without disabilities and the unemployment rate rose dramatically to levels exceeding that of other workers (Kaye, 2010). Without a doubt, lack of employment opportunities excludes people with disabilities from full community participation, significantly affecting the quality of their lives.

Dunn (1974) suggested that job placement should be viewed as a program goal instead of a discrete set of activities (helping clients find jobs) that occur in the final stage of the vocational rehabilitation process. Rehabilitation counselors must be familiar with labor market information, job requirements, and employer demands to help consumers develop appropriate vocational goals consistent with their job performance and capacity early in the vocational rehabilitation process. Importantly, employment demand is changing and projected to shift due to fundamental structural economic changes (Chan, Strauser, Gervey, & Lee, 2010). The organizational structures of American companies are also changing. The organizational chart is now flatter and team based, and the emphasis is on flexibility, productivity, and workplace socialization skills. Therefore, rehabilitation professionals must have a thorough understanding of the real concerns of employers about hiring and retention of persons with disabilities and be able to address their concerns and needs. Helping people with disabilities develop flexible, versatile, and adaptable work skills to meet employer expectations and requirements for jobs in the new economy will improve their odds of obtaining employment.

Employers are less risk averse in occupations where the demand is high and the supply of qualified workers is low. Preparing people with disabilities for these occupations will increase their chance of being hired. As a result, a demand-side employment approach is gaining considerable attention in vocational rehabilitation. To improve employment rates and employment quality for individuals with disabilities, rehabilitation counselors must be able to identify the largest or fastest growth areas of employment opportunities and be knowledgeable about the skill sets needed for these demand occupations. It is important for rehabilitation counselors to be familiar with occupational information and analysis.

OCCUPATIONAL INFORMATION SYSTEMS

Overview

A variety of systems have been developed for classifying occupational information. Classification generally refers to (a) industries, (b) occupations, and/or (c) instructional programs. In this section, we will provide a description of several major job classification systems that are important to the professional practice of rehabilitation counseling.

▓ LEARNING OBJECTIVES

By the end of this unit you should be able to:

1. Understand the function of occupational information systems.
2. Identify commonly used occupational information systems and their designated purposes and features.

▓ KEY CONCEPTS

A variety of systems have been developed for classifying occupational information. Classification generally refers to (a) industries, (b) occupations, and/or (c) instructional programs. The following is a description of several major job classification systems that are important to the professional practice of rehabilitation counseling.

Dictionary of Occupational Titles

The revised fourth edition of *Dictionary of Occupational Titles* (DOT, http://www.occupationalinfo.org) was published by the U.S. Department of Labor (1991). It is one of the most comprehensive occupational information resources that covers over 12,000 jobs representative of the U.S. labor market. The DOT uses a nine-digit code to classify occupations with each digit bearing a specific meaning. The first digit provides information on one of the nine broad *Occupational Categories* (see Table 4.1, column 1). *Occupational Divisions* (83 divisions) within each of the occupations are denoted by the first two digits, whereas the *Occupational Groups* (564 groups) within each of the divisions are defined by the first three digits. The middle three digits provide information on the worker function (functional demand) ratings for tasks performed in the occupation. The fourth digit refers to worker functions in relationship to *Data*; the fifth digit refers to worker functions in relationship to *People*; and the sixth digit refers to worker functions in relationship to *Things*. The numerical assignments for each of these relationships are shown in Table 4.1, columns 2–4.

TABLE 4.1 ▓ **Categories of Occupations and Worker Function Ratings (Data–People–Things)**

Category (1st digit)	Data (4th digit)	People (5th digit)	Things (6th digit)
0/1 Professional, technical, and managerial	0 Synthesizing	0 Mentoring	0 Setting up
	1 Coordinating	1 Negotiating	1 Precision working
2 Clerical and sales	2 Analyzing	2 Instructing	2 Operating-controlling
3 Service	3 Compiling	3 Supervising	3 Driving-operating
4 Agricultural, fishery, forestry, and related	4 Computing	4 Diverting	4 Manipulating
5 Processing	5 Copying	5 Persuading	5 Tending
6 Machine trades	6 Comparing	6 Speaking-signaling	6 Feeding-offbearing
7 Benchwork	7 Serving	7 Handling	
8 Structural work		8 Taking instructions-helping	
9 Miscellaneous			

Finally, the last three-digit set aids in discriminating among closely related jobs within the same occupational group. Note that there are no two occupations having the same nine-digit code. Each occupation in DOT is analyzed based on job analysis. DOT variables are analyzed in terms of necessary or desirable characteristics of the worker that derived from job analysis schedules which include (1) worker functions; (2) vocational aptitudes (see Table 4.2 for the 11 aptitude levels); (3) temperaments (see Table 4.2 for the 11 temperaments); (4) interests; (5) physical demands; (6) working conditions; (7) general educational development, and (8) specific vocational preparation (Mayall, 1994). The physical demands factor is particularly important in job matching as it provides information on the extent that how impairments/functioning can affect job performance and the kinds of accommodations are needed to enable the person with a disability to perform the essential functions of a particular job. There are seven basic parts to an occupational definition, which present data about a job in a systematic fashion (U.S. Department of Labor, 1991). The parts are listed in the order in which they appear in every definition: (1) Occupational Code Number; (2) Occupational Title; (3) Industry Designation; (4) Alternate Titles (if any); (5) Body of the Definition; (6) Undefined Related Titles (if any); and (7) Definition Trailer. Table 4.3 provides an example to illustrate the structure of DOT coding.

Occupational Information Network

Occupational Information Network (O*NET) is a database of occupational requirements and worker attributes developed using a modern empirically based framework and

TABLE 4.2 ■ Vocational Aptitudes and Temperaments

Vocational Aptitude	Temperament
(G) General learning ability	(D) Directing, controlling, or planning activities of others
(V) Verbal aptitude	(R) Performing repetitive or short-cycle work
(N) Numerical aptitude	(I) Influencing people in their opinions, attitudes, and judgments
(S) Spatial aptitude	(V) Performing a variety of duties
(F) Form perception	(E) Expressing personal feelings
(Q) Clerical perception	(A) Working alone or apart in physical isolation from others
(K) Motor coordination	(S) Performing effectively under stress
(F) Finger dexterity	(T) Attaining precise set limits, tolerances, and standards
(M) Manual dexterity	(U) Working under specific instructions
(E) Eye–hand–foot coordination	(P) Dealing with people
(C) Color discrimination	(J) Making judgments

TABLE 4.3 ■ Sample DOT Code and Its Coding Structure

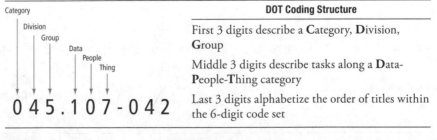

Category	DOT Coding Structure
Division Group Data People Thing 0 4 5 . 1 0 7 - 0 4 2	First 3 digits describe a **C**ategory, **D**ivision, **G**roup
	Middle 3 digits describe tasks along a **D**ata-**P**eople-**T**hing category
	Last 3 digits alphabetize the order of titles within the 6-digit code set

methodology for obtaining occupational information. It is developed as a replacement for the DOT. O*NET describes occupations in terms of the skills and knowledge requirements, how the work is performed, and typical work settings. The O*NET database is a comprehensive source of descriptors, with ratings of importance, level, relevance, or extent, for more than 1,000 occupations that are key to the U.S. economy. O*NET descriptors for jobs include skills, abilities, knowledge, tasks, work activities, work context, experience levels required, job interests, work values/needs, and work styles. New tools and technology (T2) data provide information on machines, equipment, tools, and software that workers may use for optimal functioning in a high-performance workplace.

Standard Occupational Classification System

The 2010 Standard Occupational Classification (SOC) system is used by federal statistical agencies to classify workers into occupational categories for the purpose of collecting, calculating, or disseminating data. All workers are classified into one of 840 detailed occupations according to their occupational definition. To facilitate classification, detailed occupations are combined to form 461 broad occupations, 97 minor groups, and 23 major groups. Detailed occupations in the SOC with similar job duties, and in some cases skills, education, and/or training, are grouped together. There are, at the most specified level, 840 *Detailed Occupations*. Each worker is classified into only one of the 840 detailed occupations based on the tasks he or she performs. Each item in the SOC is designated by a six-digit code. The hyphen between the second and third digit is used only for clarity (BLS, U.S. Department of Labor, 2011b). Table 4.4 provides an example of SOC code to illustrate the structure of coding.

The U.S. Department of Labor's BLS produces employment and wage estimates using the SOC system. Similarly, each O*NET occupational title and code is based on the updated O*NET-SOC 2009 taxonomy. This ensures that O*NET information links directly to other labor market information, such as wage and employment statistics that are important to rehabilitation counselors.

North American Industry Classification System

North American Industry Classification System (NAICS) is the standard used by federal statistical agencies in classifying business establishments for the purpose of collecting, analyzing, and publishing statistical data related to the U.S. business economy. It was developed under the auspices of the Office of Management and Budget (OMB), and adopted in 1997 to replace the Standard Industrial Classification (SIC) system. NAICS is based on a production-oriented concept. The first two digits designate a *Major Economic Sector* (formerly *Division*), the third digit designates an *Economic Subsector* (formerly *Major Group*), the fourth digit designates an industry group, and the fifth digit designates the *Specific*

TABLE 4.4 ■ **Sample SOC Code and Its Coding Structure**

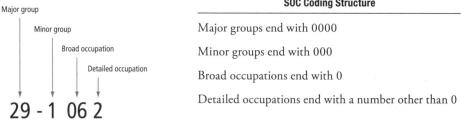

	SOC Coding Structure
Major group	Major groups end with 0000
Minor group	Minor groups end with 000
Broad occupation	Broad occupations end with 0
Detailed occupation	Detailed occupations end with a number other than 0

29 - 1 06 2

TABLE 4.5 ■ Sample NAICS Code and Its Coding Structure

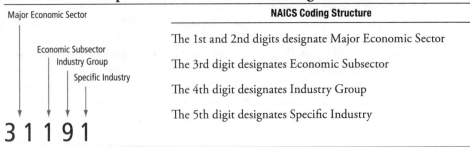

	NAICS Coding Structure
Major Economic Sector	The 1st and 2nd digits designate Major Economic Sector
Economic Subsector	The 3rd digit designates Economic Subsector
Industry Group	The 4th digit designates Industry Group
Specific Industry	The 5th digit designates Specific Industry

3 1 1 9 1

TABLE 4.6 ■ Economic Sectors Under NAICS

Code	Title
11	Agriculture, forestry, fishing, and hunting
21	Mining
22	Utilities
23	Construction
31–33	Manufacturing
41–43	Wholesale trade
44–46	Retail, trade
48–49	Transportation and warehousing
51	Information
52	Finance and insurance
53	Real estate and rental and leasing
54	Professional, scientific and technical services
55	Management of companies and enterprises
56	Administrative and support and waste management and remediation services
61	Educational services
62	Health care and social assistance
71	Arts, entertainment, and recreation
72	Accommodation and food services
81	Other services (except public administration)
91–93	Public administration

Industry. Table 4.5 provides an example of NAICS code to illustrate the structure of coding. Table 4.6 contains a list of all 20 NAICS sectors and their codes.

Occupational Outlook Handbook

The Occupational Outlook Handbook (OOH, http://www.bls.gov/OCO) is developed by the U.S. Department of Labor and its latest edition was revised and updated in 2010. It provides information for over 250 different occupations, which are clustered into 19 broad occupational categories. Information contained in the OOH includes nature of work; typical functions; working conditions; employment prospect; education preparation, training, and other qualifications; employment outlook; wage or salary levels; related occupations; and sources of additional information (BLS, U.S. Department of Labor, 2011a). The information is obtained from trade associations, professional associations, educational institutions, and governmental agencies. The OOH is an excellent resource for rehabilitation counselors to provide job requirements information to their clients to help them make informed vocational decisions (Rubin & Roessler, 2008).

JOB ANALYSIS

Overview

Job analysis is a commonly employed assessment and vocational process used in gathering information and recommending work accommodation in rehabilitation counseling. This section will discuss the purpose of job analysis and introduce its key elements.

▨ LEARNING OBJECTIVES

By the end of this unit you should be able to:

1. Understand the purpose and process of job analysis.
2. Identify key elements and steps involved in job analysis.
3. Identify possible resources for conducting job analysis.

▨ KEY CONCEPTS

Job Analysis

The U.S. Department of Labor (1972) defined job analysis as a systematic study of the worker in terms of what the worker does, the methods and techniques one employs, the resulting products or services one produces, and the traits necessary to accomplish the job. It is an important skillset used by rehabilitation counselors to analyze the essential functions of a job to determine transferrable skills, job accommodation needs, and job placement (selective placement) of people with disabilities (Rubin & Roessler, 2008). Job analysis involves breaking the total job down into tasks and/or subtasks, determining how the job is performed, what is accomplished, where it is performed, and why it is performed. It also involves determining the tools, equipment, machines, work aids and materials used in performing the job. The analysis also involves determining the physical requirements, environmental conditions and special vocational preparation required to perform the job. Specifically, a comprehensive job analysis involves a careful analysis of the following factors that are associated with performing the job well: (1) purpose; (2) DOT data; (3) hiring requirements; (4) salary; (5) tasks and elements; (6) vocational aptitudes; (7) temperaments; (8) physical demands; (9) interests; (10) working conditions; (11) general educational development; (12) specific vocational preparation; (13) tools and machines used; (14) interpersonal interactions; (15) unscheduled demands; (16) architectural barriers. To compare different occupational options, the *Worker Traits Data Book* can be used, which provides ratings on every job found in the DOT in regard to minimal vocational aptitudes, physical demands, environmental conditions, and worker temperaments associated with performing the job well (e.g., temperament for adapting to a variety of work situations; Mayall, 1994).

CAREER DEVELOPMENT THEORIES

Overview

Rehabilitation counselors are involved in providing career assessment, counseling, and planning services to people with disabilities. Career counseling can help people with disabilities crystallize their vocational goals and help them obtain career-based occupations consistent with their interest and abilities. In this section, we will provide an overview of career development theories and their applications in rehabilitation counseling.

▓ LEARNING OBJECTIVES

By the end of this unit you should be able to:

1. Gain basic understanding of theories related to career development.
2. Identify the commonly used assessment instruments and other applications related to each specific theory.

▓ KEY CONCEPTS

Career Development

Rehabilitation counselors are involved in providing career assessment, counseling, and planning services to people with disabilities. Career counseling can help people with disabilities crystallize their vocational goals and help them obtain career-based occupations consistent with their interest and abilities. In this subsection, we will provide an overview of career development theories and their applications in rehabilitation counseling.

Trait and Type Theories

Parsons's (1909) is regarded as the founder of the career development movement. He developed the trait and factor theory. Parsons described trait as an operational characteristic of an individual and factor as a characteristic necessary for successful job performance. Parsons outlined three career development stages, which counselors should support clients to accomplish: (1) self-understanding, (2) awareness of work requirements and conditions, and (3) reasoning on the interaction of self-knowledge and vocational information. These trait and factor concepts strongly influenced other trait and type theories. Trait and type theories assess traits of individuals to match these traits to specific job requirements. This section will discuss the following trait and type theories: person–environment interaction theory (previously trait and factor theory), work adjustment theory, and Holland's typological theory.

Person–Environment Interaction Theory

Parsons's (1909) conceptualization of trait and factor theory is now described as a person–environment interaction theory (Szymanski, Enright, Hershenson, & Ettinger, 2003). The original theoretical underpinnings were that (1) individuals have stable traits; (2) occupations require specific characteristics; and (3) matches can be found between the person and job (Brown, 1990). Yet, current person–environment interaction theories are based on new assumptions: individuals seek out and create environments; degree of fit between person and environment is related to outcomes that can significantly impact the individual and environment; and the process of the person–environment fit is reciprocal (Szymanski et al., 2003).

According to Parsons (1909), it is imperative for the career-selection process to have an evaluation of the client's awareness of self. To assess a client's self-understanding, clinicians can select from an array of assessment instruments. These instruments can evaluate five basic traits and factors: values, personality, interests, aptitudes, and achievement. Table 4.7 provides assessment samples for four of the traits and factors. Achievement samples are not provided as these tests are typically provided after specific classes or training programs to assess level of information learned (Aiken, 2003). Specific examples of aptitude tests are available as these assessments are designed to reveal an individual's expected future ability and performance.

The second critical factor of the person–environment interaction theory is to assess the environment through occupational information. Occupational information can be obtained on working conditions, salary, and job duties (Szymanski et al., 2003). There are several classification systems that can enable a counselor and client to acquire this information. The OOH (2004) has detailed information for over 250 occupations. The handbook is available by book or online. However, the most comprehensive information can be found within the DOT published in 1991 by the Department of Labor. This classification system describes about 12,000 occupations. Designed as a substitute to the DOT, the O*NET, the Occupational Information Network, was recently created as an online occupational classification system. The O*NET only has information for over 1,000 occupations, but new occupations will continue to be added.

The third and final step in the person–environment interaction theory is to synthesize information derived from the client and his or her occupation assessments into a job analysis (Brown, 1990). If the occupational information is related to a client's traits, there may be an optimal match found between person and career environment.

Work Adjustment Theory

The Minnesota Theory of Work Adjustment (MTWA) was originally developed in the 1960s to improve the work adjustment of vocational rehabilitation clients. Lofquist and Dawis (1969, 1991) define work adjustment as a dynamic, ongoing process by which the worker seeks to achieve and maintain congruity with the environment. Thus, work adjustment underscores job tenure and performance, differentiating work adjustment theory from other trait and type theories (Sharf, 2006).

There are two predicting variables of work adjustment, satisfaction, and satisfactoriness (Dawis & Lofquist, 1984). Satisfactoriness refers to the employer's satisfaction with the person's performance. In contrast, satisfaction describes an individual's satisfaction with his or her own work performance. Satisfaction is a key indicator of work adjustment as individuals who are satisfied will demonstrate better overall performance and longer job tenure. Similarly, a worker must demonstrate that he or she has the abilities to meet the demands

TABLE 4.7 ■ **Instruments Used in Person–Environment Interaction Theory**

Area of Measurement	Assessment Instrument
Values	Study of values (SV) Values scale (VS)
Personality	California psychological inventory (CPI) Sixteen personality factor questionnaire (16 PF)
Interests	Kuder career search (KCS) Strong interest inventory (SII) California Occupational Preference Survey (COPS)
Aptitude	Differential aptitude tests (DAT) U.S. Employment Service General Aptitude Test Battery (GATB)

TABLE 4.8 ■ Instruments Used in Work Adjustment Theory

Measurement Area	Assessment of Individual	Assessment of Occupations
Abilities	General Aptitude Test Battery (GATB)	Occupational ability patterns
Values	Minnesota Importance Questionnaire (MIQ)	Minnesota Job Description Questionnaire (MJDQ)
Personality	Instruments are being developed	Instruments are being developed

of the job requirements to achieve job tenure. Congruence between job satisfaction and job satisfactoriness is therefore combined to predict job tenure.

Similar to other trait and type theories, work adjustment theory focuses on assessments of the individual's abilities, values, personality, and interests (Sharf, 2006). Dawis, Lofquist, and colleagues have developed or are working on the development of a variety of assessment instruments described in Table 4.8. However, since Dawis and Lofquist (1984) interpret an individual's interests as an expression of abilities and values, their primary focus is on ability and value assessment.

The next step of work adjustment theory is measuring the abilities and values needed for particular occupations. The Minnesota Job Description Questionnaire (MJDQ; Borgen, Weiss, Tinsley, Dawis, & Lofquist, 1968) was developed to assess how much an occupation reinforces the value patterns of individuals. For instance, individuals may prefer environments where they are busy all the time. As a result, this type of job value would reinforce their personal values. Finally, measurements of abilities are available through the Occupational Ability patterns developed by the U.S. Department of Labor to define abilities that are needed for a multiplicity of jobs.

When matching the individual abilities and values to vocational abilities and values, clinicians have a variety of tools available to them (listed in Table 4.2). If a close match is formed, an individual has an increased chance for job satisfaction and satisfactoriness (Dawis & Lofquist, 1984). The main objective of work adjustment theory is to assist the individual to find permanent and satisfying work adjustment.

Work Personality Theory

Holland's (1966, 1973, 1985, 1992, 1997) theory proposes that an individual's career choice is based on his or her personality type. He also believes that an individual's beliefs, worldviews, generalizations, and stereotypes are usually accurate. By investigating these beliefs and stereotypes, Holland assigns both people and work environments to specific category types (Sharf, 2006).

Holland proposes that personality types and environments in which people live and work can resemble six types of categories: realistic, investigative, artistic, social, enterprising, and conventional (see Figure 4.1). (The Holland types closest to each other are more alike than those farther away, try to compare the types opposite each other on the hexagon.) The coupling of individuals and environments allows for a prediction of vocational, social, and educational outcomes (Holland, 1997).

Assessment instruments can be included in Holland's approach to career counseling to provide additional vocational assistance to individuals. The Self-Directed Search (SDS; Holland, Fritzsche, & Powell, 1994) and the Vocational Preference Inventory (VPI; Holland, 1985) provide objective assessments of personality types. The Career Attitudes and Strategies Inventory (CASI; Holland & Gottfredson, 1994) and the Environmental Identity Scale (EIS; Gottfredson & Holland, 1996) assess work attitudes. Finally, the Position Classification Inventory (Gottfredson & Holland, 1991) classifies positions by

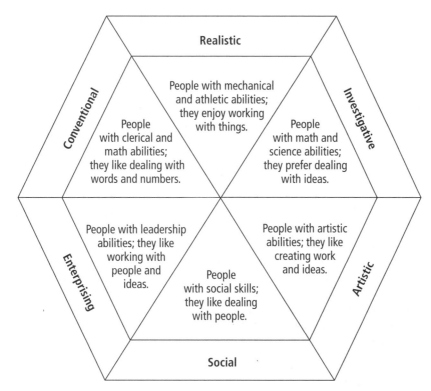

FIGURE 4.1 ■ Holland's personality types.

Holland personality type. These assessment instruments can provide objective information to clinicians when assessing individuals and their environments.

SPECIAL FOCUS THEORIES

Overview

A number of theories have been developed that describe career development in distinctive ways. Many of these theories have applied psychological theory or constructs to the career decision-making process. This section will review the following special focus theories: Super's theory, Krumboltz's theory, and social cognitive theory.

■ LEARNING OBJECTIVES

By the end of this unit you should be able to:

1. Understanding the other special focus theories related to career development.
2. Identify the assessment instruments and intervention strategies developed for each specific theory.

■ KEY CONCEPTS

Life-Span Theory

Super's research (1970, 1994) has explained the career developmental stages of the life span and has infiltrated most of the current career counseling in the United States (Szymanski et al., 2003). The key tenets of this developmental theory for adults encapsulate two major concepts: (1) life role and (2) life stage.

The six major life roles are: child, student, leisurite, citizen, worker, and homemaker (see Figure 4.2). Super (1990) hypothesizes that individuals will identify importance of work differently at varying periods in their life. Clinicians can administer the Salience Inventory (Super & Nevill, 1986) to assess the saliency of roles at any given point in time.

Not only do roles change because of saliency, roles also change due to nature of involvement. Involvement can be assessed by participation, commitment, knowledge, and values expectations. Super et al. developed specific assessment instruments to measure knowledge and values expectations. The Career Development Inventory (Super, Thompson, Lindeman, Jordan, & Myers, 1981) measures knowledge about work roles, and the Values Scale (Super & Nevill, 1986) and Salience Inventory measure values expectations for work roles (Super & Nevill, 1986).

The concept of life stages is the second component of Super's life-span theory (1990). The life stages are age related as individuals typically go through a temporal order of the stages of exploration, establishment, maintenance, and decline or disengagement. Yet, it is possible that an individual can experience a stage at any time in life. The Adult Career Concerns Inventory (Super, Thompson, Lindeman, Myers, & Jordan, 1986) can assist counselors in identifying life stages. After life stage and role assessment, counselors are able to provide appropriate and individualized career development services.

Social Learning Theory

Krumboltz's social learning theory reflects one of the earlier applications of Bandura's (1977) social learning concepts to career development (Hackett & Lent, 1992). This social learning

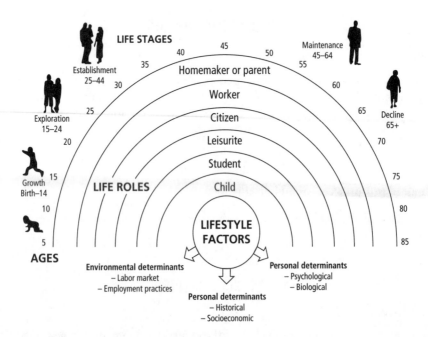

FIGURE 4.2   ■   The life roles rainbow.

theory describes how individuals make career decisions based on cognition and behavior. The following four categories of factors influence career decision making: genetic endowment environmental conditions and events; learning experiences and task approach skills. The subsequent outcomes of learning experiences may include: (1) self-observation generalizations, (2) worldview generalizations, (3) task approach skills, and (4) actions (Mitchell & Krumboltz, 1990, 1996). Although many other career development theories emphasize abilities and environmental events, social learning theory emphasizes the significance of learning experiences and task approach skills (Mitchell & Krumboltz, 1996).

In recent work, Krumboltz and associates have emphasized the change within the individual and environment. Thus, the second part of the theory is that clients need to expand their capabilities and interests, clients need to prepare for changing work tasks, clients need to be empowered to take a stance, and counselors need to provide vocational counseling at all career development stages (Mitchell & Krumboltz, 1996). Therefore, Krumboltz (1996) believes that career counselors should implement initial, ongoing, and follow-up vocational services.

Cognitive and behavioral strategies have been developed to assist clients with career development (Sharf, 2006). Behavioral strategies may integrate the following techniques: reinforcement, role models, role-playing, and simulation (Krumboltz, 1970). Cognitive strategies may include goal clarification, reframing, resolving discrepancies, and cognitive rehearsal (Krumboltz, 1996). Krumboltz's theory suggests that counselors integrate cognitive and behavioral interventions into career counseling to assist clients with career selection.

Social Cognitive Career Theory

In the 1980s, theorists began applying Bandura's (1982) concepts of self-efficacy to career development (Sharf, 2006). Self-efficacy is the belief that one can accomplish tasks successfully. Most recently Lent and Hackett (1994) and Lent, Brown, and Hackett (2000) emphasized self-efficacy, outcome expectancies, and personal goals as essential variables in an interaction system of (1) personal attributes, (2) external environmental factors, and (3) overt behavior. Therefore, social cognition plays a pivotal role in the career decision-making process.

Assessment instruments are an essential factor of social cognitive theory (Sharf, 2006). Clients can acquire important information for career decision making from interest, values, and performance measures. Moreover, clinicians can utilize information to support self-efficacy and discuss outcome expectancies.

CAREER COUNSELING

Overview

In this section, we will provide rehabilitation counselors with a framework for the implementation of career development theories and suggest strategies for providing career counseling to individuals with disabilities.

LEARNING OBJECTIVES

By the end of this unit you should be able to:

1. Identify important considerations when providing career counseling to individuals with disabilities.
2. Identify the stages of the career development process and the relationship with career counseling.

▓ KEY CONCEPTS

Applications for Individuals With Disabilities

Person–environment interactions, the fundamental components of trait and type theory, have long been a focus of assessment and planning approaches to vocational rehabilitation (e.g., Rubin & Roessler, 1994). More recently, both trait and type theories and special focus theories have been described to have great potential applications to individuals with disabilities (Szymanski et al., 2003). However, clinicians should not solely utilize career development theoretical approaches when providing vocational rehabilitation services to individuals with disabilities. Although career development theories have been suggested to be applicable to individuals with disabilities, these theories must be applied with an understanding of the limitations resulting from disability and possible need for accommodations. These theoretical approaches and related assessment instruments can be included in a rehabilitation counselor's toolkit, but counselors should still consider the whole person, including the disability impact.

Salomone (1988) has suggested strategies for providing career counseling to individuals with disabilities. Salomone (1988) delineated the career development process in ordinal stages. He suggested adding two stages to Parsons's original three stages. This career counseling approach posits helping clients to reach the following steps: (1) understand self; (2) understand work and work environments; (3) understand the decision-making process; (4) implement career and educational decisions; and (5) adjust and adapt to the world of work and school. These stages may provide rehabilitation counselors with a framework for the implementation of career development theories. Rehabilitation interventions may need to combine career development theories and psychosocial adaptation strategies to help clients develop coping skills, increase community participation, and achieve higher levels of work adjustment.

VOCATIONAL CONSULTATION AND JOB PLACEMENT

Overview

Job placement is one of the most important services in rehabilitation counseling. In this section, we will provide an overview of job placement and discuss the essential skill sets to be considered.

▓ LEARNING OBJECTIVES

By the end of this unit you should be able to:

1. Understand the concept of job placement.
2. Identify the difference between specific employability, general employability, and placeability skills needed for job placement.

▓ KEY CONCEPTS

Job Placement

To obtain and retain competitive employment in integrated settings, individuals with disabilities must develop appropriate specific employability, general employability, and placeability skills (Chan et al., 1997; Chan, Leahy, & Saunders, 2005). *Specific employability skills* (e.g., intelligence, aptitudes, temperament, physical capacity, job knowledge, and skills) are job specific and vary from one job class to another. Vocational behavior and skills in specific employability are important in predicting job performance. Conversely, *general employability skills*, also known as general work personality, are not job specific. General employability skills are required in every job. Examples of these behaviors include grooming and hygiene, attendance, punctuality, safety consciousness, interpersonal relationships, frustration tolerance, work stamina, productivity, and so on (Chan et al., 1997). General employability behaviors and skills are important in the prediction of job maintenance behavior. *Placeability* is often referred to as the degree of sophistication in job-acquiring skills. Although placeability has little to do with the person's ability to perform a job, it is an important factor to evaluate in rehabilitation, because it addresses a person's ability to obtain a job. Job-seeking behaviors are evaluated in terms of the client's resourcefulness, motivation, skills in writing resumes and cover letters, interview behavior, and so on (Chan et al., 1997, 2005). As a process, job placement is referred to as a set of activities involved in locating a suitable job for VR consumers and getting them hired for the job (Rubin & Roessler, 2008). Specifically, job placement assistance include job-seeking skills training, direct placement, job development, supported employment, and demand-side job placement.

Job-Seeking Skills Training

Rubin and Roessler (2008) indicated that poor job-seeking skills is the main culprit for poor-quality employment outcomes for people with disabilities. Some of the job-seeking skills deficits of rehabilitation clients include (a) lack of awareness of techniques needed to secure job leads, (b) difficulty explaining employment significance of educational background, job skills, and job history; (c) inability discussing disability-related issues and accommodation needs appropriately in job interviews; (d) deficiency in completing job applications and preparing job resumes; and (e) failure to look for work frequently and dress appropriately for the job interview. Job-seeking skills training is designed to provide practice opportunity and to teach clients to:

a. determine job suitability
b. identify vocational strengths and limitations
c. prepare a resume
d. perform in a job interview
e. secure job leads

One of the most successful job-seeking skills training programs is the "job club" approach. In addition to providing clients with typical job seeking skills training, the job club approach seeks to enhance motivation by using techniques such as a buddy system, family support, role models, and ample practices in completing job application, writing resumes, and performing job interviews. Azrin and Philips (1979) reported that in their experimental study, 95% of the job club members were employed compared with 28% of the rehabilitation clients in a traditional job-seeking skills program. However, high drop-out rate (70%) for people with severe mental illness was reported as a problem by Corrigan et al. (1995).

Direct Placement Intervention

Selective placement is defined as the precise and detailed matching of the person's abilities with the work environment and the requirements of the job. Direct placement intervention requires the aggressive marketing of the benefits of hiring people with disabilities to employers and the ability to supply employers with qualified candidates with disabilities using selective placement. Job analysis is essential to successful selective placement and is used to determine person–job fit and the modifications that can be used to enhance the appropriate fit.

JOB PLACEMENT ASSISTANCE

Overview

Job placement assistance includes job-seeking skills training, direct placement, job development, supported employment, and demand-side job placement. This section will provide an overview of job placement assistance and discuss different supported employment approaches.

◼ LEARNING OBJECTIVES

By the end of this unit you should be able to:

1. Identify various types of job placement assistance and the difference between direct placement and client-centered placement.
2. Understand the concepts related to the supported employment model.
3. Identify the major components of various supported employment approaches, such as the train–place–train–follow-up (TPTF) and the place–train–follow-up (PTF) approaches.
4. Understand the relationship of disability to job analysis and job placement.

◼ KEY CONCEPTS

Supported Employment

The supported employment model is a wide-ranging selective placement approach (Salomone, 1996). This type of placement highlights job preparation for individuals with severe disabilities (e.g., schizophrenia and mental retardation) in competitive employment settings and continued follow-up of services during the course of employment. Rubin and Roessler (2001) stated that supported employment's main focus with on job-site training, advocacy, long-term job retention, and follow-up services is what distinguishes this work model from other job placement approaches. The supported work approach places clients who do not have all the needed work and social skills necessary for immediate job success, which is a noteworthy variation from conventional placement approaches that involve that before placement can occur, the client must be job ready (Wehman & Kregel,1985).

There are a number of variations of the supported employment model. Among the most prevalent are the train–place–train–follow-up (TPTF; Lagomarcino, 1986) and the place–train–follow-up (PTF; Wehman, 1986) approaches. The TPTF is composed of four major parts: (1) surveying potential employers to establish significant vocational and social survival skills that require training, (2) training individuals with the purpose of performing such skills, (3) placing trainee clients in competitive employment settings, and (4) supplying long-term follow-up training (Lagomarcino, 1986). The first part of this approach stresses the identification of prospective job placements within the community and conducting a job analysis for the available positions. The second part focuses on training by means of time-limited pre-employment training programs. Individuals are placed within community-based training programs in local industries, for a period of time no longer than 6 months, where they learn the necessary and required skills for competitive employment. The third part of the approach, placement, provides clients with the necessary services to transition from training to competitive employment. The last part of the TPTF approach centers on providing follow-up services after placement and is characterized by being shorter in duration and more intense than the training phase.

The PTF approach is composed of four major components: (1) job placement, (2) job-site training, (3) ongoing assessment, and (4) job retention (Wehman, 1986). Each component of this approach involves particular activities that must be performed by staff. In job placement, staff activities should include: (a) structuring job search attempts for the client and matching his or her strengths to the job's needs, (b) on behalf of clients, interacting with employers, (c) arranging transportation for travel related to training, and (d) encouraging the involvement of client's families to assist in identifying suitable jobs. During job-site training, staff activities should include: (a) providing clients with training in behavioral skills and social skills at the job site as needed, (b) working with the client's employer and coworkers to provide help to the client, and (c) aiding the client and coworkers in their adjustment to each other. In ongoing assessment, staff activities should include: (a) attaining feedback on the client's development from the employer, (b) supervising the client's progress in learning the job through observation directly, and (c) occasionally assessing the client and the client's family satisfaction with the program. In the last component, job retention, staff activities should include: (a) systematically fading the staff intervention at the job placement, (b) following-up with the client's employer, and (c) helping the client to find a new job if needed (Wehman, 1986). In both the approaches discussed above, as well as for all other approaches with a selective placement orientation, job analysis plays a fundamental role. The TPTF approach emphasizes job training before placing the client in a permanent competitive job; whereas, the PTF approach centers on placing the client at a specific job setting where she or he can attain on-the-job training and can also expect long-term employment (Rubin & Roessler, 2001).

Client-Centered Placement

Salomone (1996) advocated the use of client-centered placement because the selective placement approach of doing things for clients may impair the dignity, independence, and self-confidence of clients. He indicated that it is more effective to teach clients job-seeking and job-retaining skills. Client-centered placement is a subset of psychoeducational counseling with the goal of helping clients to become self-directed, self-motivated individuals with a can-do attitude. It is an empowerment model that encourages clients to take charge of their own lives and to develop requisite attitudes and skills to succeed in obtaining and maintaining meaningful employment. Client-centered placement is not independent job seeking because it requires frequent meetings with the counselor to develop effective job search strategies. However, the client is responsible for acting as his or her own agent in making contacts with employers and setting up job interviews.

▦ INTERNET RESOURCES

Occupational Information
American's Career InfoNet
http://www.acinet.org/

O*NET Online
http://www.onetonline.org/

Labor Market Information
Bureau of Labor Statistics—Employment Projections (Occupational Data)
http://www.bls.gov/emp/ep_data_occupational_data.htm

The Riley Guide—Employment and Industrial Trend
http://www.rileyguide.com/trends.html#gov

Career Development

Minnesota's Career, Education, and Job Resources
http://www.iseek.org

National Career Development Association
http://associationdatabase.com/aws/NCDA/pt/sp/home_page

Quintessential Careers: College, Careers, and Jobs Guide
http://www.quintcareers.com

Job Placement

Career & Job News, Work, Employment Salary Trend
http://online.wsj.com/public/page/news-career-jobs.html

Susan Ireland's Resume Site
http://susanireland.com

The Riley Guide—Using Employment Kiosks and Online Job Applications
http://www.rileyguide.com/kiosk.html

Job Banks

America's Job Bank Transition
http://www.ajb.dni.us

Job Search, Employment, and Career Site
http://www.careerbuilder.com
http://monster.com
http://www.gettinghired.com

▦ MULTIPLE CHOICE QUESTIONS AND ANSWER KEY

1. What is the first digit of the DOT represents?
   A. Occupational category
   B. Occupational group
   C. Occupational division
   D. Occupational cluster

2. The North American Industry Classification System (NAICS) is the standard used by Federal statistical agencies in classifying business establishments. NAICS covers how many business sectors?
   A. 12
   B. 20
   C. 30
   D. 40

3. The founder of the vocational guidance movement was:
   A. Donald Super
   B. Frank Parsons
   C. Albert Bandura
   D. John Holland

4. Person–environmental interaction and work adjustment theory are BOTH what kind of career development theory?
   A. Trait and factor theory
   B. Developmental theory
   C. Special focus theory
   D. Trait and type theory

5. What career development theories originally described the career development process in three stages that involve self, work, and the interaction between self and work?
   A. John Holland

B. Albert Bandura
C. Gail Hackett
D. Frank Parsons

6. Which of the following assessment instruments would be considered a measure for personality?
    A. California Psychological Inventory (CPI)
    B. Kuder Career Search (KCS)
    C. Strong Interest Inventory (SII)
    D. General Aptitude Test Battery (GATB)
    E. None of the above

7. What career development theory was initially designed for vocational rehabilitation clients in Minnesota?
    A. Trait and factor theory
    B. Social cognitive theory
    C. Work adjustment theory
    D. Krumboltz's theory
    E. None of the above

8. The place-train-follow-up (PTF) is composed of four major components, which one of the next elements is not a component of the PTF.
    A. Job placement
    B. Job-site training
    C. Ongoing assessment
    D. Supplying long-term follow-up training

9. The train-place-train-follow-up (TPTF) is composed of four major parts, which of the following components is a component of the TPFF:
    A. The first component of this approach stresses the identification of prospective job placements within the community and conducting a job analysis
    B. Structuring job search efforts for the client and matching his or her strengths to the job's needs
    C. Supervising the client's progress in learning the job through observation directly
    D. The States Rights Rehabilitation Act of 1902

10. Sophistication in job-acquiring skills is referred to as:
    A. Placeability skills
    B. Specific employability skills
    C. General employability skills
    D. Job interviewing skills

ANSWER KEY

1. A; 2. B; 3. B; 4. D; 5. D; 6. A; 7. C; 8. C; 9. A; 10. A

ADVANCED MULTIPLE CHOICE QUESTIONS

1. The DOT covers over ___ jobs in the U.S. economy?
    A. 800
    B. 1,000
    C. 5,000
    D. 12,000

2. A rehabilitation counselor is working with a client to find him or her a job, the counselor has explored the client's work values, has some idea of his or her skill levels and has identified some of his or her career interests. Now, it is time for the counselor and client to examine the employment prospects of these career paths. Which of the following should they use?

    A. *Dictionary of Occupational Titles* (DOT)
    B. Worker Traits Data Book (WTD)
    C. Standard Occupational Classification System (SOC)
    D. Occupational Outlook Handbook (OOH)

3. The first career development theory was:
    A. Super's life-span theory
    B. Work adjustment theory
    C. Trait and factor theory
    D. Social learning theory

4. The two main concepts of work adjustment theory are:
    A. Life role and developmental stage
    B. Satisfaction and satisfactoriness
    C. Self-efficacy and outcome expectancies
    D. Trait and factor

5. True or False: According to Holland's theory, personality types and work environments can resemble six types: realistic, investigative, artistic, social, enterprising, and conventional

6. Which one the following categories of factors DO NOT influence career decision making in Krumboltz's theory?
    A. Personality type
    B. Genetic endowment
    C. Learning experiences
    D. Task-approach skills
    E. Environmental events and conditions

7. What concepts of the social-cognitive theory of career development are borrowed from Albert Bandura?
    A. Social learning experiences
    B. Self-efficacy and outcomes expectancies
    C. Social relationship patterns
    D. Societal values

8. Job seeking skills training seek to teach clients
    A. Prepare resume
    B. Secure job leads
    C. Perform interviews
    D. All the above

9. What is the main features of the "job club" that is different from other job seeking skills program?
    A. The use of a "buddy" system
    B. The use of selective placement
    C. The use of client-centered placement
    D. All the above

10. According to Paul Salomone, the negative consequences of selective placement include:
    A. Increase client dependence
    B. Decrease self-confidence
    C. Impair dignity
    D. All the above

▥ ANSWER KEY AND EXPLANATION OF ANSWERS

1-D: The DOT includes description for over 12,000 jobs in the U.S. economy. However, the DOT has been replaced by O*NET that analyzes jobs using an empirical framework and methodology.

2-D: Besides nature of work, typical functions, working conditions, education preparation, and other qualifications needed, OOH also includes information about employment prospect, employment outlook, wage or salary levels, and additional information of other related occupations.

3-C: Frank Parsons developed trait and factor theory in 1909. This was the first career development theory and it has had a significant impact on other trait and type theories (e.g., work adjustment theory).

4-B: Satisfaction and satisfactoriness are the two key concepts of work adjustment theory. Satisfaction describes an individual's job reinforce needs. Satisfactoriness is the employer's satisfaction with the individual's performance.

5-True: Holland developed six types of personality types and work environments. He believed that individuals would have more successful vocational outcomes if their types of environments and personality resembled each other.

6-A: Personality type does not influence career decision making in Krumboltz's theory. The four factors that influence decision making are genetic endowment, environment conditions and events, learning experiences, and task–approach skills.

7-B: Self-efficacy and outcome expectancies were represented in the social cognitive theory of career development. These constructs are theorized to impact career decision making. This distinguishes social cognitive theory from Krumboltz's social learning theory. Krumboltz's theory incorporates Bandura's concept of social learning experiences. Krumboltz believes that prior learning experiences will impact career decision making.

8-D: Poor job seeking skills is the main culprit for poor-quality employment outcomes for people with disabilities. Helping client determines job suitability, identify vocational strengths, prepare resume, perform interviews, and locating job leads are key contents in job-seeking skills training.

9-A: Job club has a strong emphasis on motivational factors including the use of a buddy system, family support, and role models.

10-D: Selective placement is commonly used to connect VR consumers to employment. The basic assumption is that skills and aptitudes of workers can be measured reliably and accurately and that job requirements could also be measured accurately and reliably, allowing the rehabilitation counselor to use a match or selling approach to connect people with disabilities to employment. However, selective placement fosters dependency and discourage skill building leading the client to return to the counselor for additional selective placement services.

▧ REFERENCES

Aiken, L. R. (2003). *Psychological testing and assessment* (11th ed.). Boston: Allyn & Bacon.

Azrin, N. H., & Philip, R. A. (1979). Job club method for the handicapped: A comparative outcome study. *Rehabilitation Counseling Bulletin, 23*, 144–155.

Bandura, A. (1977). *Social learning theory*. Englewood Cliffs, NJ: Prentice Hall.

Bandura, A. (1982). Self-efficacy mechanism in human agency. *American Psychologist, 37*, 122–147.

Borgen, F. H., Weiss, D. J., Tinsley, H. E., Dawis, R. V., & Lofquist, L. H. (1968). *Minnesota Job Description Questionnaire*. Minneapolis, MN: University of Minnesota, Psychology Department, Vocational Psychology Research.

Brown, D. (1990). Trait and factory theory. In D. Brown & L. Brooks (Eds.), *Career choice and development: Applying contemporary theories to practice* (2nd ed., pp. 13–36). San Francisco, CA: Jossey-Bass.

Bureau of Labor Statistics, U.S. Department of Labor. (2010). The employment situation: July 2010 [Press release]. Retrieved from http://www.bls.gov/schedule/archives/empsit_nr.htm#2010

Bureau of Labor Statistics, U.S. Department of Labor. (May 8, 2011a). *Occupational outlook handbook* (2010–2011 Edition). Retrieved from http://www.bls.gov/oco

Bureau of Labor Statistics, U.S. Department of Labor. (May 8, 2011b). *Standard occupational classification* (2010 Edition). Retrieved from http://www.bls.gov/soc

Chan, F., Leahy, M. J., & Saunders, J. L. (Eds). (2005). *Case management for rehabilitation health professionals (2nd ed.).* Osage Beach, MO: Aspen Professional Services.

Chan, F., Shaw, L., McMahon, B. T., Koch, L., & Strauser, D. (1997). A model for enhancing consumer-counselor working relationships in rehabilitation. *Rehabilitation Counseling Bulletin, 41,* 122–137.

Chan, F., Strauser, D., Gervey, R., & Lee, E. (2010). Introduction to demand-side factors related to employment of people with disabilities. *Journal of Occupational Rehabilitation, 20*(4), 407–411.

Corrigan, P. W., Reedy, P., Thadani, D., & Ganet, M. (1995). Correlates of participation and completion in a job club for clients with psychiatric disability. *Rehabilitation Counseling Bulletin, 39,* 42–53.

Dawis, R. V., & Lofquist, L. H. (1984). *A psychological theory of work adjustment.* Minneapolis, MN: University of Minnesota Press.

Dictionary of occupational titles (4th ed.). (1991). Washington, DC: U.S. Department of Labor, Employment and Training Administration.

Dunn, D. J. (1974). *Placement services in the vocational rehabilitation program.* Menomonie: University of Wisconsin-Stout, Dept. of Rehabilitation & Manpower Services, Research & Training Center.

Dutta, A., Gervey, R., Chan, F., Chou, C. C, & Ditchman, N. (2008). Vocational rehabilitation services and employment outcomes of people with disabilities: A United States study. *Journal of Occupation Rehabilitation, 18,* 326–334.

Gottfredson, G. D., & Holland, J. L. (1991). *Position Classification Inventory professional manual.* Odessa, FL: Psychological Assessment Resources.

Gottfredson, G. D., & Holland, J. L. (1996). *Dictionary of Holland occupational codes* (3rd ed.). Odessa, FL: Psychological Assessment Resources.

Hackett, G., & Lent, R. W. (1992). Theoretical advances and current inquiry in career psychology. In S. D. Brown & R. W. Lent (Eds.), *Handbook of counseling psychology* (2nd ed., pp. 419–451).

Holland, J. L. (1966). *The psychology of vocational choice.* Waltham, MA: Blaisdell.

Holland, J. L. (1973). *Making vocational choices: A theory of careers.* Englewood Cliffs, NJ: Prentice-Hall.

Holland, J. L. (1985). *Making vocational choices: A theory of vocational personalities and work environments* (2nd ed.). Englewood Cliffs, NJ: Prentice-Hall.

Holland, J. L. (1992). *Making vocational choices: A theory of vocational personalities and work environments.* Odessa, FL: Psychological Assessment Resources.

Holland, J. L. (1997). *Making vocational choices: A theory of vocational personalities and work environments* (3rd ed.). Odessa, FL: Psychological Assessment Resources.

Holland, J. L., Fritzsche, B. A., & Powell, P. G. (1994). *The Self-Directed Search (SDS) technical manual.* Odessa, FL: Psychological Assessment Resources.

Holland, J. L., & Gottfredson, G. D. (1994). *The career attitudes and strategies inventory.* Odessa, FL: Psychological Assessment Resources.

Kaye, S. H. (2010). The impact of 2007-09 recession on workers with disabilities. *Monthly Labor Review, 133,* 19–30.

Krumboltz, J. D. (1970). *Job experience kits.* Chicago: Science Research Associates.

Krumboltz, J. D. (1996). A learning theory of career counseling. In M. L. Savickas & W. B. Walsh (Eds.), *Handbook of career counseling theory and practice* (pp. 55–80). Palo Alto, CA: Consulting Psychologists Press.

Lagomarcino, T. (1986). Community services. In F. Rusch (Ed.), *Competitive employment issues and strategies* (pp.65–75). Baltimore: Brookes.

Lent, R. W., Brown, S. D., & Hackett, G. (2000). Contextual supports and barriers to career choice: A social cognitive analysis. *Journal of Counseling Psychology, 47,* 36–49.

Lent, R. W., & Hackett, G. (1994). Sociocognitive mechanisms of personal agency in career development: Pan theoretical prospects. In M. L. Savickas & R. W. Lent (Ed.), *Convergence in career development: Implications for science and practice* (pp. 77–101). Palo Alto, CA: Consulting Psychologists Press.

Lofquist, L. H., & Dawis, R. V. (1969). *Adjustment to work: A psychological view of man's problems in a work-oriented society.* New York, NY: Appleton-Century-Crofts.

Lofquist, L. H., & Dawis, R. V. (1991). *Essentials of person-environment correspondence counseling.* Minneapolis, MN: University of Minnesota Press.

Mayall, D. (1994). *The worker trait data book.* Indianapolis, IN: JIST.

Mitchell, L. K., & Krumboltz, J. D. (1990). Social learning approach to career decision making: Krumboltz's theory. In D. Brown & L. Brooks (Eds.), *Career choice and development: Applying contemporary theories to practice* (2nd ed., pp. 145–196). San Francisco, CA: Jossey-Bass.

Mitchell, L. K., & Krumboltz, J. D. (1996). Krumboltz's learning theory of career choice and counseling. In D. Brown & L. Brooks (Eds.), *Career choice and development* (3rd ed., pp. 233–280). San Francisco: Jossey-Bass.

Occupational outlook handbook. (2004). Washington, DC: U.S. Department of Labor.

Parsons, F. (1909). *Choosing a vocation.* Boston, MA: Houghton Mifflin.

Rubin, S. E., & Roessler, R. T. (1994). *Foundations of the vocational rehabilitation process* (4th ed.). Austin, TX: Pro-Ed.

Rubin, S. E., & Roessler, R. T. (2001). *Foundations of the vocational rehabilitation process.* Austin, TX: PRO-ED.

Rubin, S. E., & Roessler, R. (2008). *Foundations of the vocational rehabilitation process* (6th ed.). Austin, TX: Pro-Ed.

Salomone, P. R. (1988). Career counseling: Steps and stages beyond Parsons. *Career Development Quarterly, 36,* 218–221.

Salomone, P. R. (1996). Career counseling and job placement: Theory and practice. In E. M. Szymanski & R. M. Parker (Eds.), *Work and disability: Issues and strategies in career development and job placement* (pp. 365–420). Austin, TX: Pro-Ed.

Sharf, R. S. (2006). *Applying career development theory to counseling.* Belmont, CA: Brooks/Cole.

Super, D. E. (1970). *Work values inventory.* Boston, MA: Houghton Mifflin.

Super, D. E. (1990). A life-span, life-space approach to career development. In D. Brown & L. Brooks (Eds.), *Career choice and development: Applying contemporary theories to practice* (2nd ed., pp. 197–261). San Francisco, CA: Jossey-Bass.

Super, D. E. (1994). A life span, life space perspective on convergence. In M. L. Savickas & R. W. Lent (Eds.), *Convergence in career development theories: Implications for science and practices* (pp. 63–74). Palo Alto, CA: Consulting Psychologists Press.

Super, D. E., & Nevill, D. D. (1986). *The salience inventory.* Palo Alto, CA: Consulting Psychologists Press.

Super, D. E., Thompson, A. S., Lindeman, R. H., Jordan, J. P., & Myers, R. A. (1981). *The career development inventory, school and college forms.* Palo Alto, CA: Consulting Psychologists Press.

Super, D. E., Thompson, A. S., Lindeman, R. H., Myers, R. A., & Jordan, J. P. (1986). *Adult Career Concerns Inventory.* Palo Alto, CA: Consulting Psychologists Press.

Szymanski, E. M., Enright, M. S., Hershenson, D. B., & Ettinger, J. (2003). Career development theories, constructs, and research: Implications for people with disabilities. In E. M. Szymanski & R. M. Parker (Eds.), *Work and disability: Issues and strategies in career development and job placement* (2nd ed., pp. 91–153). Austin, TX: Pro-Ed.

U.S. Department of Labor. (1991). *Dictionary of occupational titles* (4th ed.). Washington, DC: U.S. Government Printing Office.

U.S. Department of Labor. (1972). *Handbook for analyzing jobs.* Washington, DC: U.S. Government Printing Office.

Wehman, P. (1986). Competitive employment in Virginia. In F. Rusch (Ed.), *Competitive employment issues and strategies* (pp. 23–33). Baltimore, MD: Brookes.

Wehman, P., & Kregel, J. (1985). A supported work approach to competitive employment of individuals with moderate and severe handicaps. In P. Wehman & J. Hill (Eds.), *Competitive employment for persons with mental retardation* (pp. 20–45). Richmond, VA: Rehabilitation Research and Training Center, Virginia Commonwealth University.

Counseling Approaches and Principles

5

JULIE CHRONISTER, ARLENE BAGAIN, MAUREEN FITZGERALD, JEFFREY F. THOMAS, AND MISTY TRUJILLO

This chapter reviews the fundamental counseling approaches and principles that are critical to the counseling process. Areas reviewed in this chapter include:

- Individual counseling and personality theory
- Mental health counseling
- Counseling skills and techniques development
- Gender issues in counseling
- Conflict resolution and negotiation strategies
- Termination of counseling relationships
- Consumer empowerment and rights
- Boundaries of confidentiality
- Ethics in the counseling relationship
- Multicultural issues in counseling
- Counselor supervision

INDIVIDUAL COUNSELING AND PERSONALITY THEORY

Overview

This section reviews the major counseling theories including psychodynamic (psychoanalytic, analytic, and individual psychology), humanistic (client-centered, existential, and Gestalt), and behavioral and cognitive-behavioral approaches (cognitive-behavioral, social learning theory, rational emotive behavior therapy [REBT], and reality therapy).

■ LEARNING OBJECTIVE

By the end of this unit you should be able to:

1. Communicate a basic understanding of established counseling theories and their relationship to personality theory.

■ KEY CONCEPTS

Psychoanalytic Counseling Theory

Psychoanalytic counseling theory is most notably linked to Sigmund Freud. In Freud's drive theory, psychological functioning is based on sexual and aggressive urges that are molded by early body and family experiences (Livneh & Siller, 2004). Personality structure comprised three components including the id, ego, and superego. The id is driven by the pleasure principle and needs immediate gratification regarding all needs such as eating, sleeping, and sex. The ego is driven by the reality principle that attempts to deal with the realities of the world. The ego also serves as the mediator between the id and the moralistic superego. The superego is a person's moralistic component and thus strives toward perfection. These components of a person's mind drive every behavior and emerge at different developmental points. For example, the superego develops as a person receives messages of right and wrong from parents and others. A child's ego develops as they learn that the world has limited resources. The id is present at birth and is considered innate and wants its needs met from the moment of birth (Halbur & Halbur, 2006).

Freud identified specific psychosexual stages that all people experience. These stages are described in Chapter 3 and include the anal, phallic, latency, and genital stages. As people develop, they move through these developmental stages; if they successfully move through and meet these developmental challenges, psychological health occurs. If psychological struggles are significant, an individual may get stuck at a stage or become fixated at the stage. To avoid and manage psychological pain, people use defense mechanisms to bury the pain deep into the unconsciousness. Defenses such as projection, repression, rationalization, sublimation, reaction formation, regression, and compensation keep traumatic thoughts and emotions from interrupting people's conscious life (Halbur & Halbur, 2006; Livneh & Siller, 2004). The goals of therapy are for the client to work through repressed memories and repair or remove unhealthy defense mechanisms. Because this approach conceptualizes current difficulties as rooted in experiences, helping clients re-experience and move beyond experiences are critical to effective psychoanalytic counseling. As such, a primary focus is to bring the unconscious forward and work through it (Halbur & Halbur, 2006). The techniques commonly used include allowing the client to free associate, which brings the unconscious forward. In addition, confrontation, clarification, interpretation, and working through are distinct techniques in psychoanalysis (Livneh & Siller, 2004). Confrontation involves making explicit to the client the phenomenon in question; clarification refers to activities that place the psychic phenomenon being analyzed into sharp focus; interpretation is "the ultimate and decisive instrument . . . to make conscious the unconscious meaning, source, history, mode or cause of a given psychic event" (Greenson, 1967, p. 39). Finally, working through involves a complex set of techniques and processes that take place after an insight has been given that include ongoing, repetitive explanations of the resistances that prevent change from occurring (Livneh & Siller, 2004).

Analytic Counseling Theory

Analytic counseling theory was developed by Carl Jung. Jung believed that people are holistic individuals connected at an ancestral level. While he agreed with Freud that people possess physical drives, he believed that one's main life pursuit was to move intentionally toward individuation (wholeness). Jung's view of humans was positive. Although Jung did acknowledge that peoples' past influenced their current situation, he was less deterministic and assumed people actively moved toward their potential and development occurs throughout the lifespan. Jung coined the term psyche, which comprised three major systems: the ego, personal unconscious, and the ancestral collective unconscious. The ego, people's current thoughts, feelings, and reflections, is readily accessible and contains current experiences. The personal unconscious holds those memories and thoughts that are more difficult to reach but accessible. The collective unconscious is the deepest level of the psyche and is difficult to access. Jung believed that all cultures have common themes and stories that comprise a deeper, ancestral level of our psyche. He posited that deep within this ancestral level people contain archetypes, which are the basic building blocks of personality. For example, all people contain a shadow, the wise one, healer, anima (female side), animus (male side), and hero images. When people have life experiences, they build on these archetypes to shape their personality (Halbur & Halbur, 2004). The main goal of therapy is to integrate the psyche. The integrated self allows individuals to ultimately become fully functioning individuals. The techniques most prominent in this approach include a warm relationship between the client and counselor, dream analysis, and archetypal analysis.

Individual Psychology

Individual psychology, was founded by Alfred Adler. Adler believed that humans are motivated primarily by socialization. *Gemeinschaftsgefuhl*, typically translated as social interest, is the core tenet of individual psychology. Like Freud, Adler believed that one's primary personality was constructed and determined at an early age; however, he focused on the development and role one plays in the family. Adler believed that people are teleological (goal-directed) organisms and that people have free will, free choice, and the power to choose their behavior. Consequently, individuals can choose new goals and behaviors. Adler described humans' constant striving to become their ideal person in terms of fictional finalism. Adler also believed that people are born with a natural sense of inferiority, or a feeling of being "less than." This is a normal experience and serves as a powerful motivator of human behavior. As such, people strive to achieve superiority to compensate for feelings of inferiority. If individuals do not have a sense of superiority, an inferiority complex may develop. Conversely, people may develop a superiority complex, or an attempt to overcompensate for inferiority feelings with grandiose opinions of oneself (Halbur & Halbur, 2006). The primary goal of therapy is to increase the social interest of clients and to assist clients in changing disruptive private logic, inferiority/ superiority complexes, mistaken goals, and develop healthy goals and accomplish tasks in socially responsible ways. The primary techniques include a therapeutic alliance and lifestyle assessments that allows the counselor to learn about the client's family constellation, private logic, and fictional finalism. In addition, Adlerians focus on gathering early recollections and look at these recollections to find patterns and themes (Halbur & Halbur, 2006).

Client-Centered Theory

Client-centered theory (also known as Rogerian or person centered) exemplifies the humanistic approach and focuses on the client as the primary agent of change. The client-centered counselor views humans as positive and striving to reach their full potential (Rogers, 1961). Thus, this approach posits that humans naturally strive toward self-actualization, which is the process of moving toward one's greatest potential. This actualization process involves constant growth and experience but is never fully achieved (Halbur & Halbur, 2006). This approach views clients from a phenomenological perspective, meaning that counselors see the world as the client sees the world. Client-centered counselors believe that clients ultimately know themselves better than counselors and therefore client-centered counselors typically offer minimal advice or directives (Halbur & Halbur, 2006). The primary goal of therapy is to assist individuals in moving toward self-actualization. At times, growth toward actualization is hindered and therefore counseling is about removing these barriers. A common barrier faced by individuals is a distorted view of self. Specifically, the difference between who people perceive themselves to be and who they actually are can cause psychological difficulties and barriers toward actualization (Halbur & Halbur, 2006). Therefore, counselors assist clients in finding greater self-understanding and increased congruence between one's perceived self and one's real self. The primary technique is the therapeutic relationship. Specifically, genuineness, a non-judgmental attitude, and the provision of empathy are the core conditions of counseling and are considered necessary and sufficient for change to occur (Rogers, 1957). Genuineness or the ability to be authentic requires counselor transparency. Counselors must be aware of their own feelings and allow this awareness to enter the counseling relationship. Genuineness requires self-knowledge and self-understanding and requires the counselor to know and share one's self. Being nonjudgmental or offering unconditional positive regard requires counselors to completely accept their clients (Rogers, 1957). Counselors cannot have a conditional relationship with clients because this will impact trust and acceptance. Finally, counselors must convey empathy. Empathy is the ability to see the world through the eyes of another individual and to be able to relay this insight to the individual (Halbur & Halbur, 2006).

Existential Theory

Existential theory is based on the fundamental issues related to the human condition including death, isolation, and existence (Yalom, 1995). Therefore anxiety is related to coping with these human conditions. Specifically, the unknown related to death is believed to be the most fundamental issue that people are facing (Yalom, 1995). This approach focuses on facilitating meaning and purpose in life. The primary goal of therapy is awareness (Corey, 2004). Similar to client-centered counseling, existential counseling focuses on moving toward actualization. However, existentialists also believe that it is important to assist clients in confronting issues associated with existence, meaning, and the human condition (Hansen, Cramer, & Rossberg, 1993). More specific goals include understanding the freedom to choose, taking responsibility for personal choices, acknowledging the limitations and barriers associated with freedom, and increasing awareness around available possibilities (Halbur & Halbur, 2006). The primary technique associated with this approach is the counseling relationship. The counselor uses acceptance, authenticity (genuineness), and empathy. It is critical that the counselor facilitate empathy by entering the client's world and understanding the client's worldview (Corey, 2004). Additionally, the counselor's role is to be present while clients confront issues, assist client in accepting responsibility for their choices and to not problem solve (Corey, 2004). Existential counseling is not technique oriented, it is relationship focused but may use techniques from other supporting, counseling approaches.

The Gestalt approach was founded by Fritz Perls and has strong roots in German philosophy and perceptual psychology. Gestalt, which refers to a unified whole, is the basis of this approach. A fundamental assumption of this approach is that the whole is greater than the sum of the parts and humans function best as a whole. Thus, the Gestalt approach posits understanding humans as products of the interrelationship between thoughts, feelings, perceptions, mind, soul, and sensations as opposed to understanding each separate part of an individual. Gestalt counselors also believe that individuals have the capability to shape reality and make their own choices (Coven, 1979; Halbur & Halbur, 2006). Emotional difficulties occur when people, who begin as whole individuals, lose their integrated self. As such, therapeutic change includes gaining insight and re-integrating aspects of their selves. The major goals of therapy are to increase awareness and self-responsibility to facilitate integration (Halbur & Halbur, 2006). Techniques associated with the Gestalt approach include focusing on the here and now as the past is relevant only as it facilitates bringing the individual to the present. In addition, like other humanistic schools, the Gestalt counselor uses a phenomenological approach to see the world as the client see it. While Perls is known for a variety of techniques, he did not believe that a counselor should be wed to any one particular technique. Some of Perls's most popular techniques include: "Empty chair," which is a technique to assist clients in moving beyond any "unfinished business" with another person and requires the client to imagine that the other individual is sitting in the other chair and have a dialogue with the person. Typically, the counselor will instruct the client to assume both roles—moving to the other (empty) chair at times. "Pronouns" is a technique that involves assisting clients in using personal pronouns such as "I" or "me" versus third person such as "you" when talking about themselves. This technique facilitates personal growth by becoming more aware of their particular feelings and thoughts versus detaching themselves. "Sharing hunches" is a technique that involves the counselor sharing the potential meaning of nonverbal messages or facilitating the client to share a possible meaning of nonverbal messages to help the client gain greater self-awareness. Finally, "dream work" is a technique that involves a client playing out roles or completing conversations that occurred in a dream (Halbur & Halbur, 2006).

Behavioral Therapy

The behavioral approach posits that human behavior is shaped by the environmental conditioning and reinforcement. While traditional behavioral approaches are grounded in empiricism and focus primarily on tangible behaviors, goals, and techniques, there are contemporary variations that also attend to emotions and the counseling relationship (Halbur & Halbur, 2006). Behavioral therapy is a compilation of approaches and techniques used to reduce maladaptive behaviors and increase adaptive behaviors (Stoll, 2004). Behavioral therapy emphasizes current behavior rather than past behavior and relies on scientific methods to assess the effectiveness of the techniques through objective, measureable goals (Corey, 2001). Behavioral therapies use multiple assessments throughout treatment (Corrigan & Liberman, 1994) and views behavioral problems as a consequence of learning negative behaviors (Halbur & Halbur, 2006). There are two major theoretical underpinnings that describe traditional behavioral approaches: classical conditioning and operant conditioning.

Classical conditioning was founded by Ivan Pavlov. Classical conditioning is a learning process that occurs through associations between an environmental stimulus and a naturally occurring stimulus. Pavlov showed that a stimulus that should not cause an automatic reaction could be made to cause an automatic reaction through the following experiment: Pavlov rang a bell, provided dogs with food, and then the dogs salivated; following this, he rang the bell again, gave the dogs food, and the dogs salivated again. He repeated this process yet again and the dogs salivated. He then rang the bell without giving the dogs food and the dogs salivated. The food therefore served as the unconditioned stimulus (US)—meaning it caused an automatic reaction (salivating) that is the unconditioned response (UR). When a neutral stimulus (the bell) was repeatedly paired with the US (food), the bell became a conditioned stimulus (CS) that elicited a response on its own, or the conditioned response (CR), and thus, learning occurred (Halbur & Halbur, 2006). Importantly, once the CS and CR relationship is established, the association will disappear if the CS is repeatedly presented without the US. This process is referred as classical extinction (Schloss & Smith, 1994).

Operant conditioning was described by E. L. Thorndike and B. F. Skinner (Wilson, 2000). Thorndike developed the law of effect, which posits that behaviors leading to satisfaction will be reinforced, whereas behaviors leading to dissatisfaction will not be reinforced. In the same vein, Skinner believed that complex behaviors resulted from how an organism interacted with or operated on the environment because of the consequences (Corey, 2001). The key components of operant conditioning are reinforcement and punishment. Reinforcement is anything that increases the frequency of a behavior and punishment is anything that reduces the frequency of a behavior (Craighead, Craighead, Kazdin, & Mahoney, 1994). Reinforcement and punishment involve the provision of a positive reward for adaptive behavior (Craighead et al., 1994) and negative reinforcement occurs when the frequency of behavior increases through the elimination of a negative stimulus (Papajohn, 1982). Punishers may also be positive or negative; positive punishment occurs when an undesired behavior decreases following the provision of a particular stimulus and negative punishment occurs when a positive stimulus is removed following an undesired behavior (Kiernan, 1975).

There are two types of reinforcers: (a) primary reinforcers, which are inherently reinforcing, and (b) secondary reinforcers, which are reinforcing through learning and experience (e.g., tokens earned in a token economy). For operant conditioning to be effective, however, reinforcers must be meaningful for the client (Mueser, 1993). In addition, reinforcers can be delivered through a variety of reinforcement schedules including: a continuous schedule (client is reinforced after each occurrence of the desired behavior); a fixed interval schedule (provides reinforcement to the client after a consistent time interval regardless of how many times the desired behavior occurred within the time interval); a fixed ratio schedule (when the client is reinforced after he or she makes a specified number of the desired responses); a variable interval schedule (provides reinforcement after an unpredictable period of time); and finally, a variable ratio schedule (the provision of reinforcement after a client demonstrates a variable number of desired responses) (Halbur & Halbur, 2006; Stoll, 2004). Operant conditioning can also include extinction. This occurs when reinforcement is withheld from a previously reinforced behavior to decrease the undesired behavior (Wilson, 2000).

The goals of behavioral therapy include helping clients change their environment and reinforce more adaptive behaviors. The focus of behavior therapy is corrective learning, which involves the development of new coping skills, the improvement of communication, and overcoming maladaptive emotional issues (Wilson, 2000). There are many operant techniques used to increase the frequency of adaptive behavior including shaping, differential reinforcement, behavioral contracts, token economies, and social skills training (Stoll, 2004). Shaping involves reinforcing closer approximations of the desired target behavior until the target behavior is shown. Differential reinforcement occurs when all behaviors except the target behavior are positively reinforced. Behavioral contracts are agreements between the counselor and the client (Kazdin, 2000). The contract includes behaviors that need to be changed and the reinforcers and punishers needed for behavior change. Token economies are typically implemented in structured environments where desirable behaviors (taking medication, participating in activities) are reinforced with tokens, which can then be used to "buy" more desired reinforcers (Corrigan & Liberman, 1994). Finally, social skills training is used to enhance communication, assertiveness, problem solving, and other desired social skills (Corrigan & Liberman, 1994).

Cognitive–Behavioral Therapy

Attributed primary to A. T. Beck (1976) and R. L. Beck (1991), cognitive–behavioral therapy (CBT) views emotional and behavioral consequences as a result of cognitions. Specifically, this approach posits that people's feelings and behaviors are based on how they think (cognitions). As such, psychological distress is largely due to one's thought processes that are based on faulty ineffective thinking. From this approach, personality is seen as an enduring set of behavioral and emotional responses to stimuli that stem from ingrained, idiosyncratic ways of thinking. CBT holds that individuals have innate dispositions that interact with the environment to shape their responses and worldviews (Beck & Weishaar, 2000). The primary goal of therapy is to teach clients about how they think so they can correct faulty reasoning (Nelson-Jones, 2000). The primary technique is psychoeducation and the emphasis is on developing skills for managing specific problems (Hansen et al., 1993). Five common CBT techniques include (a) identification of dysfunctional and distorted cognitions; (b) self-monitoring of negative thoughts, or "self-talk"; (c) identification of the relationships between thoughts, underlying beliefs, and feelings; (d) identification of alternative thinking patterns; and (e) personal hypothesis testing regarding the validity of basic assumptions about self, world, and future (Craighead et al., 1994). Other popular techniques include skills training, assertiveness training, relaxation techniques, and training in areas such as life skills, social skills, communication, role-play, systematic desensitization, flooding, thought-stopping, and cognitive modification (Halbur & Halbur, 2006). CBT counselors typically work collaboratively with clients and develop a mutual relationship with therapeutic rapport. Empathy, genuineness, and unconditional positive regard are considered necessary for change, but not sufficient. A therapeutic alliance is needed for change but technique is needed as well.

Social Learning Theory

Social learning theory was developed by Bandura, Underwood, and Fromson (1975). Bandura et al. also considered the role of cognitive processes in behavior change and posited that the influence of environmental events on behavior is largely determined by cognitive processes. This approach is based on a reciprocal determinism model that suggests that there are three interacting factors that contribute to behavior: (a) external stimulus events, (b) external reinforcement, and (c) cognitive meditational processes (Corsini & Wedding, 1989). Simply put, psychological functioning involves the reciprocal interaction between behavior, cognition, and the environment. In social learning theory, the person is the agent of change, emphasizing that individuals have the ability for self-directed behavior change (Corsini & Wedding, 1989).

Rational Emotive Behavior Therapy (REBT)

Rational emotive behavior therapy (REBT) was developed by Albert Ellis (1962). REBT posits that humans are fundamentally inclined toward growth, actualization, and rationality; yet, at the same time, humans experience opposing irrational and dysfunctional tendencies (Ellis, 1962). Both these conflicting tendencies are considered to stem from biological, social, and psychological influences (Garske & Bishop, 2004). According to this theory, irrational thoughts become ingrained at an early age and manifest later in life (Gilliland & James, 1998). However, Ellis believed that humans are capable of changing these irrational thoughts by "attacking" the beliefs to reduce self-defeating, irrational thinking. Thus, the primary goal of therapy is to change the way people think, because thoughts (vs. events and emotions) cause emotional problems (Gilliland & James, 1998). The goals and process of REBT are often summarized using the ABC method: *A* refers to the activating event or adversity; *B* is the individual's beliefs about the event, which may be rational and helpful or irrational and maladaptive; *C* refers to the emotional and behavioral consequences of those beliefs; *D* refers to the responsibility of the counselor to dispute the irrational beliefs and assist the client to obtain more rational, adaptive belief; and *E* refers to when a client develops new behavioral and emotional consequences (Gilliland & James, 1998). REBT attempts to change the client's basic value system (Hansen et al., 1993) and the ultimate consequence is for the client to live a rational life, independent from the counselor (Halbur & Halbur, 2006).

The most common REBT technique is education. Counselors teach clients about REBT assumptions and the ways in which consequences of irrational beliefs impact functioning. Common techniques include confrontation, disputing irrational beliefs, and bibliotherapy (Halbur & Halbur, 2006). Affective and behavioral aspects are also addressed and may include techniques such as imagery, role-playing, homework assignments, and skills training (Gilliland & James, 1998). REBT is an active, directive, and problem-focused counseling approach that can be brief and uses tools such as questionnaires, self-help forms, and homework (e.g., reading of or listening to psychoeducational materials). While it is common for REBT counselors to convey unconditional acceptance, a warm relationship is not considered necessary and certainly not sufficient for change. Similar to CBT, techniques are considered paramount for change.

Reality Therapy

Reality theory was developed by William Glasser (1998) and is based on the fundamental assumption that human beings strive to have their needs met including the need to survive, need to love and be loved, need to have power, need to have freedom, and need to have fun. Glasser posits that people consistently seek to have their needs met in a world where it is not possible to have all their needs met completely. Accordingly, emotional difficulties occur when individuals meet their needs in socially inappropriate or destructive ways. Glasser proposed that people are presented with various choices and the ability to make choices that meets one's basic needs in adaptive and socially responsible ways determines their level of health (Halbur & Halbur, 2006). Glasser emphasized two important themes: (a) individual responsibility and (b) the inability to change other people to make them meet one's own personal needs. The goals of reality therapy are to assist clients in understanding their needs, making healthy choices that will meet their basic needs, and accepting responsibility for the choices made. Glasser (1965) believed that making choices requires that clients accept that they are the agent of change and have control over their life (Halbur & Halbur, 2006).

Reality therapy techniques include contracts and plans that assist clients in delineating specifically how they plan to make changes. Other techniques include pinning down and adopting positive-addicting behaviors. Pinning down refers to helping clients specify how and when they will execute a plan. Adopting positive-addicting behaviors involves adopting behaviors that are so critical to a person's life and leave a person feeling empty when they do not exist. For example, prayer, meditation, exercise, helping others, and volunteering are examples of positive addicting behaviors that serve people in socially appropriate ways that contributes to a more meaningful life (Halbur & Halbur, 2006).

MENTAL HEALTH COUNSELING

Overview

The focus of this section is to review psychological or mental health–related concerns as they intersect with disability and the procedures and sources used to make a mental health diagnosis including a review of the *Diagnostic and Statistical Manual of Mental Disorders* (APA, 2000).

▨ LEARNING OBJECTIVES

By the end of this unit you should be able to:

1. Recognize clients who demonstrate psychological or mental health–related concerns and make appropriate referrals.
2. Explain and utilize standard diagnostic classification systems for mental health conditions within the limits of the role and responsibilities of the rehabilitation counselor.

▨ KEY CONCEPTS

Disability and Mental Health

A mental disorder is defined as a clinically significant behavioral or psychological syndrome or collection of symptoms that causes an individual distress, disability, or an increased risk of suffering death, disability, pain, or the loss of freedom (American Psychiatric Association [APA], 2000; Morrison, 2006). Mental illness is a significant health problem in the United States and around the world (National Institute of Mental Health) and there are high rates of co-occurring mental health problems among people with disabilities (PWDs). In addition, there are increasing numbers of individuals with psychiatric disabilities being served in the rehabilitation system (Tschopp & Frain, 2009). There are several ways in which mental disorders interface with disability. A mental disorder may be a co-morbid or co-existing condition that exists in conjunction with another disability; for example, a person with a spinal cord injury who also experiences depression. The degree to which depression is disabling in such a situation depends on the diagnosis, functional limitations, and duration (Tschopp & Frain, 2009). However, treating the co-morbid condition is critical, because it directly influences response to disability and rehabilitation success. Studies suggest that a significant portion of PWDs experience co-existing depression (Lee, Chan, Chronister, Chan & Romero, 2009). Second, a mental illness may be the primary disabling condition. In this case, disability associated with the psychiatric condition occurs because of "significant role impairments affecting social relationships, work, leisure, and self-care" (Bond & Resnick, 2000, p. 235). Mental disorders such as major depression, bipolar disorder, schizophrenia, and obsessive–compulsive disorders constitute four of the 10 leading causes of disability in developed regions, including the United States (Murray & Lopez, 1996). Third, those with dual diagnosis have a psychiatric disability and substance abuse disorder (Falvo, 2009). Substance abuse may co-exist with any type of disability, yet it is uniquely referred to as dual diagnosis when it co-exists with a psychiatric disability.

Diagnostic Procedures in Mental Illness

Mental illness is a complex condition that requires many professionals to be involved in the evaluation and treatment process (Falvo, 2009). In addition to the rehabilitation counselor, other professionals who may be involved include a psychiatrist, clinical psychologists, and social worker. A diagnosis of mental illness occurs through information gathered from a variety of sources including psychological tests/surveys including intelligence, neuropsychological, personality, behavioral, and emotional functioning instruments (Falvo, 2009). Data from these sources are used in conjunction with clinical judgment and clinical interviews. The *Diagnostic and Statistical Manual of Mental Disorders, Fourth Edition, Text Revision* (*DSM-IV-TR*; APA, 2000) is the classification system used most frequently for the diagnosis of mental disorders (Tschopp & Frain, 2009) and is described below.

Diagnostic and Statistical Manual of Mental Disorders

The *DSM-IV-TR* (APA, 2000) contains broad definitions of psychiatric diagnoses. The basic structure of *DSM-IV-TR* includes 17 major mental disorders grouped according to their diagnostic class (APA, 2000), including such group as, disorders usually first diagnosed in infancy, childhood, or adolescence; substance-related disorders; mood disorders; somatoform disorders; sleep disorders; adjustment disorders; and personality disorders. For a complete list of the mental disorder classification groups, please refer to the *DSM-IV-TR* (APA, 2000).

To warrant a specific diagnosis, individuals must meet certain criteria as indicated by each mental disorder. For example, for Major Depressive Episode, individuals must meet five or more of the *DSM-IV-TR* criteria such as depressed mood, decreased interest or pleasure in all or almost all activities, insomnia, fatigue, and poor concentration (APA, 2000). For Generalized Anxiety Disorder, examples of criteria used to determine this disorder include such symptoms as restlessness or feeling on edge, easily fatigued, irritability, muscle tension, and difficulty concentrating or mind going blank (APA, 2000). For a complete list of the criteria required for Major Depressive Episode, Generalized Anxiety Disorder, and other mental disorders, please refer to the *DSM-IV-TR* (APA, 2000). Additional associated features, such as general medical conditions, culture, age, gender, prevalence, course, and familial patterns, are noted as well.

The *DSM-IV-TR* provides a multiaxial classification system that includes four axes to assist with the biopsychosocial assessment of clients (Morrison, 2006). Axis I includes clinical disorders and other conditions that may be a focus of clinical attention. All mental diagnoses and their accompanying diagnostic codes are recorded under Axis I, except for mental retardation and personality disorders. Axis II includes personality disorders and mental retardation. Axis III includes general medical conditions (with ICD-9-CM codes). Axis IV includes psychosocial and environmental problems that may impact diagnosis, treatment, and prognosis for individuals with Axis I and/or Axis II disorders (APA, 2000). The *DSM-IV-TR* outlines nine categories that fall under Axis IV and include such problems in areas related to primary support group, education, occupation, housing, economic, health care, and legal issues. Axis V includes a global assessment of functioning (GAF). The GAF score reflects an individual's overall psychological, occupational, and social functioning using a single number on a 100-point scale (Morrison, 2006). Subjectivity may pose a problem, thus the GAF is most useful for tracking an individual's progress. For example, for Axis V, GAF = 40 (on admission) and GAF = 65 (at discharge).

COUNSELING SKILLS AND TECHNIQUES DEVELOPMENT

Overview

The focus of this section is to review the key skills and techniques critical to developing a counseling relationship. These include developing the working alliance, establishing the core conditions of counseling (empathy, warmth, genuineness), developing attending and listening skills, and learning basic interviewing skills.

■ LEARNING OBJECTIVES

By the end of this unit you should be able to:

1. Develop and maintain confidential counseling relationships with individuals with a disability using established skills and techniques.
2. Establish, in collaboration with the consumer, individual counseling goals and objectives.
3. Apply basic counseling and interviewing skills.

■ KEY CONCEPTS

Working Alliance

Developing and maintaining a confidential, collaborative counseling relationship with rehabilitation clients requires the use of key counseling and interviewing skills. The effectiveness of these skills is predicated on the development of a strong working alliance. The working alliance has been identified as a critical factor in delivering effective rehabilitation counseling services and is established throughout the course of the counseling relationship (Chan, Berven, & Thomas, 2004). The working alliance is also referred as the rehabilitation counselor's ability to "connect with" clients and other rehabilitation team members. A "connection" can be a positive bond or personal attachment and typically involves a mutual sense of trust, respect, and acceptance (Chan et al., 2004). Participation from clients, rehabilitation professionals, and other team members is essential for the coordination of rehabilitation services and for the development of a working alliance. This collaboration helps to build the working alliance by mutual agreements between all parties to create equality and a shared responsibility during the rehabilitation process. The planning of rehabilitation services and outcomes of services depends on the bonds, goals, and tasks, which are agreed upon through this collaboration. Agreed upon goals and interventions that help facilitate change are also an essential part of creating the connection that builds the working alliance between all members of the rehabilitation team.

Core Conditions of Counseling

The core conditions of counseling are known as empathy, warmth, and genuineness (Chan et al., 2004). Empathy is an act of knowing and understanding the experience of another. It is the ability to convey support and acceptance by understanding the client's experience via the client's perspective. Warmth is a way to show that there is respect between counselor, client, and other members of the rehabilitation team by being nonjudgmental, showing praise when appropriate, and expressing appreciation for work put in by all people involved in the rehabilitation process. Genuineness is the act of being authentic and honest via effective communication methods, such as self-disclosure, that does not detract from attention to client and uses language that is accessible to clients and rehabilitation team members (Chan et al., 2004).

Attending and Listening Skills

Attending and listening skills provide the basic platform for which all counseling skills are built and are typically nonverbal in nature (Chan et al., 2004). These nonverbal skills involve the physical orientation of the rehabilitation counselor toward the client as a means of communication with a goal of showing attentiveness and availability (Chan et al., 2004). Effective posturing of counselors is usually achieved through an open and nondefensive body position, with a slight lean forward. Eye contact with a steady gaze, not staring is also important. However, the normative standard for eye contact varies depending on the client's cultural background. Moments of silence that give the client time to focus his or her thoughts and give space for client to experience emotions is also another commonly used nonverbal skill. Attention to the client's nonverbal cues is also an important way to show attentiveness to clients (Chan et al., 2004; Ivey & Ivey, 2007).

Interviewing Skills

Interviews are conducted as a part of the counseling process. They are used to gather information about the client in either a highly structured or unstructured way and involve a wide array of techniques to help gather pertinent information (Chan et al., 2004). Encouragers can be both verbal and nonverbal cues that show the counselor is hearing the client and prompts the client to say more (Ivey & Ivey, 2007). These include head nods, "uh huhs," repetition of key words, and other similar gestures. These convey warmth, which allow the client to open up and gain comfort during the interview. Paraphrasing is an interviewing technique, where the counselor restates what the client has said using counselor's own words and key words from the client (Chan et al., 2004). This gives the counselor an opportunity to make sure he or she understands what the client is saying. This also allows the client to hear the counselor's interpretation of what the client is saying and verify accuracy. Summarizing is an interviewing technique that allows the counselor to provide an overview of a part of or an entire counseling session (Chan et al., 2004). The counselor briefly summarizes what was said, typically at the end or beginning of a meeting. This technique similar to paraphrasing allows for the client to hear the counselor's interpretation and make corrections if miscommunications have occurred. Reflection of feeling is a verbal statement whereby there is recognition of the client's emotions by the counselor (Ivey & Ivey, 2007). The counselor can use the key emotional words stated by the client to exhibit a reflection of feeling. There may also

TABLE 5.1 ■ Counseling Skills and Techniques Key Concepts

Working alliance	A connection involving trust, respect and acceptance among counselor, client, and all members of the rehabilitation team
Core conditions of counseling	Empathy, warmth, and genuineness
Attending and listening skills	Nonverbal skills involving physical orientation of counselor toward client: open and nondefensive body position, with a slight lean forward, moments of silence, and eye contact
Encouragers	Verbal and nonverbal cues that show the counselor is hearing the client and prompts the client to say more
Paraphrasing	Interviewing technique where the counselor restates what the client has said using counselor's own words and key words from the client
Summarizing	Interviewing technique that allows the counselor to provide an overview of a part of or an entire counseling session
Reflection of feeling	Verbal statement whereby there is a recognition of the client's emotions by the counselor using key emotional words stated by the client
Open-ended questions	Questions are questions that allow the client to respond using more than one word and encourage the client to elaborate and say more
Closed-ended questions	Questions that are specific and typically have short or one word answers
Clarifying questions	Questions that allow the counselor to gain a fuller understanding of a topic in which the client has provided vague information

be unspoken feelings expressed by a client of which the counselor can also recognize and use in reflection of feeling statements.

Open-ended questions are questions that allow the client to respond using more than one word, such as "yes" or "no" (Chan et al., 2004). These questions encourage the client to talk more and usually begin with "how," "where," "when," or "who." These types of questions allow the counselor to gain more information about the client's situation and understand the client's point of view. Closed-ended questions are specific and typically have short or one-word answers (Chan et al., 2004). These questions should be used minimally and woven into the conversation between open-ended questions. These questions limit client response and may cause the client to pull back and not open up to the counselor. These questions provide limited opportunity for the client to express emotion. Clarifying questions allow the counselor to gain a fuller understanding of a topic in which the client has provided vague information. The use of these questions will help the counselor avoid confusion and misunderstanding of information in question. These questions also allow for a re-discussion of information, which may facilitate client insight (Chan et al., 2004; Ivey & Ivey, 2007). See Table 5.1 for definitions of key counseling skills and techniques concepts.

GENDER ISSUES IN COUNSELING

Overview

The focus of this section is to review the role of gender in the rehabilitation process. Specifically, this section will examine the biological and evolutionary gender differences, the socialization influences related to gender roles, lesbian and gay sexual orientations, and the importance of considering gender identity in the rehabilitation process and societal response to those identities considered to be "different" from societal norm.

LEARNING OBJECTIVES

By the end of this unit you should be able to:

1. Assist clients in making lifestyle choices that may involve gender or multicultural issues.
2. Identify gender differences that can affect the rehabilitation counseling and planning processes.

KEY CONCEPTS

Gender issues are important to consider within the counseling context. Gender is a multidimensional construct that has been defined through biological, evolutionary, and socialization influences. Specifically, biological differences between men and woman include chromosomes, hormonal production, and reproductive capabilities. Evolutionary differences include historic familial roles fulfilled by men and woman, with women assuming roles that involve creating an environment that ensures protection and survival of offspring, while men assume hunter–gatherer roles that involve strength, aggression, and competition with other men. Socialization influences occur through the internalization of societal norms that influence children as early as 8 years old. Specifically, behaviors are shaped and learned from social experiences that reward girls for showing behaviors considered desirable for women and reward boys for behaviors that are appropriate for men (Gardiner & Kosmitzi, 2008). Behaviors that are rewarded are often characterized as feminine and masculine "traits" and include gentle, tender, sensitive, nurturing, maternal, and anima for females and toughness, courageous, strong, protecting, and animus for males. Individuals who do not conform to these societal norms and display nontraditional gender-specific behaviors often receive negative feedback from their environment, which in turn, contributes to negative emotions (Gardiner & Kosmitzi, 2008).

Because of these socially reinforced "traits" and expected roles, women are often socialized into lower-status roles and positions of dependency that results in power differences between men and women (Gardiner & Kosmitzi, 2008). For example, within the context of work, women and men frequently have more access to occupations and careers that are consistent with gender traits and roles, limiting occupational options. Examples of male-dominated occupations include laborer jobs and executive positions (strength or assertiveness), and women-dominated positions include teachers, nurses, and caregivers (nurturance). Men often have access to occupations that have higher pay, status and power, and women therefore are placed at an economic disadvantage and have less power and status (Gardiner & Kosmitzi, 2008).

In most cultures, the philosophies of gender and sexuality are closely interrelated. Cultural and societal norms dictate how men and women should act, look, and dress. For example, in the United States, women are expected to be attracted to and engaging in sexual relationships with men, demonstrating deference to them and their decisions related to family. In the United Kingdom, however, relationships are more egalitarian. Individuals whose sexual orientation deviates from societal norms such as lesbian women or gay men often experience stigma, prejudice, and discrimination in social, vocational, and educational spheres. Similarly, individuals who are perceived as assuming nontraditional roles or exhibiting opposite gender behaviors may be perceived as having a nontraditional sexual orientation and therefore stigmatized. For example, men who exhibit effeminate behaviors or choose careers more commonly held by a woman may be perceived as gay, even if the person is heterosexual. Indeed, deviating from gender and/or sexual norms may result in serious social and psychological consequences. For example, transgendered and intersex individuals may be misunderstood and seen as part of a "freak show." Rehabilitation counselors need to be sensitive to issues related to gender identity and be prepared to refer individual to help professionals in the community if unable to adequately address this aspect of the individual's life.

CONFLICT RESOLUTION AND NEGOTIATION STRATEGIES

Overview

The focus of this section is to define conflict and review five important conflict resolution steps necessary to take to assist rehabilitation consumers and counselors in resolving conflict.

■ LEARNING OBJECTIVES

By the end of this unit you should be able to:

1. Apply conflict resolution skills on behalf of consumer interests and negotiate alternative solutions to conflict situations.
2. Assist consumers in developing skills to effectively respond to conflict and negotiate in support of their interests.

■ KEY CONCEPTS

Conflict takes place when an individual's actions or goals are perceived as incompatible with the actions or goals of another individual (Fisher & Brown, 1988). Conflicts may occur when rehabilitation counselors and clients experience discrepancies between their expectations and their perceptions (Koch, McReynolds, & Rumrill, 2004). For example, conflicts might occur due to expectations about roles and responsibilities, client eligibility, service delivery method and timeliness, program policies, and counselor error (Holmes, Hall, & Karst, 1989; Koch et al., 2004). It is important to address conflict and facilitate resolution at the early stages of counseling to relay to clients their value as members of the rehabilitation team and that they will be treated and receive quality services (Koch et al., 2004). Conflict resolution involves the following steps: First, myths about "good" working relationship must be addressed such as the best working relationship occurs when no discrepancies are present, individuals in the relationship have shared values and expectations, and the goal of the relationship is to avoid conflict. Working relationships work best when the individuals deal with conflicts, try to understand the other's values and perceptions of the situation, and work through the disagreements in a way that it works for both parties (Koch et al., 2004). Next, conflict needs to be accurately defined and reframed as differences related to interests and goals versus a negative will (Koch et al., 2004). Third, the misperceptions should be clarified regarding what one has stated and how the information has been interpreted prevents miscommunications (Koch et al., 2004). Fourth, the individuals should discuss ideas that will contribute to the development of a set of shared expectations by reconciling differences. During this step, it is important for rehabilitation counselors to clearly delineate the guidelines and boundaries within which the team works (Koch et al., 2004). The final step involves implementing and evaluating resolutions that involve agreement on what the roles and responsibilities of each will be, and a written agreement outlining these roles and responsibilities is recommended. The individuals should review the agreement throughout the counseling relationship and revise the agreement as needed to reduce the risk of future conflicts (Koch et al., 2004; Curl & Sheldon, 1992).

TERMINATION OF COUNSELING RELATIONSHIPS

Overview

The focus of this section is to review the strategies and actions necessary for ethically terminating a counseling relationship. This section will review appropriate reasons for termination, specific termination procedures to follow with an individual client, and termination within a group setting.

▧ LEARNING OBJECTIVE

By the end of this unit you should be able to:

1. Develop a plan of action in collaboration with the consumer for strategies and actions at the conclusion of the counseling process.

▧ KEY CONCEPTS

According to the Code of Professional Ethics for Rehabilitation Counselors (CRCC, 2010), rehabilitation counselors may not abandon clients and must make appropriate referrals for clients being terminated. Appropriate reasons for termination include: (a) client is not benefitting from counseling; (b) client no longer needs counseling; (c) counseling may harm client or persons related to client; and (d) client is not paying agreed upon fees (CRCC, 2010). If a rehabilitation counselor is transferring a client, it must be done in a timely manner and procedures should be in place to ensure that communication occurs with both the client and the practitioner to whom the client is being referred. In addition, in the case of a counselor's incapacitation, death, or leaving of practice, a note should be filed in the client's records regarding such (CRCC, 2010) and communication by another professional shall occur with the client regarding the situation and a transfer process set in place immediately.

Termination Procedures With an Individual Client

Termination with an individual client should be a collaborative process between the client and counselor and should include (at minimum) the following strategies. First, a discussion with the client about the termination process well before the termination date should occur. This will emotionally prepare the client for the transition or cessation of the client–counselor relationship. Second, discuss with the client the positive changes that have occurred since the start of counseling, any memorable moments or obstacles in the counseling process, and generally express positive feelings regarding the client. Third, acknowledge any limitations associated with the parameters of rehabilitation counseling and review resources available to the client to address any areas that were not adequately addressed within the rehabilitation context. Fourth, provide the client with information about the process of returning for services if needed. Finally, address the limits of the counselor–client relationship upon termination. For example, if the client wants to be friends (e.g., Facebook), make clear the limits of the client–counselor relationship with a former client (Teyber, 2006).

Termination in a Group Setting

Termination procedures within a group context also include addressing the issue of termination prior to the last meeting of the group. Rehabilitation counselors need to realize that group members may be anxious about the group ending and losing the established social network. It is important to reassure group members that the type of connections formed in the group can be replicated outside the group (Corey & Corey, 2006). In addition, rehabilitation counselors should recognize their own feelings related to endings and separation (Corey & Corey, 2006). According to Corey and Corey (2006), the following are specific tasks that should be performed for group termination. First, the facilitator must discuss any unfinished business related to the group and complete what can be accomplished and discuss what cannot be accomplished. Second, review what the group has learned and acknowledge the behavioral changes. Third, discuss ways in which group members can bring the new behaviors learned and knowledge gained to the outside world. Fourth, ask the group to give concrete feedback about the group to the facilitator and to specific individual members.

CONSUMER EMPOWERMENT AND RIGHTS

Overview

The focus of this section is to review the definition and basic tenets of empowerment to provide rehabilitation counselors with a guide toward facilitating an empowering relationship that is ethical and consistent with the consumer's culture, values, and beliefs. This section reviews the importance of focusing on client abilities and opportunities rather than deficits, and the importance of valuing unique client experiences and the varying levels of control that consumers have over their lives.

▧ LEARNING OBJECTIVES

By the end of this unit you should be able to:

1. Promote ethical decision making and personal responsibility that is consistent with the consumer's culture, values, and beliefs.
2. Assist consumers in applying behavior management practices as a part of implementing personal changes.

▧ KEY CONCEPTS

The rehabilitation counselor should facilitate client empowerment and client rights. Empowerment is defined as a process of increasing personal, interpersonal, or political power, so that individuals can take action to improve their life situation (Gutierrez, 1990). Basic tenets of empowerment include: (a) every individual has worth and dignity; (b) every individual should have the same opportunity to maximize his or her potential; (c) people generally strive to grow and change in positive directions; and (d) individuals should be free to make their own decisions about the management of their lives (Kosciulek, 2000). To facilitate an empowering counseling relationship, rehabilitation counselors need to focus on client capabilities, capacities, and opportunities rather than their deficits. In addition, rehabilitation counselors need to value unique client experiences and recognize that clients come with different levels of control over their lives and their environments.

BOUNDARIES OF CONFIDENTIALITY

Overview

The focus of this section is to review the boundaries of confidentiality including sharing with parents/guardians, acknowledging when a client is at risk to self or others and, due to a legal mandate, when to release information by a court order. This section will also review mandatory reporting laws, the duty to protect, the Tarasoff Decision, and privileged communication.

■ LEARNING OBJECTIVES

By the end of this unit you should be able to:

1. Explain the legal limits of confidentiality for rehabilitation counselors for the state in which they practice counseling.
2. Identify established rehabilitation counseling ethical standards for confidentiality and apply them to actual case situations.

■ KEY CONCEPTS

Boundaries of Confidentiality

Confidentiality is considered essential to the counselor–client relationship because clients need assurance that personal information will remain with the counselor (Woody, 2001). Unless informed otherwise, most clients assume that everything shared with counselors will remain confidential (Shaw & Tarvydas, 2001). Although rehabilitation counselors often share information about a client with physicians and allied health professionals, supervisors, parents, or guardians, case audits by regulatory bodies, third-party payers such as insurance companies, and other treatment team members (Campbell, 1994; Cobia & Boes, 2000; Cooper, 2000; Tarvydas, 1995; Shaw, 2004) permission should always be obtained in writing and should articulate clearly what information is to be released, to whom, and for what reason. Additionally, the document should specify a time frame for how long permission is granted and have a space for the client's signature (Shaw, 2004). Situations in which rehabilitation counselors will need to break confidentiality include: (a) sharing information with parents/guardians of a minor or a person with an intellectual or psychiatric disability; (b) when a client is at risk of harm to self or others including the risk of exposing another to a life-threatening disease; and (c) when a counselor is legally mandated to release information by a court order (CRCC, 2010).

Mandatory Reporting Laws

Mandatory reporting laws are designed to protect those members of society who are considered to be vulnerable and unable to protect themselves (Shaw, 2004). In these situations, rehabilitation counselors are not allowed the choice to use their own judgment. If a counselor fails to report in such a situation, they are in violation of state law. Although the types of information that must be reported vary from state to state, at the very least, most states have mandatory laws that require reporting child abuse, older adult abuse, and abuse of PWDs.

Duty to Protect

The law states that rehabilitation counselors should violate confidentiality in situations where they believe the client poses a risk to themselves or to others. This includes when a client is at risk of harm to self (e.g., suicide) or others (e.g., homicide) and includes the risk of exposing another to a life-threatening disease (CRCC, 2010; Shaw, 2006). In these situations, the state's obligation to protect others is viewed as outweighing the importance of confidentiality.

Tarasoff Decision

The counselor's duty to protect another person from his or her client when the client has disclosed an intention to commit such an act is highlighted following the outcome of a controversial malpractice case, *Tarasoff v. Regents of the University of California* (1976). In this case, a psychologist at UC-Berkeley was treating a graduate student, Prosenjit Poddar who became obsessed with an undergraduate student, Tatianna Tarasoff. Poddar reported to the psychologist that he intended to kill Tarasoff and the psychologist reported the information to the police; the police detained Poddar, but after questioning him, he was released. Shortly after, Poddar murdered Tarasoff. The court decided that confidentiality should be breached when there is a foreseeable victim of harm perpetrated by the individual with whom the helping professional has a special relationship, defining the duty as "the duty to exercise reasonable care to protect the foreseeable victim of that danger" (*Tarasoff v. Regents of the University of California*, 1976; p. 345). As a result, the California Supreme Court adopted the principles regarding duty and limitations on confidentiality as a rule of law and other states adopted "duty" laws, each of which vary in the interpretation and definition of "foreseeability" (Shaw, 2006).

Privileged Communication

The right of clients to have their communication with their rehabilitation counselors kept confidential is legally referred as privileged communication or testimonial privilege (Shaw, 2006). In many states, this right is extended to client–counselor relationships in recognition of the importance of confidentiality in the counseling relationships. Several are important issues related to privileged communication. First, the right to privileged information is owned by the client, not the counselor; and second, in situations where confidentiality cannot be protected, counselors are required to inform clients of potential situations in which confidentiality may need to be breeched (Shaw, 2004).

Breaking confidentiality always poses a risk to the client–counselor relationship. When breaking confidentiality, counselors should only disclose the minimum amount of information required. In addition, counselors should be aware that the boundaries of confidentiality may differ from culture to culture. If the counselor is unfamiliar with the boundaries of another culture, the counselor should seek consultation from an expert on that culture. Finally, counselors are responsible for keeping accurate and up-to-date client records that are kept in a confidential and safe environment, and they should include even those records of deceased clients unless there is a legal mandate to disclose (CRCC, 2010).

ETHICS IN THE COUNSELING RELATIONSHIP

Overview

The focus of this section is to review the Code of Professional Ethics for Rehabilitation Counselors. This section reviews the basic principles upon which the Code is based and provides highlights of the 12 sections of the Code.

▓ LEARNING OBJECTIVES

By the end of this unit you should be able to:

1. Describe the practical implications of the CRCC Code of Ethics as part of the rehabilitation counseling process.
2. Confirm competency in applying an established ethical decision-making process to rehabilitation counseling case situations.

▓ KEY CONCEPTS

The Code of Professional Ethics for Rehabilitation Counselors

Professional organizations have established codes of behavior for their members to protect clients, professionals, the profession itself, and the larger community. The CRCC developed and administers the Code of Professional Ethics for Rehabilitation Counselors (the Code). The most recent edition of this code can be accessed at www.crccertification.com. The CRCC has authority to make decisions and impose consequences for code violations. The CRCC Code of Ethics is based on six principles: (a) *Autonomy,* which involves respecting the rights of clients to be self-governing within their social and cultural framework; (b) *Beneficence,* which means doing good to others and promoting the well-being of clients; (c) *Fidelity,* which involves being faithful to the client by keeping promises and honoring the trust placed in rehabilitation counselors; (d) *Justice,* which is defined as being fair in the treatment of all clients and to provide appropriate services to all; (e) *Nonmaleficence,* which involves doing no harm to others; and (f) *Veracity,* which means to be honest. The standards of practice in the Code are divided into 12 sections and highlights are outlined below.

Section A: The Counseling Relationship

The primary responsibility of rehabilitation counselors is to respect and promote the welfare of their clients. As such, rehabilitation counselors must work with clients to develop employment plans and goals that respect the client's decision making, while considering the capabilities of the client. Clients have the right to informed consent, and when there is a reduced capacity to give consent because of age or disability, consent may be granted by a parent or guardian but assent or agreement should be given from the client. Rehabilitation counselors need to balance the guardian's responsibility to protect the client with the client's rights to make decisions (CRCC, 2010).

The Code prohibits sexual relationships with current clients, their immediate family, or romantic partners. Sexual relationships with former clients or their immediate family members or romantic partners are prohibited for at least 5 years after the end of the counseling relationships. If a sexual relationship with anyone that would directly or indirectly harm the client, the counselor must avoid it. Finally, counselors cannot ethically take on a new client with whom they have been romantically involved in the past (CRCC, 2010). Counselors must communicate in a manner that is understandable by the client. Communication may be modified for cultural sensitivity reasons or in response to language or communication differences between the client and the counselor (i.e., using an interpreter). In the same vein, counselors must incorporate respect for the client's cultural background in all aspects of the client–counselor relationship.

Section B: Confidentiality, Privileged Communication, and Privacy

Clients have the right to privacy and confidentiality regarding the information they share with a counselor. In most instances, counselors are not allowed to share client information without consent from the client first (Shaw, 2006). Circumstances in which confidentiality may be breached must be explained to clients at the start of counseling. These circumstances may include: (a) sharing information with parents/guardians of a minor or a person with an intellectual or psychiatric disability; (b) when a client is at risk of harm to self or others including the risk of exposing another to a life-threatening disease; and (c) when a counselor is legally mandated to release information by a court order (CRCC, 2010). Finally, counselors are responsible for keeping accurate and up-to-date client records. Records must be kept in a confidential and safe environment and include even those records of deceased clients unless there is a legal mandate to disclose.

Section C: Advocacy and Accessibility

Rehabilitation counselors work with clients who face being stereotyped and discriminated against because of their disability (CRCC, 2010). As such, counselors must remain up to date on laws and systems that affect the rights of people with disabilities including: the American's with Disabilities Act, public benefits systems, medical services, transportation, and housing (CRCC, 2010). In addition, counselors must increase their own knowledge about disabilities and assist clients in self-advocacy strategies.

Section D: Professional Responsibility

Rehabilitation counselors must practice within their own limits of competency and represent their credentials accurately and truthfully. In addition, rehabilitation counselors shall monitor their own effectiveness and seek peer consultation and evaluation on a regular basis. Counselors must continually strive to increase their training and education in the field which includes learning cultural perspectives different from their own. Rehabilitation counselors must also use techniques that have empirical support, and if a technique is being used that is new or lacks empirical evidence, risks shall be disclosed to the client. Rehabilitation counselors shall not provide services to clients if the counselor has a physical or psychological problem that will prevent ethical, competent, and consumer-focused counseling. Rehabilitation counselors should also make provisions for continued client care in case of emergency or disaster (CRCC, 2010).

Section E: Relationships With Other Professionals

Rehabilitation counselors shall be respectful of their co-workers, which include having knowledge of and respect for different cultures and beliefs. Counselors shall also abide by the rules of their agency and suggest changes in a constructive manner. When consulting with other entities about a client, rehabilitation counselors shall be certain that there is client consent and that the consulting sources are competent. When working as part of a consultation team, rehabilitation counselors shall abide by the decision of the team, and if the counselor feels the team decision violates an ethical code, the counselor must seek a solution that is in best interest of the client (CRCC, 2010).

Section F: Forensic and Direct Services

When working in the forensic capacity of giving expert witness, rehabilitation counselors shall produce an unbiased, objective written report based on evidence. Individuals being evaluated, or their assigned guardian, must give written consent except if there is a sound clinical or cultural reason, there is a legal mandate, or the individual being evaluated is deceased. Rehabilitation counselors cannot serve in a forensic capacity for current or former clients unless legally mandated (CRCC, 2010).

Section G: Evaluation, Assessment, and Interpretation

Rehabilitation counselors shall explain assessment procedures, purposes, and results of assessment tools in a way that is culturally appropriate and understandable to the client. If there is a psychiatric diagnosis, counselors shall recognize that culture affects how psychiatric disorders manifest. Rehabilitation counselors must also be aware that certain groups (i.e., women) have been misdiagnosed and pathologized, and may refrain from giving a diagnosis if the counselor believes it will cause harm to the client or others. Counselors shall use psychological tests that have sound psychometric properties, are appropriate for the specific client, and for which the counselor has competence in administering, scoring, and interpreting. Counselors shall recognize that some tests may not be valid for certain individuals or cultural groups, and when tests have not been normed on the population to which the client belongs, counselors shall interpret the scores with caution. Finally, rehabilitation counselors shall adhere to the testing procedures required and maintain the integrity of the test by not disclosing protected aspects of a testing device (CRCC, 2010).

Section H: Teaching, Supervision, and Training

Rehabilitation counselor supervisors protect the welfare of the supervisee by (a) ensuring supervisee knowledge of client's rights; (b) ensuring the client is aware of the supervisee's experience and status; (c) ensuring the client understands that confidential information will be shared with the supervisor; and (d) regularly meeting with a supervisee and monitoring clinical work and case notes. In addition, rehabilitation counseling supervisors shall maintain knowledge of cultural diversity issues and address areas of cultural conflict between supervisee and client. Supervisors shall not engage in sexual or nonprofessional roles with supervisees. They shall be aware of the power differential between themselves and their supervisee and are cautious when entering nonprofessional relationships with former supervisees. Supervisors shall not supervise close relatives, friends, or romantic partners. The welfare of rehabilitation counseling students is the responsibility of counselor educators; as such, the benefits and risks of self-disclosure by counseling students shall be safeguarded by counselor educators. Supervisors and counseling educators do not assume the role of "counselor" for their student/supervisee, with the exception of assisting in resolving immediate issues that emerge (CRCC, 2010).

Section I: Research and Publication

Precautions must be taken to prevent injury to human research participants. Institutional and scientific standards for research with human participants must be followed and consultation should be sought when necessary. Participation in research experiments must be voluntary and participants are allowed to withdraw consent to participate at any time. Any test results gathered from a research study must be kept confidential and used only for research purposed. Researchers shall share research data to qualified professionals for replication studies. Manuscripts may only be submitted to one journal at a time and must include accurate reporting of results and proper crediting of other researchers (CRCC, 2010).

Section J: Technology and Distance Counseling

Professional rehabilitation counselor conduct is held to the same ethical standards when technology is used in counseling. Use of the Internet, cell phones, fax machines, video phones, and message machines require rehabilitation counselors to employ extra caution to protect client confidentiality. Counselors must inform clients of the risks to confidentiality associated with any technology used. Security measures include using encrypted internet sites, limiting the use of email/phone communication to in-person communication, and using code words to ascertain identities. Although new technologies make distance counseling more accessible for many clients, rehabilitation counselors must be aware of the laws that restrict practice across local, state, or national boundaries. When participating in online consultations or discussion groups, rehabilitation counselors must adhere to ethical guidelines and limit disclosure of confidential information. Rehabilitation counselors using technology for distance counseling must make an alternative resource or reference to an alternate resource available for situations in which technology fails or the counselor is not available through technology. Finally, rehabilitation counselors shall not assume that technology used to keep client records protects confidentiality (CRCC, 2010).

Section K: Business Practices

Rehabilitation counselors are expected to be honest and accurate in business advertising, and are not permitted to solicit private practice clients from their places of employment. Records must be kept for the amount of time legislated by the laws and regulations governing the rehabilitation counselor's practice and then destroyed. Fees must be fair and reasonable and explained clearly to the client. Bartering is discouraged, but if requested by the client, it may be culturally appropriate if no harm is done to the client. Bartering arrangements should, however, be recorded on paper (CRCC, 2010).

Section L: Resolving Ethical Conflict

Rehabilitation counselors must be prepared to make ethical decisions by using an ethical decision making model. One such model is the Integrative Decision Making Model (Parker, Szymanski, & Patterson, 2005). This model has four steps: (1) interpret the situation; (2) formulate an ethical decision; (3) select and action; and (4) plan and execute the course of action. A transcultural integrative model adds to Step 3 looking at the situation from different cultural perspectives (Garcia, Winston, & Borzuchowska, 2003). If rehabilitation counselors are working in an organization with conflicting codes of ethics, rehabilitation counselors must follow the CRCC code. If a counselor believes that another counselor has violated an ethical code, the counselor shall first try to resolve the situation informally unless confidentiality would be violated. If an informal resolution is not feasible or not successful, rehabilitation counselors shall report the violation to the appropriate regulatory body, unless a client refuses to allow the information to be shared. If in doubt, the rehabilitation counselor shall confer with a colleague with expertise in the area. If ethical considerations conflict with legal mandates, rehabilitation counselors shall make known their commitment to the code, and try to resolve the matter. If a resolution cannot be reached upon taking the code into consideration, counselors shall follow the law (CRCC, 2010).

MULTICULTURAL ISSUES IN COUNSELING

Overview

The focus of this section is to review the critical multicultural issues in rehabilitation counseling practice and highlight some of the multicultural factors that may influence the rehabilitation process among particular cultural groups. Specifically, this section will review key concepts such as individualism and collectivism, followed by a brief review of some of the values and experiences that may be important to consider when working with persons who are African American, Asian American, Latino, or Native American.

▨ LEARNING OBJECTIVES

By the end of this unit you should be able to:

1. Identify critical multicultural issues in rehabilitation counseling practice.
2. Describe multicultural differences that can affect the rehabilitation counseling and planning processes.

▨ KEY CONCEPTS

According to the U.S. Census Bureau (2010), ethnic minority cultures accounted for more than one third of the U.S. population. Approximately 19% of the U.S. population has a disability and nearly 13% are aged 65 years or older (U.S. Census Bureau, 2008). A large majority of PWDs are cultural minorities, and thus, rehabilitation counselors will work with those who are culturally different from themselves. To respond to the multicultural landscape of PWDs, rehabilitation counselors must continually work toward cultural competency. Culturally competency standards have been developed that provide a roadmap for developing cultural beliefs and attitudes, knowledge, and skills of self, client, and intervention. In brief, culturally competent rehabilitation counselors need to be (a) cognizant of their own cultural worldview; (b) cognizant of their attitude toward cultural differences, including biases; (c) knowledgeable of different cultural practices and worldviews, especially those of client populations that they work that are different from their own; and

TABLE 5.2 ▨ **Differences Between Western and Non-Western Cultural Values**

Western Cultural Value	Non-Western Cultural Value
Individualism	Collectivism/group
Verbal/high-context	Non-verbal/low-context
Equality/egalitarianism	Hierarchy
Informal	Formal
Guilt (internal self-control)	Shame (external control)
Directness/assertiveness	Indirectness
Respect for results	Respect for status/ascription
Respect for competence	Respect for elders
Time is money	Time is life
Action/doing	Being/acceptance
Systematic/mechanic	Humanistic
Tasks	Relationship/loyalty
Winning	Collaboration/harmony
Pride	Saving face
Future/change	Past/tradition
Control	Fate
Specific/linear	Holistic
Achievement	Modesty

Adapted from Kohls (1981).

(d) develop cross-cultural skills through research and practice. Multicultural competence is an ongoing process throughout one's career.

At the most basic level of cultural knowledge is the fundamental value differences between Western and non-Western cultures. Specifically, individualism is the primary cultural mode of mainstream Western culture (e.g., United States) and collectivism is the primary cultural model of non-Western cultures (e.g., China). See Table 5.2 for an outline of the value differences of Western and non-Western culture. Rehabilitation counselors should be mindful that differences exist from one ethnic group to another—even when they are members of the dominant cultural group. For example, some Asian Americans, African Americans, and Native Americans have collectivist cultural ways of being despite their acculturation to the larger dominant group for which they are also a member.

African Americans

According to Rowe and Rowe (2009), African Americans tend to be wary and suspicious of mental health treatment because of enduring racism and may present as guarded and cautious. Rehabilitation counselors must therefore create trust by conveying openness while encouraging questions about themselves—including being more open to self-disclosure. Rehabilitation counselors must also convey a willingness to answer questions regarding the therapeutic process, theoretical approaches, length of treatment time, involvement of important others, role expectations defined, and the corresponding responsibilities laid out. Particular attention is often paid by African Americans to metacommunication, or what the rehabilitation counselor says and how they say it, their comfort with stylist nuances (intonation, volume, speed, and gesturing), and their comfort in discussing real and perceived experiences of racism and discrimination. Rehabilitation counselors should develop familiarity with linguistic nuances. African Americans are commonly higher energy people, are more demonstrative, use gesturing to highlight communication, and respond faster and with less-emotional restraint. In addition, many African Americans are highly religious or spiritual. Thus, rehabilitation counselors should be prepared to support enlistment of their client's religious/spiritual affiliate (i.e., minister, pastor, church deacon) to aid in problem solving if needed (Rowe & Rowe, 2009).

Asian Americans

The term Asian American is often utilized to reference indigenous persons of the Asian continent residing in the United States. This term often results in viewing persons of Asian descent as a single homogenous group despite the vast heterogeneity among Asian cultures. In general, the Asian culture places group needs and wants above individual needs (collectivist vs. an individualistic perspective). They place extraordinary emphasis on relationships and the harmony within these relationships. According to Brightman Asian heritage encompasses filial piety, shame as a method of reinforcement of desirable behaviors, self-control, consensus, fatalism, and inconspicuousness. In Asian cultures, men who have roles as husband and father are considered the patriarch of the family and thus the fiscally responsible head-of-household, whereas women who have roles as wife and mother are responsible for the home. In regards to counseling, many Asians do not seek mental health/social services because of their belief of bringing shame to their families. When working with Asian men in particular, rehabilitation counselors should be cognizant that counseling may be considered nonmasculine (e.g., showing emotion when culture dictates saving face). Rehabilitation counselors should be cognizant of family first values in the Asian culture and therefore consider exploring with the client including family in the therapeutic process. Finally, when making referrals to other allied helping professions, rehabilitation counselors should be sure that the referral source is cultural appropriate to work with Asian persons.

Latino

Latino culture also includes Hispanic American culture. The Hispanic and Latino population is the fastest growing population within the United States (U.S. Census Bureau, 2010). These labels, however, like others, can be problematic, as a Mexican American born in the United States may refer to himself or herself as a Chicano, for example. Thus, rehabilitation counselors must understand how clients ethnically and culturally identify to avoid monolithic viewpoints. Hispanic and Latino Americans who reside in the Eastern United States prefer to identify as Hispanic, whereas those residing in the Western United States tend to prefer Latino. According to Smart and Smart (1992), many Latino/Hispanic individuals view themselves as bicultural. They wish to maintain their native culture while adding American culture, which is important to consider when conceptualizing clients and introducing culturally appropriate counseling interventions. In addition, rehabilitation counselors need to separate the effects of culture from socioeconomic status (SES). For example, Latino/Hispanic individuals who appear uncooperative may in fact be feeling helpless and powerless due to economic deprivation, thus dropping out of services because of lack of economic resources. Most Latino/Hispanic cultures have a collectivist culture and place emphasis on family (to depend on one another), deference to age, gender, and authority, and have an informal way of interpersonal communication (Mejia, 2009). They also tend to view disability from the moral model based on their religious beliefs (Gibson, 2009). Many Latino/Hispanic individuals maintain devout religiousness/spirituality. Latino/Hispanic cultures place emphasis on maleness (machismo) and gender role norms. Women are responsible for child rearing and the household, and men are often the sole provider working long hours or holding multiple jobs to provide for family. Thus, taking off work to attend a counseling session would likely conflict with gender role and impact income. Latino/Hispanic cultures commonly deemphasize mental health services because they are typically accustomed to seeing physicians only; thus, explaining the role of counseling is highly important. Moreover, as with other cultures, seeking mental health services is stigmatized ("loco") and a sign of weakness especially in the more hypermasculine (machismo) Latinos/Hispanic men.

Native American

Native American culture is vastly different from that of mainstream society. According to King (2009), there are many different beliefs among the 500+ federally recognized tribes in the United States, yet there is one commonly held worldview regardless of tribal affiliation, which is, humans are seen as equal to the rest of creation. Views of self, society, nature, time, and communication are drawn from this basic worldview, which contrast significantly from other worldviews. In addition, there is a significant difference between mainstream theories and American Indian psychology. For example, the American Indian worldview focuses more on process rather than product, relationship over expertise, indigenous healing methods versus empirical-based outcomes, willingness to journey with clients within their worldview and views of healing, and an equal power dynamic in the therapeutic relationship (King, as cited in Trimble & Gonzalez, 2008). Effective practice of Indian psychology takes into practice the reversal of "the pain of the people," the recognition of historical trauma, dynamics of racism, White supremacy, and oppression (King, 2009). Greater emphasis is placed on the healing itself as opposed to common techniques for treatment effectiveness. Presenting problems are seen as preparatory hardships to strengthen the individual for the next step in their journey. In summary, treatment is considered successful when an individual becomes more fully who they are meant to be as both a tribal member and complete cultural being.

King (2009) offers the following therapeutic recommendations for working with Native Americans: (a) be flexible (e.g., visit clients at their homes; self-disclose); (b) be genuine (e.g., say so when you do not know about a tribe); (c) be knowledgeable about the worldview and history of tribal people and their differences; (d) be aware of acculturation issues. Native people range from being traditional to fully assimilated to White culture; (e) be aware of traditional and nontraditional healing (i.e., sometimes herbs are prescribed by medicine men who can interact with prescribed medications); (f) use attending behaviors such as silence, maintaining eye contact, dressing casually (dressing professionally is seen as a barrier to communication as represents White culture); (g) make room for mystery (Traditional Native thinking is not the same logical, linear communication style found in mainstream society. Also, seeing spirits is common for Native people; although it is not necessary for rehabilitation counselors to believe this to be true, this must be allowed to be true for the client); (h) have humor. Despite the stoic American Indian stereotype, Native Americans have a good sense of humor—even at their own expense. Humor is used as a coping mechanism during difficult times.

COUNSELOR SUPERVISION

Overview

The focus of this section is on concepts that are related to rehabilitation counselor supervision, including definition, supervisory activities (support, consultation, counseling, training and instruction, and evaluation), clinical supervision formats (self-supervision, individual supervision, team supervision, group supervision, and peer supervision), methods to evaluate supervisee development (indirect delayed, direct delayed, direct present, and indirect present), and supervisee developmental level which includes a review of the integrated development model.

▨ LEARNING OBJECTIVE

By the end of this unit you should be able to:

1. Explain the purpose, roles, and need for counselor supervision to enhance the professional development, clinical accountability, and gate-keeping functions for the welfare of individuals with a disability.

▨ KEY CONCEPTS

Definition of Supervision

Supervision is an essential component of the rehabilitation counseling discipline and involves qualified, experienced, and trained rehabilitation counselors overseeing supervisees' clinical experiences to ensure that supervisees demonstrate satisfactory knowledge and skills in performing the fundamental duties of a rehabilitation counselor. Herbert (2004) defined clinical supervision as a process by which supervisors (a) use clinical techniques to provide supervision, (b) focus on supervisee professional and personal development, and (c) direct the clinical work of front-line staff, so that client services can be provided to meet organizational goals and professional standards. Herbert identified how rehabilitation counselor supervision differs from other helping profession supervision stating that it (a) fosters skill development in psychosocial interventions; (b) encourages supervisees' personal growth and self-efficacy; and (c) establishes supervisees' case conceptualization skills around disability issues. Herbert emphasizes that psychosocial aspects of disabilities and chronic illnesses should be the primary focus of rehabilitation counseling supervision.

Supervisory Activities

Support, consultation, counseling, training and instruction, and evaluation have been identified as five primary supervisory activities (Bradley & Ladany, 2001). Supervisors support supervisees by creating a safe environment to process anxiety, fears, uncertainty, and confusion. Consultation pertains to supervisors and supervisees working collaboratively to address challenges faced when working with clients to determine diagnoses, interventions, and treatment plans. Counseling refers to supervisors showing empathy to supervisees on a professional level; however, precaution must be taken to ensure no dual relationship exists. Training and instruction involves supervisors determining the best approach when educating supervisees on skills, knowledge, and theories. Training and instruction must be tailored to meet supervisees' needs and developmental level. Evaluation occurs when supervisors provide supervisees with constructive feedback around effectiveness with clients and professional development.

Clinical Supervision Formats

Herbert (2004) recognized five basic formats of clinical supervision—self-supervision, individual supervision, team supervision, group supervision, and peer supervision. In self-supervision, counselors review their own clinical work, assess for needs, and intervene when necessary; however, this approach poses problems as issues may be overlooked without reviews from peers. Individual supervision is a widely used approach in mental health settings, where experienced professionals monitor, evaluate, and mentor counselors-in-training. In team supervision, professionals from multiple disciplines consult about clients. Group supervision consists of professionals consulting with others from the same discipline, affording supervisees the opportunity to present cases and receive feedback about their clinical work and possible interventions. For professionals with advanced knowledge, experience, and skills, peer supervision is used for consultation and evaluation of clinical work with peers where no power differential exists. Peer supervision is often used among professionals who own their own private practice.

Methods to Evaluate Supervisee Development

Assessment of counselors-in-training competency requires evaluations of client–counselor interactions (Herbert, 2001). Herbert describes four methods to evaluate supervisee development—indirect delayed, direct delayed, direct present, and indirect present. The indirect delayed method includes self-reports of client progress, case conceptualizations, and reflections of interactions between supervisees and their clients through written documentations, such as process notes, case presentations, and case reviews. Direct delayed methods directly monitor counselor–client interactions through the use of audio and video recordings, which allow supervisors to make inferences about counselor–client interactions, assess how supervisees attend to presenting issues during the session, examine supervisee interventions, and formulate supervisory interventions tailored to improve supervisee skills and competence with clients (Herbert, 2004). Direct present methods involve "live" supervision where supervisors evaluate sessions in real-time and intervene if necessary. Two specific types are co-counseling and live supervision. Supervisors and supervisees provide counseling services collaboratively in co-counseling, so supervisees have the opportunity to observe experienced counselors. Live supervision is when supervision occurs with clients present. Indirect present methods include direct observations of counselor–client interactions with less intrusiveness. The most popular technique involves supervisees wearing a "bug-in-the-ear" while counseling sessions are in progress. Supervisors provide input and feedback for adjustments without disrupting the session.

Supervisee Developmental Level

Supervision outcomes depend on the degree to which supervisors adjust their roles and behaviors to match the developmental level of supervisees. Herbert (2004) states that beginning supervisees generally prefer encouragement, support, and space to examine personal concerns that may impact client interactions and a structured framework where direct and clear suggestions are provided. In contrast, experienced counselors prefer greater autonomy, space to address personal issues such as countertransference, increased self-efficacy, and a structured framework devoted to case consultation (Herbert, 2001). The integrated developmental model (IDM) provides a structured framework to better understand the developmental process of counseling trainees to competent, experienced, and skilled professionals (Herbert, 2001).

The IDM structure is based on supervisory interventions that are chosen based on the supervisee's affective and cognitive needs. The primary supervisory activities cover eight dimensions (Herbert, 2001) including (a) assessment techniques; (b) case conceptualization; (c) individual differences; (d) interpersonal assessment; (e) intervention skills competence; (f) professional ethics; (g) theoretical orientation; and (h) treatment plans and goals. In the IDM, supervisees continuously progress from Level 1, counselors with limited experience, to Level 3 Integrated, counselors who successfully move through the eight dimensions. Growth and successful movement across the eight dimensions are assessed within each level by evaluating supervisees' on three basic structures—awareness, motivation, and autonomy (Herbert, 2001; Maki & Delworth, 1995).

▨ MULTIPLE CHOICE QUESTIONS

1. Breaching client confidentiality must occur in which of the following situations:
   A. The client informs you that he or she is going to kill his or her girlfriend
   B. The client tells you that he/she feels pretty sad and depressed
   C. The client tells you that he/she hit his/her son a couple times
   D. A and C

2. Sexual relationships with former clients are prohibited for at least ___ years following termination.
   A. 2
   B. 5
   C. 10
   D. 20

3. Irrational thinking is most closely aligned with which counseling theory:
   A. REBT
   B. Existential
   C. Gestalt
   D. Client-centered

4. Cultural competency includes all the following EXCEPT:
   A. Understanding of one's own worldview
   B. Understanding of one's attitudes and biases
   C. Knowledge of different cultural practices and worldviews from one's own
   D. A diverse workplace

5. Rehabilitation counselor supervision differs from other types of clinical supervision in which of the following ways:
   A. Its primary focus is on psychosocial aspects of disabilities and chronic illness
   B. Occurs in Public Vocational Rehabilitation settings
   C. Typically occurs in a group setting
   D. Often is performed by multiple supervisors

6. The "empty chair" technique is associated with which of the following counseling theories?
   A. CBT
   B. Gestalt

    C. Client-centered

    D. Psychodynamic

7. Reinforcement and punishment are key components of which form of learning:

    A. Classical conditioning

    B. Modeling

    C. Operant conditioning

    D. A and C

8. Which of the following occurs when reinforcement is withheld from a previously reinforced behavior to decrease the undesired behavior?

    A. Unconditional stimulus

    B. Law of effect

    C. Conditioned response

    D. Extinction

9. When the following three factors (external stimulus, external reinforcement, and cognitive mediation processes) interact to explain behavior, this is called:

    A. Social learning theory

    B. Reciprocal determinism

    C. Operant conditioning

    D. CBT

10. This is defined as a clinically significant behavioral, psychological syndrome, or collection of symptoms that causes an individual stress, disability, or an increased risk of suffering death, disability, pain, or the loss of freedom.

    A. Psychiatric disability

    B. Serious mental illness

    C. Mental disorder

    D. Health condition

▓ ANSWER KEY

1. D; 2. B; 3. A; 4. D; 5. A; 6. B; 7. C; 8. D; 9. B; 10. C

▓ ADVANCED MULTIPLE CHOICE QUESTIONS

1. This counselor theory posits that humans are primarily motivated by socialization.

    A. CBT

    B. Social learning theory

    C. Individual psychology

    D. REBT

2. Empathy, genuineness, and unconditional positive regard are considered necessary and sufficient for change to occur in which counseling theory:

    A. Client-centered

    B. Gestalt

    C. CBT

    D. Psychoanalysis

3. The "ABC" method was developed from which counseling theory:

    A. CBT

    B. Existential

    C. Gestalt

    D. REBT

4. Dual diagnosis refers to:

    A. Comorbid physical and mental disorder

    B. Comorbid psychiatric and substance abuse disorder
    C. Differential diagnosis
    D. Co-existing physical disabilities

5. This is the most frequently used classification system and diagnostic tool used for determining mental disorders is:
    A. Psychological tests
    B. Personality measures
    C. *DSM-IV-TR*
    D. Institute of Medicine Classification System

6. This is considered fundamental to the development of a counseling relationship and involves a "connection" or positive bond with clients and other treatment team members that involve mutual trust, respect, and acceptance.
    A. Empathy
    B. Working alliance
    C. Attending
    D. Reflection

7. Biological differences between men and woman include all the following EXCEPT:
    A. Chromosomes
    B. Hormonal production
    C. Reproductive capabilities
    D. Cellular production

8. The final step in conflict resolution is:
    A. Dispelling myths about "good" relationships
    B. Defining the conflict
    C. Generating options for resolving the conflict
    D. Implementing solutions for resolving conflict

9. Which of the following represents an appropriate reason to terminate a client–counselor relationship?
    A. Counselor has negative feelings toward the client
    B. Client is resistant to counseling treatment
    C. Client is not paying agreed upon fees
    D. Counselor is experiencing countertransference

10. Which of the following approaches to rehabilitation counseling requires a focus on a client's capabilities, capacities, and opportunities versus deficits and limitations?
    A. Ecological approach
    B. Empowerment approach
    C. Biopsychosocial approach
    D. Humanistic approach

ANSWER KEY AND EXPLANATION OF ANSWERS

1-C: Individual psychology, which is based on Alfred Adler's theory, posits that humans are primarily motivated by socialization. Alternatively, CBT believes that people's feelings and behaviors are based on how they think (cognitions) and personality is seen as an enduring set of behavioral and emotional responses to stimuli that stem from ingrained, idiosyncratic ways of thinking. Social learning theory posits that psychological functioning involves the reciprocal interaction between behavior, cognition, and the environment, and REBT believes that individuals are constantly striving toward growth but are often stuck because of irrational thinking.

2-A: The client-centered approach is based on the role of empathy, genuineness, and unconditional positive regard as the fundamental conditions necessary and sufficient for change to occur. Specific techniques above and beyond these conditions are not considered from this theoretical perspective. The Gestalt approach, while also humanistic, is known for a variety of techniques such as empty chair, pronouns, sharing hunches, and dream work. The CBT approach focuses primarily on psychoeducation and developing skills for managing specific problems, and includes the use of a variety of techniques. While empathy, genuineness, and unconditional positive regard are considered necessary for change, they are not considered sufficient. Finally, psychoanalysis relies heavily on free association, interpretation, confrontation, and working through as primary techniques.

3-D: The goals and process of REBT are often summarized using the ABC method: *A* refers to the activating event or adversity; *B* is the individual's beliefs about the event, which may be rational and helpful or irrational and maladaptive; *C* refers to the emotional and behavioral consequences of those beliefs; *D* refers to the responsibility of the counselor to dispute the irrational beliefs and assist the client to obtain more rational, adaptive belief, and *E* refers to when a client develops new behavioral and emotional consequences.

4-B: "Dual diagnosis" is reserved specifically for those who have both a psychiatric disability and a substance abuse disorder.

5-C: The *DSM-IV-TR* is the most frequently used classification system and diagnostic tool used for determining mental disorders. This system was developed by the APA and provides users with criteria for a wide array of mental conditions using a five-level Axis system.

6-B: Working alliance is considered fundamental to the development of a counseling relationship and involves a "connection" or positive bond with clients and other treatment team members that involve mutual trust, respect, and acceptance. Empathy is an act of knowing and understanding the experience of another. It is the ability to convey support and acceptance by understanding the client's experience via the client's perspective. Attending are nonverbal skills that involve the physical orientation of the rehabilitation counselor toward the client as a means of communication with a goal of showing attentiveness and availability. Reflection of feeling is a verbal statement whereby there is recognition of the client's emotions by the counselor.

7-D: Biological differences between men and women include chromosomal differences, hormonal production differences, and reproductive capability differences. Cellular production does not differ by gender per se.

8-D: The final step in conflict resolution is implanting solutions for resolving conflict. Specifically, the steps suggested to follow for conflict resolution occurs in the following sequence: (1) myths about "good" working relationship must be addressed such as the best working relationship occurs when no discrepancies are present, individuals in the relationship have shared values and expectations, and the goal of the relationship is to avoid conflict; (2) conflict needs to be accurately defined and reframed as differences related to interests and goals versus a negative will; (3) misperceptions should be clarified regarding what one has stated and how the information has been interpreted prevents miscommunications; (4) individuals should discuss ideas that will contribute to the development of a set of shared expectations by reconciling differences; and (5) implementing and evaluating resolutions that involve agreement on what the roles and responsibilities of each will be and a written agreement outlining these roles and responsibilities is recommended.

9-C: Client resistance, counselor countertransference, and counselor negative feelings toward a client are not sufficient reasons to terminate immediately. The latter reasons do suggest the need for immediate consultation but not termination. If a client does not pay for agreed upon fees, termination is an appropriate solution.

10-B: The empowerment approach involves focusing on a client's capabilities, capacities, and opportunities versus deficits and limitations. Empowerment is defined as a process of increasing personal, interpersonal, or political power, so that individuals can take action to improve their life situation. To facilitate an empowering counseling relationship, rehabilitation counselors need to focus on client capabilities, capacities, and opportunities rather than their deficits. Ecological approach refers to considering the person × environment interaction in understanding disability and chronic illness; biopsychosocial approach is an approach that emphasizes understanding the biological, psychological, and social aspects of health and disability used by all contemporary health and allied health professionals is response to the reliance on a biomedical explanation of illness. The humanistic approach, while generally posits that individuals are moving toward growth, this broad umbrella refers to a counseling school of thought and includes such counseling theories as client-centered, Gestalt, and existential theories of counseling.

■ REFERENCES

American Psychiatric Association. (2000). *Diagnostic and statistical manual of mental disorders* (4th ed.), *Text Revision* (*DSM-IV-TR*). Washington DC: Author.

Bandura, A. et al. (1977). Self-efficacy: Toward a unifying theory of behavioral change. *Psychological Review, 84*(2), 191–215.

Bandura, A., Underwood, B., & Fromson, M. E. (1975). Disinhibition of aggression through diffusion of responsibility and dehumanization of victims. *Journal of Research in Personality, 9*(4), 253–269.

Beck, A., & Weishaar, M. (2000). Cognitive therapy. In R. Corsini & D. Wedding (Eds.), *Current psychotherapies*. Itasca, IL: F. E. Peacock Publishers.

Beck, A. T. (1976). *Cognitive therapy and the emotional disorders*. Oxford England: International Universities Press.

Beck, R. L. (1991). The hearing impaired psychotherapist: Implications for process and practice. *Clinical Social Work Journal, 19*(4), 417–426.

Bond, G. R., & Resnick, S. G. (2000). Psychiatric rehabilitation. In R. G. Frank & T. R. Elliot (Eds.), *Handbook of rehabilitation psychology* (pp. 235–258). Washington DC: American Psychological Association.

Bradley, L. J., & Ladany, N. (2001). *Counselor supervision: Principles, process and practice* (3rd ed.). Philadelphia, PA: Brunner-Routledge.

Campbell, T. W. (1994). Psychotherapy and malpractice exposure. *American Journal of Forensic Psychology, 12*, 4–41.

Chan, F., Berven, L., & Thomas, K. R. (2004). *Counseling theories and technologies for rehabilitation health professionals*, New York, NY: Springer Publishing.

Cobia, D. C., & Boes, S. R. (2000). Professional disclosure statements and formal plans for supervision: Two strategies for minimizing the risk of ethical conflicts in post-master's supervision. *Journal of Counseling and Development, 78*, 293–296.

Commission on Rehabilitation Counselor Certification (CRCC). (2010). Code of Professional Ethics for Rehabilitation Counselors. *Journal of Applied Rehabilitation Counseling, 32*, 38–61.

Cooper, C. C. (2000). Ethical issues with managed care: Challenges facing counseling psychology. *Counseling Psychologist, 28*, 179–236.

Corey, G. (2001). *Theory and practice of counseling and psychotherapy* (4th ed.). Pacific Grove, CA: Brooks/Cole.

Corey, G. (2004). *Theory and practice of counseling and psychotherapy* (5th ed.). Pacific Grove, CA: Wadsworth.

Corey, M. S., & Corey, G., (2006). *Groups: Process and practice*. Belmont, CA: Thomson Brooks/Cole.

Corrigan, P. W., & Liberman, R. P. (1994). Overview of behavior therapy in psychiatric hospitals. In P. W. Corrigan & R. P. Liberman (Eds.), *Behavior therapy in psychiatric hospitals* (pp. 1–38). New York, NY: Springer Publishing.

Corsini J. R., & Wedding, D. (1989). *Current psychotherapies* (2nd ed.). Itasca IL: Peacock.

Coven, A. B. (1979). The Gestalt approach to rehabilitation of the whole person. *Journal of Applied Rehabilitation Counseling, 9*, 144–147.

Craighead, L. W., Craighead, W. E., Kazdin, A. E., & Mahoney. M. J. (Eds.). (1994). *Cognitive and behavioral interventions: An empirical approach to mental health problems*. Boston, MA: Allyn & Bacon.

Curl, R. M., & Sheldon, J. B. (1992). Achieving reasonable choices: Balancing the rights and responsibilities of consumers with those of rehabilitation counselors. *Rehabilitation Education, 6*, 195–205.

Ellis, A. (1962). *A reason and emotion in psychotherapy.* New York, NY: Lyle Stuart.

Falvo, D. (2009). *Medical and psychosocial aspects of chronic illness and disability* (4th ed.). New York, NY: Jones and Bartlett.

Fisher, R., & Brown, S. (1988). *Getting together: Building a relationship that gets to yes.* Boston, MA: Houghton Mifflin.

Garcia, J. G., Winston, S. M., & Borzuchowska, B. (2003). A transcultural integrative model for ethical decision making in counseling. *Journal of Counseling and Development, 81*, 268–277.

Gardiner, H. W., & Kosmitzi, C. (2008). *Lives across cultures: Cross cultural human development.* Boston: Pearson Educational, Inc.

Garske, G. G., & Bishop, M. (2004). Rational-emotive behavior therapy. In F. Chan, N. L. Berven, K. R. Thomas, F. Chan, N. L. Berven, & K. R. Thomas (Eds.), *Counseling theories and techniques for rehabilitation health professionals* (pp. 177–195). New York, NY: Springer Publishing.

Gibson, J. (2009). Clinical competency and culturally diverse clients with disabilities: The case of Linda. In M. E. Gallardo & B. W. McNeill (Eds.), *Intersections of multiple identities* (pp. 277–307). New York, NY: Routledge.

Gilliland, B. E. & James, R. K. (1998). *Theories and strategies in counseling and psychotherapy.* Boston, MA: Allyn & Bacon.

Glasser, W. (1965). *Reality therapy: A new approach to psychiatry.* New York, NY: Guilford.

Glasser, W. (1998). *Choice theory: A new psychology of personal freedom.* New York, NY: Harper-Perennial.

Greenson, R. (1967). *The technique and practice of psychoanalysis* (Vol. 1). New York, NY: International Universities Press.

Gutierrez, L. M. (1990). Working with woman of color: An empowerment perspective. *Social Work, 35*, 149–153.

Halbur, D. A., & Halbur, K. V. (2006). *Developing your theoretical orientation in counseling and psychotherapy.* Boston, MA: Pearson Educational, Inc.

Hansen, J. H., Cramer, S. H., & Rossberg, R. H. (1993) *Counseling: Theory and process* (5th ed.). Upper Saddle River, NJ: Allyn and Bacon, Inc.

Herbert, J. H. (2004). Clinical supervision in rehabilitation settings. In F. Chan, L. Berven, & K. R. Thomas, *Counseling theories and techniques for rehabilitation health professionals* (pp. 405–422). New York, NY: Springer Publishing.

Holmes, G. E., Hall, L., & Karst, R. H. (1989). Litigation avoidance through conflict resolution: Issues for state rehabilitation agencies. *American Rehabilitation, 15*, 12–15.

Ivey, A. E., & Ivey, M. B. (2007). *Intentional interviewing and counseling: Facilitating client development in a multicultural society* (2nd ed.). Pacific Grove, CA: Wadsworth.

Kazdin, A. E. (2000). *Behavior modification in applied settings* (6th ed.). Belmont, CA: Wadsworth.

Kiernan, C. (1975). Behaviour modification. In D. Bannister (Ed.), *Issues and approaches in the psychological therapies* (pp. 241–260). New York, NY: Wiley.

King, J. (2009). Psychotherapy within an American Indian perspective. In M. E. Gallardo & B. W. McNeil (Eds.), *Intersections of multiple identities: A casebook of evidence-based practices with diverse populations* (pp. 113–136). New York, NY: Routledge.

Koch, L. C., McReynolds, C., & Rumrill, P. D. (2004). Basic counseling skills. In F. Chan, N. L. Berven, K. R. Thomas, F. Chan, N. L. Berven, & K. R. Thomas (Eds.), *Counseling theories and techniques for rehabilitation health professionals* (pp. 227–243). New York, NY: Springer Publishing.

Kohls, L. R. (1981). *Developing intercultural awareness.* Washington, DC: Sietar.

Kosciulek, J. F. (2000). Implications of consumer direction for disability policy development and rehabilitation service delivery. *Journal of Disability Policy Studies, 11*, 82–89.

Lee, E. J., Chan, F., Chronister, J., Chan J. Y. C., & Romero, M. (2009). Models, research and treatment of co-existing depression for people with chronic illness and disability. In F. Chan, E. Da Silva Cardoso, & J. A. Chronister (Eds.), *Understanding psychosocial adjustment to chronic illness and disability: A handbook for evidence-based practitioners in rehabilitation* (pp. 75–107). New York, NY: Springer Publishing.

Livneh, H. & Siller, J. (2004). Psychodynamic therapy for rehabilitation professionals. In F. Chan, N. L. Berven, & K. R. Thomas (Eds.), *Counseling theories and techniques for rehabilitation health professionals* (pp. 20–52). New York, NY: Springer Publishing.

Maki, D. R., & Delworth, U. (1995). Clinical supervision: A definition and model for the rehabilitation counseling profession. *Rehabilitation Counseling Bulletin, 38*, 282–303.

Mejia, O. L. (2009). Struggling with research and practice with a Mexican American family: The case of Robert. In M. E. Gallardo & B. W. McNeil (Eds.), *Intersections of multiple identities: A casebook of evidence-based practices with diverse populations* (pp. 29–58). New York, NY: Routledge.

Morrison, J. (2006). *DSM-IV made easy: The clinician's guide to diagnosis.* New York, NY: Guildford Press.

Mueser, K. T. (1993). Designing new psychosocial treatments for schizophrenia: Comment. *Psychiatry: Interpersonal and Biological Processes, 56*(3), 250–253.

Murray, C. J. L., & Lopez, A. D. (Eds.). (1996). *The global burden of disease: A comprehensive assessment of mortality and disability from diseases, injuries, and risk factors in 1990 and projected to 2020.* Cambridge, MA: Harvard University Press.

Nelson-Jones, R. (2000). *Six key approaches to counseling and therapy.* New York, NY: Continuum.

Papajohn, J. C. (1982). *Intensive behavior therapy.* New York, NY: Pergamon Press.

Parker, R. M., Szymanski, E. M., & Patterson, J. B. (2005). *Counseling: Basics and beyond* (4th ed.). Austin, TX: Pro-Ed.

Rogers, C (1961). *On becoming a person.* Boston, MA: Houghton-Mifflin.

Rogers, C. (1957). The necessary and sufficient conditions of therapeutic personality change. *Journal of Consulting Psychology, 21*, 95–103.

Rowe, D. M., & Rowe, S. L. (2009). Conversations in marriage: An African-centered marital intervention. In M. E. Gallardo & B. W. McNeil (Eds.), *Intersections of multiple identities: A casebook of evidence-based practices with diverse populations* (pp. 59–84). New York, NY: Routledge.

Schloss, P. J., & Smith, M. A. (1994). *Applied behavior analysis in the classroom.* Boston, MA: Allyn & Bacon.

Shaw, L. (2004). Risk management for rehabilitation counseling and related professions. In F. Chan, N. L. Berven, K. R. Thomas, F. Chan, N. L. Berven, & K. R. Thomas (Eds.), *Counseling theories and techniques for rehabilitation health professionals* (pp. 423–443). New York, NY: Springer Publishing.

Shaw, L. & Tarvydas, V. M. (2001). The use of professional disclosure in rehabilitation counseling. *Rehabilitation Counseling Bulletin, 45*, 40–47.

Smart, J. F., & Smart, D. W. (1992). Cultural issues in the rehabilitation of Hispanics. *Journal of Rehabilitation, 58*, 29–37.

Stoll, J. L. (2004). Behavior Therapy. In F. Chan, N. L. Berven, K. R. Thomas, F. Chan, N. L. Berven, & K. R. Thomas (Eds.), *Counseling theories and techniques for rehabilitation health professionals* (pp. 136–158). New York, NY: Springer Publishing.

Stuntzner, S. (unpublished manuscript). *Counseling supervision within the field of rehabilitation counseling: An important aspect of the profession emerging.*

Tarasoff v. Regents of the University of California, 529 P.2d 553, 118 Cal. Rptr. 129 (1974), *vacated,* 17 Cal. 3d 425, 551 P.2d 334, 131 Cal. Rptr. 14 (1976).

Tarvydas, V. M. (1995). Ethics and the practice of rehabilitation counselor supervision. *Rehabilitation Counseling Bulletin, 38*, 294–306.

Teyber, E. (2006). *Interpersonal process in psychotherapy: A relational approach* (5th ed.). Pacific Grove, CA: Brooks/Cole.

Trimble, J. E., & Gonzalez, J. (2008). Cultural considerations and perspectives for providing psychological counseling for Native American Indians. In P. Pedersen, J. Draguns, W. Lonner, & J. Trimble (Eds.), *Counseling across cultures* (6th ed., pp. 93–111). Thousand Oaks, CA: Sage.

Tschopp M. & Frain, M. (2009). Psychiatric rehabilitation. In F. Chan, E. Da Silva Cardoso, & J. A. Chronister (Eds.), *Understanding psychosocial adjustment to chronic illness and disability: A handbook for evidence-based practitioners in rehabilitation* (pp. 371–398). New York, NY: Springer Publishing.

U.S. Census Bureau. (2010). *National population by race United States: 2010*. Retrieved from http://2010.census.gov/2010census/data/

Wilson, K. B. (2000). Predicting vocational rehabilitation eligibility based on race, education, work status, and source of support and application. *Rehabilitation Counseling Bulletin, 43*, 97–105.

Woody, R. H. (2001). *Psychological information: Protecting the right to privacy: A guidebook for mental health practitioners and their clients*. Madison, CT: Psychosocial Press.

Yalom, I. D. (1995). *The theory and practice of group psychotherapy* (4th ed.). New York, NY: Basic Books.

Group Work and Family Dynamics

Eun-Jeong Lee and Kristin Sokol

6

The composition of groups in group counseling ranges from couples to families to large groups of individuals (Hueber, 2004). Across this range of compositions, common goals include self-understanding, personal growth, and building on inner resources (Corey & Corey, 2006). Group counseling involves individuals coming together to form a social system with norms and expectations, interacting with each other as well as with the leader, sharing needs and experiences, exchanging support, and forming an identity as members of the group. In group counseling, the group context and the group process constitute the treatment intervention (Hueber, 2004). The therapeutic effects originate within the group context and are based on the fundamental assumption that the presence of others provides a unique opportunity for self-exploration and learning that is not present in individual approaches (Corey & Corey, 2006; Hueber, 2004). This chapter will review the following topics related to group and family counseling:

- Group dynamics and counseling theory
- Group process
- Group leadership styles and techniques
- Family dynamics and counseling theory
- Ethical and legal issues impacting group process

GROUP DYNAMICS AND COUNSELING THEORY

Multiple theoretical approaches may apply to group counseling. Huebner (2004) reviewed four categories of therapeutic approaches in group counseling. In this section, those four broach categories of therapeutic approaches will be briefly reviewed, and the fundamental differences between theoretical approaches will be discussed.

LEARNING OBJECTIVES

By the end of this unit you should be able to:

1. Understand the core assumptions and values of each theoretic approach.
2. Understand how each theoretical approach can be uniquely applied in group settings.

KEY CONCEPTS

Psychodynamic Approaches

Psychodynamic approaches include psychoanalysis, object relations, and interpersonal theory. The goal of psychodynamic intervention is to provide a climate in which clients may reexperience relationships with others. The group process itself may elicit transference and defense mechanisms in group members. Transference elicits interaction patterns that may be dysfunctional in the current context. Through identification, analysis, and interpretation of such patterns in group, members are provided the opportunity to develop insights into the origins of flawed psychological development and expectations in relationships (e.g., self-defeating, self-fulfilling, personal strengths, and weaknesses). Developing insight into the origins of dysfunctional patterns of interaction reduces the shame associated with recognizing weaknesses, because weaknesses are understood as logical adaptive responses to experiences (Huebner, 2004).

Applications

Persons with disabilities experience the same life issues as individuals without disabilities such as relationship challenges, emotional distress, cultural issues, and abuse, to name a few (Patterson, McKenzie, & Jenkins, 1995). In addition, experiences with disability may elicit stereotypical responses, including misperceptions of abilities, the spread of disability to all aspects of life, lowered expectations for adaptation, and social isolation (Marshak & Seligman, 1993). Effective group leaders recognize that these expectations and stereotypical responses may be enacted in the group, providing opportunities to practice alternative responses to develop social competence and proper social skills.

Experiential Approaches

Gestalt therapy, reality therapy, existential therapy, and person-centered therapy are characterized as experiential approaches. The goal of these approaches is to develop a realistic and a present-centered understanding of self and to empower group members to change and take responsibility for their lives. The focus of group work is on present feelings and responses. Nonverbal behaviors are attended to as clues to masked feelings. The focus on the "here-and-now" experience is intended to increase awareness of emotions, provide catharsis, and develop congruence between actions and feelings (Huebner, 2004).

Applications

Experiential groups may help individuals experience mourning or anger related to their disabilities or others. Role playing and keeping a journal of emotions and thoughts are some of the techniques typical of experiential group work (Huebner, 2004).

Cognitive–Behavioral Approaches

Cognitive–behavioral approaches to group work include behavior therapy, rational-emotive therapy, cognitive therapy, stress inoculation, and solution-focused therapy. The goal of cognitive–behavioral approaches is to identify maladaptive behavior and patterns of thinking and to replace them with adaptive behavior and rational cognition (Huebner, 2004). The group members and leader reinforce adaptive behavior and thoughts, seek to extinguish maladaptive responses, and promote direct and vicarious learning. Group role plays, systematic desensitization, realization, meditation, assertiveness, and time management training are some common cognitive–behavioral techniques (Huebner, 2004).

Applications

Group role play, structured experiences, inoculation, reframing cognitive distortion, and a problem-solving approach may help people with disabilities to redefine a disability and assist people in identifying and expanding adaptive strategies and strengths (Huebner, 2004).

Psychoeducational Approaches

Educational groups, support groups, and self-help groups are included in these approaches. The goals are to impart and acquire knowledge, to develop pragmatic coping strategies, and to exchange social support with others who have similar experiences. The group leader may be very active in planning and running a support group. The leadership may rotate among members or there may not be a formal group leader. Group membership may also vary from session to session. The level of self-disclosure and cohesiveness may vary as well. Group members function not only as a support and knowledge base for one another but also as a source of practical solutions to problems and action planning (Huebner, 2004).

GROUP PROCESS

Group process refers to the ways in which a group develops or evolves over time from beginning to end. Group process is concerned with the dynamics that go on within the group among the members (Corey & Corey, 2006).

▧ LEARNING OBJECTIVES

By the end of this unit you should be able to:

1. Understand the stages of group development and the typical characteristics of these stages.
2. Understand how a leader may facilitate the group in moving from one stage of development to the next.
3. Understand the different styles of leadership that can be adopted during the group process.

▧ KEY CONCEPTS

Stages of Group Development

Groups can be conceptualized as progressing through a series of stages from beginning to end. According to Corey and Corey (2006), group development is divided into four stages: initial, transition, working, and final. Groups may not progress through all stages and may get stuck at a particular stage, which they may never move beyond. Each stage may be characterized or differentiated according to several things: (1) processes and tasks that members are going through or trying to accomplish, (2) responses and behaviors of members, and (3) leader behaviors (Corey & Corey, 2006) (see Table 6.1).

Initial Stage

The initial stage is a time of orientation and exploration when members are trying to find their way, learning how to relate and behave within the group, and beginning to trust the group and individual members. It is often characterized by tentativeness. This is the stage where personal goals regarding what members will gain from participation in the group are identified. The main theme in the initial stage is that members become acclimated to the group and get acquainted with one another.

Characteristic thoughts, feelings, and behaviors include (a) getting acquainted, (b) learning how the group functions, (c) developing unspoken norms to regulate group behavior, (d) exploring fears and hopes related to the group and participation in the group, (e) clarifying expectations, (f) identifying personal goals, and (g) determining the degree of safety that is present in the group.

TABLE 6.1 ■ Summary Table: Stages of Group Development

Stage of Group Development	Characteristic Activities, Thoughts, Feelings, and Behaviors	Leader Functions and Behaviors
Initial	Getting acquainted Learning how the group functions Developing unspoken norms to regulate group behavior Exploring fears and hopes related to the group and participation in the group Clarifying expectations Identifying personal goals Determining the degree of safety that is present in the group	Decide on an optimal degree of sharing of leadership responsibility between group leader(s) and members Decide on an optimal degree of structuring on the part of the group leader(s) and the nature of that structuring
Transition	Feelings, thoughts, and behaviors that may interfere with productive work on issues and problems are identified and dealt with to move into a more highly productive working stage of the group Expression of feelings and difficulties, as members work through the resistance, conflicts, mistrust that inhibit work	Challenge the resistance that is a barrier to working on issues within the group More risk taking Identification and processing of feelings, thoughts, and behaviors and facilitating self-expression to move forward with group work (working through the resistance)
Working	Working on issues and attempting to accomplish goals Commitment to deal with problems and attention to group dynamics Trust, cohesion, and a sense of inclusion Open communication, self-disclosure, and taking risks Shared leadership, with leaders carrying less of the leadership responsibility Interpersonal conflict and control and power issues recognized and effectively dealt with Direct communication among members, giving feedback freely, accepting feedback nondefensively, and confronting constructively Feelings of support and hopefulness Willingness to work outside of the group to experiment and achieve behavioral changes	Continue to encourage facilitative norms and cohesiveness Reduce activity in structuring and leading the group to allow for greater shared leadership Model direct communication, self-disclosure, feedback, and constructive confrontation Support direct communication, self-disclosure, feedback, and constructive confrontation Identify and explore common themes so as to link the work of different members Translate insight into action by encouraging the practicing of new behaviors, in the group and outside through homework assignments
Final	Feelings of anxiety, sadness, separation, fear may be evident Concerns about unfinished business; things left "hanging" with little time to resolve them Concerns about "what comes next"	Deal with member feelings surrounding the ending of the group "What has this experience meant to you?" "What are your thoughts or feelings as we begin to wrap up our time together?" Recognize and deal with unfinished business Identify and reinforce growth, changes, and achievements of members Help members transfer changes and achievements to real life Reemphasize confidentiality Evaluate member growth and change, along with strengths and weaknesses of the group

Leadership functions and behaviors in this stage include (a) deciding on an optimal degree of sharing of leadership responsibility between group leader(s) and members and (b) deciding on an optimal degree of structuring on the part of the group leader(s) and the nature of that structuring.

Transition Stage

The transition stage is characterized by beginning to challenge the resistance that is a barrier to working on issues within the group and to take more risks. A stage in group development where feelings, thoughts, and behaviors that may interfere with productive work on issues and problems are identified and dealt with to move into a more highly productive working stage of the group. This stage is also characterized by expression of feelings and difficulties, as members work through the resistance, conflicts, or mistrust that inhibit work.

Characteristic thoughts, feelings, and behaviors include (a) anxieties and fears that inhibit open communication and lead to testing for safety and trustworthiness of members and leaders; (b) defensiveness and resistance, caused by a number of anxieties and fears (e.g., fear of looking foolish, being rejected, or losing control); (c) struggle for control, between members and between members and leaders; and (d) conflict and confrontation.

Leader functions and behaviors in this stage include (a) challenge the resistance that is a barrier to working on issues within the group; (b) more risk taking; and (c) identification and processing of feelings, thoughts and behaviors, and facilitating self-expression to move forward with group work.

Working Stage

This stage is characterized by (1) working on issues and attempting to accomplish goals and (2) commitment on the part of members to explore and deal with problems, along with their attention to dynamics of the group.

Characteristic thoughts, feelings, and behaviors include (a) trust, cohesion, and a sense of inclusion; (b) open communication, self-disclosure, and taking risks; (c) shared leadership, with leaders carrying less of the leadership responsibility and group members taking on more of this role; (d) interpersonal conflict, control and power issues recognized and effectively dealt with; (e) direct communication among members, giving feedback freely, accepting feedback nondefensively, and confronting constructively; (f) feelings of support and hopefulness; and (g) willingness to work outside, the group to experiment and achieve behavioral changes.

Leader functions and behaviors in this stage include (a) continue to encourage facilitative norms and cohesiveness; (b) reduce activity in structuring and leading the group to allow for greater shared leadership; (c) model and support direct communication, self-disclosure, feedback, and constructive confrontation; (d) identify and explore common themes so as to link the work of different members; and (e) translate insight into action by encouraging the practicing of new behavior, in the group and outside, through homework assignments.

Final Stage

This stage is a time of clarifying the meaning of individuals' experiences in the group, consolidating what has been accomplished and working toward applying those accomplishments to change outside of the group.

Characteristic thoughts, feelings, and behaviors include (a) feelings of anxiety, sadness, separation, and fear may be evident; (b) concerns about unfinished business; things left "hanging" with little time to resolve them; and (c) concerns about "what comes next."

Leader functions and behaviors in this stage include (a) deal with member feelings surrounding the ending of the group (e.g., "What has this experience meant to you?"); (b) recognize and deal with unfinished business; (c) identify and reinforce growth, changes, and achievements of members; (d) help members transfer changes and achievements to real life; (e) reemphasize confidentiality; and (f) evaluate member growth and change, along with strengths and weaknesses of the group.

GROUP LEADERSHIP STYLES AND TECHNIQUES

Group procedures demand that the leader be aware of all the members in the group, focus on the group dynamics, and possess group leadership skills. According to Corey and Corey (2006) and the Association for Specialists in Group Work (ASGW) (2000, 2008), group leaders need to have (1) knowledge of human behavior, behavior change, group process, dynamics, therapeutic factors, ethical issues, and of their own strengths and limitations as a group leader; (2) skill in assessing, understanding, and responding to needs of group members, and using a variety of leader responses, styles, and roles; and (3) self-awareness of attitudes, values, beliefs, and the ways in which they may influence one's own behavior as a group leader.

■ LEARNING OBJECTIVE

By the end of this unit you should be able to:

1. Understand characteristics of various leadership styles.
2. Be aware of the skills and competencies necessary to be an effective group leader.
3. Understand the challenges and issues facing group leaders.

■ KEY CONCEPTS

Leadership Styles

There are three general leadership styles: authoritarian, democratic, and laissez-faire. The leadership styles may be shifted from time to time throughout the group process based on the perceived needs of the group and the stage in which the group is currently operating. Each style has different strengths and limitations.

Authoritarian

Group leadership and control are concentrated in the leader(s). Leaders are likely to teach or direct. Leader(s) may be friendly and persuasive, but are not necessarily "bad" leaders. Communications tend to be directed between leader(s) and members. Members may be compliant or show little enthusiasm. Members may be productive, but not particularly satisfied, and may feel little responsibility for accomplishments. Member participation may be dependent on "prodding" from leader(s) (Sampson & Marthas, 1981).

Democratic

In this approach, leadership is shared between leader(s) and members, as is the control of policies and decisions, which are matters for discussion. Leaders guide rather than direct the group, are receptive to member ideas, and leave most decisions up to the members. This style provides a problem-solving framework in which leaders attempt to create a safe environment and members express themselves freely. Communications go between leader(s) and members and between different members. Members may participate more actively and may show more enthusiasm and motivation to accomplish goals. They may show more caring toward one another and feel a greater sense of belonging. They may show more responsibility and initiative and have a greater sense of ownership of group accomplishments (Sampson & Marthas, 1981).

Laissez-Faire

Group leadership is concentrated in members, and leaders are essentially nonleaders. Leaders are nondirective, just letting the group "happen." Leader(s) may be very accepting but removed from the group process, serving more as a resource to members. Leaders are more like just a member of the group, with communications primarily between members. There are some obstacles that may be encountered in adopting this leadership style. Members may experience confusion and frustration due to lack of direction. Productivity may be low, although high-functioning members may do well with this leadership style. Participation may be uneven among members (Sampson & Marthas, 1981). Members may absolve themselves of any responsibility because of confusion and frustration.

Leadership Techniques

There is a core set of basic skills and functions that are critical for successful group leadership. These skills are active listening, restating, clarifying, summarizing, questioning, interpreting, confronting, reflecting feelings, supporting, empathizing, facilitating, initiating, goal setting, evaluating, giving feedback, suggesting, protecting, disclosing oneself, modeling, linking, blocking, and terminating (Corey & Corey, 2006).

Co-Leadership Issues

Co-leaders may divide responsibility for leadership and cover for one another. There is much to attend to as the group process goes on, and a coleadership approach allows for having two people to attend to all the interactions, discussion, and behavior going on within the group. They can cooperate in planning and rehashing/processing group sessions and provide feedback to one another. Task and maintenance roles can provide a basis for conceptualizing co-leader roles. They must function in a cooperative and close-working relationship—as a team (Corey & Corey, 2006).

FAMILY DYNAMICS, COUNSELING THEORIES, AND INTERVENTIONS

Disability affects not only the person with a disability but also his or her entire family system (Kosciulek, 2004). Coping with the impact of disability is one of the most difficult tasks that can confront a family (Power, 1995). Counselors need to have more awareness of the impact of disability on families and try to meet the needs of individual family members and entire family systems (Kosciulek, 2004). In this section, family dynamics, counseling theories, and interventions will be reviewed to assist counselors in understanding the family systems and dynamics.

◼ LEARNING OBJECTIVES

By the end of this unit you should be able to:

1. Understand family dynamics.
2. Understand how each theoretical approach can be uniquely applied in family counseling.
3. Be able to differentiate between different theoretical approaches as they apply in family counseling.

◼ KEY CONCEPTS

Family Dynamics

A "family" is a group of two or more persons related by birth, marriage, or adoption (U.S. Census Bureau, 2010). Also included in the concept of "family" are more nontraditional situations such as those who live together and never marry, those who marry and never have children, those who marry and divorce, and various other nontraditional family arrangements. According to Hill (1958), the family is not ideally set up to withstand stress, yet society has assigned to it the heaviest responsibility: the socialization of the young and the meeting of the major emotional needs of all citizens. Counselors shift perspective from trying to change individual behavior to focusing on the family system. This shift occurs in three key dimensions: (1) transition from individual to systems dynamics, (2) shift from linear to circular causality, and (3) distinction between content and process dynamics (Worden, 2003).

Individual Versus Systems Dynamics

The family is viewed as a whole that is greater than the sum of its parts, rather than a collection of individuals. The family becomes an entity of analysis in and of itself. Individual behavior is rooted within the larger family context. For example, an individual's problematic behavior is seen as an outcome of family interactions and perceived as an expression of the family's dysfunctional transactional patterns (Worden, 2003).

Linear Versus Circular Causality

Circular causality refers to the idea that everyone's behavior affects everyone else's behavior. Therapists are forced to examine the family's self-perpetuating cycles of interaction, rather than individual cause and effect relationships. Circular causality eliminates the family scapegoat (Worden, 2003).

Content Versus Process Dynamics

Content refers to the concrete issue being discussed and process refers to how the issue is portrayed in the family's interactions. Attention should be given to process issues not content issues (Worden, 2003).

Therapeutic Approaches to Family Counseling

Social Constructionism

Social constructionism is described as a narrative, solution-focused therapy. In this approach, people are seen as actively shaping how they understand the world, what meanings they create to explain the world, and how these meanings are constructed. The key concept in social constructionism is that meaning is constructed through a social interaction. The therapist is not seen as an expert but rather as a collaborator with the family (Nichols & Schawartz, 2001).

Psychoanalytic Family Therapy

Nathan Ackerman has been identified as the founder of psychoanalytic family therapy. The foundation of this theory lies in knowing where to look to discover basic wants and needs that keep individuals from interacting in a mature way. According to this approach, problems are identified within people, rather than between people. The goal is to free family members from unconscious restrictions, so that they will be able to interact with one another as a whole. Having insight is necessary for behaviors to change. Techniques include listening, empathy, interpretation, and analytic neutrality (Nichols & Schawartz, 2001).

Bowen's Family System Theory

Family system theory was introduced by Bowen (1978). It is often referred to as multigenerational or transgenerational family therapy. Analyzing the family from a three generational perspective provides good understanding. To develop a mature personality, emotional fusion to the family must be addressed. Two of the key concepts central to Bowen's theory are differentiation of self and triangulation.

1. *Differentiation of self:* Differentiation of self springs from the idea that social groups tremendously influence the way an individual thinks. The less developed and differentiated a person's self, the more they have an unhealthy dependence on and are controlled by others.
2. *Triangulation:* A triangle is the smallest stable relationship system. A two-person system is unstable and forms into a three-person system under stress. The third person can be a substitute for conversation or a messenger.

   Two of the main goals include decreasing anxiety and increasing the level of differentiation of self. Therapists must be aware of how they have been influenced by their own family.

Experiential Family Therapy

Key figures include Carl Whitaker and Virginia Satir. Emphasis is placed on the mutually shared experience of the therapist and the family. One major goal is to increase family members' capacity to experience their lives more fully by sharing their struggle with the here and now. The role of a therapist is to create turmoil and then coach family members through the experience (Napier & Whitaker, 1978). According to this approach, planned techniques are not important. As a therapist, it is important to be with a family. Therapy is often conducted with two therapists.

Behavioral and Cognitive–Behavioral Family Therapy

Key figures include Gerald Patterson and Neil Jacobson. Focus is on discrete problem areas defined by clear behavior patterns, rather than character change and insight. The goal is to modify the specific behavior or thought pattern to alleviate symptoms. Two key concepts are careful, detailed assessments and specific strategies designed to modify contingencies of reinforcement. Techniques include behavioral contracts, training in communication skills, active suggestion, and homework (Bowers, 1988).

Structural Family Therapy

The key figure for this orientation is Salvador Minuchin. Focus is on the interactions of family members as a way of understanding the structure of the family. Key concepts include (1) family structure is the invisible set of rules that organize the way members relate to each other, (2) family subsystems include spousal, parental, sibling, and extended family categories, and (3) boundaries are emotional barriers that protect and enhance the integrity of families (disengagement—enmeshment). The therapist attempts to create clear boundaries, to increase flexibility, and to modify a dysfunctional family structure. Techniques include family mapping, enactments, and reframing (Minuchin & Fishman, 1981).

Strategic Family Therapy

The key figure here is Jay Haley. The focus is on solving problems in the present. The overall goal is to resolve a problem by focusing on behavioral sequences, rather than insight. The therapist acts as a consultant and is responsible for planning a strategy to resolve problems. Techniques include using directives (advice, suggestion, and coaching), paradoxical techniques, and reframing.

Brief Family Therapy

Key figures include Luigi Boscolo and Gianfranco Cecchia. Brief therapy is increasingly popular because of economic limitations of clients and clinicians and the introduction of managed care. The goal is solution focused and encourages clients to shift from talking about problems to talking about solutions (Talmon, 1993). Therapists and clients discuss resources, goals, and exceptions to the problem. Techniques include setting limited goals and an endpoint, reinforcing family strengths, and assigning homework. Therapists may ask the "miracle question."

Family Counseling Strategies

Marshak and Seligman (1993) introduced the five-level guidance of the intervention for conceptualizing the intensity of counselor interface with the family's needs and preferences. The five levels are outlined as follows:

Level 1: Focus on the individual client
Level 2: Provide information for the family
Level 3: Provide emotional support for the family
Level 4: Provide structured assessment and intervention
Level 5: Provide family therapy (Kosciulek, 2004, pp. 275–276)

According to Roessler, Chung, and Rubin (1998), many counselors are able to provide high-quality intervention at levels 1 through 3. However, counselors must possess structural and relationship skills to provide effective family counseling at levels 4 and 5. Structural skills refer to the counselor's ability to identify problems or needs, define outcomes and alternatives, and confront family members' resistance. Relationship skills refer to the capacities to build rapport with and express empathic understanding to families.

ETHICAL AND LEGAL ISSUES IMPACTING INDIVIDUALS AND FAMILIES

Awareness and knowledge of ethical issues is as essential as a solid base of psychological knowledge and skills. They must learn to make ethical decisions, a process that can be taught in group courses and in practicum/internship supervisions. Groups designed around ethically and legally sound principles have a far greater chance of being effective than groups designed without these principles in mind. This section will review some ethical issues in group settings (Corey & Corey, 2006).

▨ LEARNING OBJECTIVES

By the end of this unit you should be able to:

1. Understand what constitutes an ethical consideration in a group setting.
2. Be aware of resources that certified rehabilitation counselors (CRC) should consult with regard to ethical dilemmas and how one may plan for ethical concerns that may arise and how to resolve them.

▓ KEY CONCEPTS

Informed Consent

Informed consent is a sound policy to provide a professional disclosure statement to group members that includes information on a variety of topics including (see Rule A.3.a in Code and Association for Specialists in Group Work [ASGW] Best Practice Guidelines):

- ▓ Nature, purposes, and goals of group
- ▓ Confidentiality, including limits of confidentiality
- ▓ Qualifications of the leader (may also include theoretical orientations)
- ▓ Services that can be provided
- ▓ Roles and responsibilities of members
- ▓ Right to withdraw from the group
- ▓ Potential risks and benefits associated with membership

Freedom to Withdraw From a Group

For groups that are voluntary, group members will typically have the right to withdraw. It is important to specify any commitments expected of group members in terms of attendance, arriving on time and not leaving early, and remaining in the group for a specified number of sessions. It is also important to specify any anticipated risks of withdrawing from a group early. If someone really wants to withdraw, it may be best to ultimately let them go. However, the decision should be made with careful consideration and explanation. Otherwise, the consequences could be negative for members remaining (Corey & Corey, 2006).

Potential Risks for Group Members That May Require Attention

Self-disclosure may not be adequately addressed, and painful things might be disclosed that might be ignored by the group, resulting in additional feelings of hopelessness or pain. Confidentiality might be violated by group members. Scapegoating may occur where members may be singled out or "ganged up on." Leaders may be inadequately prepared for the group and may find themselves operating beyond the bounds of their competence.

Multicultural Issues

In group settings, there may be effects of shared values and beliefs within a culture on a person's view of the world and events. Stereotyping may lead to invalid perceptions and attributions, and as a result, it may have a negative impact on group dynamics. It is important to consider the effects of cultural differences on group dynamics and process because cultural differences are the way that such problems can be conceptualized and solved. There are three issues to which rehabilitation counselors need to attend when working with clients from minority backgrounds (Mpofu, Beck, & Weinrach, 2004). First is knowledge of the culture(s) with which the client identifies. The client's culture provides a hypothesis to investigate in the process of conceptualizing the client's perceptual world. Second is an awareness of the client's worldview. Counselors need to listen and ask the client questions that educate them about their client's values and life meanings. Finally, as a group counselor, it is critical to be sensitive to clues such as values, rate of conversation, style of nonverbal cues, and expectations that members often give indicating that they would like to talk about some aspect of how their culture is affecting their participation in the group.

Resolving Ethical Dilemmas

When faced with an ethical question, it is essential that counselors look at the applicable professional code for guidance. For rehabilitation counselors, this is the professional code of ethics and the standards for certified rehabilitation counselors (https://www.crccertification.com/filebin/pdf/CRCC_COE_1-1-10_Rev12-09.pdf). Obtaining consultation from a colleague is also important. The most important person to consult with is one's supervisor. The goal should be to correct the situation and not resort to recrimination or punishment. Finally, it is important to think about the situation in relation to the ethical principles of autonomy, beneficence, fidelity, justice, nonmaleficence, and veracity.

▨ INTERNET RESOURCES

American Association for Marriage and Family Therapy
http://www.aamft.org/iMIS15/AAMFT

American Counseling Association
http://www.counseling.org/Resources

American Counseling Association: Ethics Q&A
http://www.counseling.org/Publications/CounselingTodayArticles.aspx?AGuid=b71c995d-8815–40d7-8459-7a91d40ff037

Association for Specialists in Group Work
http://www.asgw.org/resources.asp

Commission on Rehabilitation Counselor Certification (CRC/CCRC Code of Ethics)
http://www.crccertification.com/pages/crc_ccrc_code_of_ethics/10.php

▨ MULTIPLE CHOICE QUESTIONS

1. Thoughts, feelings, and behaviors characteristic of group members during the transition stage of the group process include:
   A. Defensiveness and resistance, anxiety and fear, struggle for control, conflict and confrontation
   B. Trust, cohesion and a sense of inclusion, open communication, self-disclosure, and taking risks, shared leadership, effectively managed interpersonal conflict, control, and power issues, direct communication among members, and giving feedback freely
   C. Defensiveness and resistance, anxiety and fear, giving feedback, and self-disclosure
   D. Anxiety, sadness, and fear, concerns about unfinished business, and questioning what comes next

2. The leadership style characterized by group leadership and control concentrated in the leader(s), with the leader functioning as a teacher/director is:
   A. Democratic
   B. Parental
   C. Dominant
   D. Authoritarian

3. A democratic leadership style is likely to impact the group by:
   A. Leading to group member compliance, little enthusiasm from group members, and no particular feelings of satisfaction or responsibility for accomplishments
   B. Resulting in more active participation, greater enthusiasm, more responsibility and initiative, and a greater sense of ownership of the group members
   C. Leading to group member compliance, greater feelings of caring about other group members, and feelings of confusion and frustration
   D. Causing feelings of confusion and frustration, lower productivity, and uneven participation among members

4. Some group building and maintenance roles that are central to the group process are:
   A. Coordinating, energizing, opinion giving, elaborating, and orienting
   B. Information seeking, recording, encouraging, and harmonizing
   C. Compromising, standard setting, encouraging, and group observing
   D. Initiating, evaluating-criticizing, procedural expediting, and harmonizing

5. The theory that states that problems within a group may serve a function for the group, may be a function of the group's inability to operate productively, and may be a symptom of dysfunctional patterns that are handed down across generations is:
   A. Bowen's family system theory
   B. Psychoanalytical family therapy
   C. Social constructionism
   D. Family system theory

6. The key figure in strategic family therapy is:
   A. Luigi Boscolo
   B. Nathan Ackerman
   C. Jay Haley
   D. Carl Whitaker

7. The ethical code to which all certified rehabilitation counselors are bound is the
   A. Hippocratic oath
   B. ASGW best practice guidelines
   C. each certified rehabilitation counselor is bound by the ethical code of their respective institution
   D. Code of professional ethics for rehabilitation counselors

8. One major goal of behavioral and cognitive–behavioral family therapy is
   A. to increase family members' capacity to experience their lives more fully by sharing their struggle with the here and now
   B. to modify the specific behavior or thought pattern to alleviate symptoms
   C. to decrease anxiety and increase the level of differentiation of self
   D. encouraging clients to shift from talking about problems to talking about solutions

9. Gestalt therapy, reality therapy, and person-centered therapy are examples of what type of approach to counseling?
   A. Experiential
   B. Cognitive–behavioral
   C. Psychoeducational
   D. Psychodynamic

10. If you are involved in group work with culturally diverse population, it will be important for you to
    A. be an expert in each of the populations
    B. accept the challenge of modifying your strategies to meet the unique needs of the members
    C. be of the same ethnic background as the members in your group
    D. conduct empirical research on your groups to validate your effectiveness

▓ ANSWER KEY

1. A; **2.** D; **3.** B; **4.** B; **5.** D; **6.** C; **7.** D; **8.** B; **9.** A; **10.** B

▓ ADVANCED MULTIPLE CHOICE QUESTIONS

1. Resolving ethical dilemmas in group practice is best done by considering the following actions:
   A. Obtaining consultation from a colleague
   B. Thinking about the situation in relation to the ethical principles of beneficence, nonmaleficence, autonomy, justice, and fidelity

    C. Looking at the applicable professional code
    D. A and C
    E. A, B, and C

2. Group counseling is most effective when leaders operate from the following theoretical orientations:
    A. Cognitive–behavioral
    B. Existential
    C. Psychodynamic
    D. None of the above—an eclectic style is recommended, taking into consideration the composition, purpose, and issues of the group.

3. The rehabilitation model addressing how a family adjusts and adapts to disability is
    A. the psychosocial model of disability
    B. family systems theory
    C. the resiliency model
    D. the family adaptation model

4. What is the theory underlying the practice of reality therapy?
    A. Holistic theory
    B. Choice theory
    C. Social learning theory
    D. Behavioral theory

5. Which of the following is NOT a key leader function/behavior during the transition stage of the group process?
    A. Challenging resistance
    B. Making decisions about degree of shared leadership
    C. Identifying and processing feelings
    D. Increasing risk taking

6. You are leading a group, which has been meeting for several weeks now and has already established a set of group rules and norms and identified some of the goals the group would like to work on. Recently, several of the group members have been very reluctant to speak in group and you overheard a conversation between two members discussing how they do not want to speak in front of the group for fear of looking foolish. Judging by this behavior, within what stage of group development is this group likely functioning?
    A. Initial stage
    B. Transition stage
    C. Working stage
    D. Final stage

7. You have received a referral to work with a same-sex couple who have 5-year-old son and are currently experiencing some relationship problems following one of the partners losing his or her job. Their son has been having some behavioral problems at school, which the school feels is linked to the problems going on at home. You are a CRC who specializes in family dynamics. Based on this information, you would make the following statement:
    A. Based on my specialization, I feel that I am prepared to assist this family to work on their issues
    B. Family dynamics applies only to traditional family structures and therefore you should refer these particular clients to someone who is prepared to handle their needs
    C. This particular group of clients does not qualify for family therapy, instead the child should receive individual counseling, and the same-sex partners should pursue either couples counseling or individual therapy
    D. None of the above

8. You are leading a group that has begun to exhibit signs of trust, cohesion, and sense of inclusion. Some individuals within the group have mentioned that they have been trying to practice some of the things that they are learning in group in their homes and communities. During group

time, you have noted that some of the members have begun to take on more of a leadership role. Based on your observations, this group is most likely currently in the _____ stage of group development.

A. Initial
B. Transition
C. Working
D. Final

9. The group that you are currently leading has recently been exhibiting a great deal of resistance to discussing and dealing with common issues, has experienced a lot of conflict between group members, and the members just do not seem to trust each other. Based on these observations, your key roles at this point in time may include

A. Recognizing and dealing with unfinished business
B. Reducing your active role in the group to allow for greater shared leadership
C. Identification and processing of feelings, thoughts, and behaviors
D. B and C

10. The group that you are currently conducting on substance abuse is in the working stage, which you have judged from the level of trust and cohesion among group members, and the presence of open communication, self-disclosure, and risk taking. You are currently operating from a democratic leadership style and feel that it would be most appropriate at this point to _____ your level of activity in structuring and leading the group. You therefore decide to adopt the _____ leadership style.

A. Maintain, democratic
B. Reduce, authoritarian
C. Increase, authoritarian
D. Reduce, laissez-faire

ANSWER KEY AND EXPLANATION OF ANSWERS

1-E: Ethical dilemmas in rehabilitation counseling must be resolved in a sensitive and professional manner to ensure protection of the client and the professional. Considering just one mode of ethical consultation in isolation may result in unsuccessful resolution of the problem.

2-D: Adopting one specific counseling orientation and rigidly applying this to all clients and all groups is not the most effective way to facilitate personal exploration and achievement of set goals. Instead, the counselor needs to be able to evaluate the needs of individual clients and the group as a whole and to apply different orientations in an eclectic manner. Flexibility and sensitivity to the clients'/group's needs are key.

3-C: The best answer here is the resiliency model, a model specifically addressing family adaptation. The psychosocial model of disability explains adaptation of the individual with the disability themselves to their disability, as opposed to addressing family adaptation. Family systems theory is not a model of adaptation, but rather a theory describing the relationships and dynamics within the family context. The family adaptation model is nonexistent—the correct title of the model describing adaptation of the family to a disability is the resiliency model.

4-B: Reality therapy is the method of counseling introduced by William Glasser. Reality therapy is based on the belief that we all choose what we do with our lives and that we are responsible for our choices. Therefore, reality therapy is firmly based on choice theory and aimed at helping individuals gain more effective control over their own lives. Choice theory posits that behavior is central to our existence and is driven by five genetically driven needs such as survival, belonging, power, freedom, and fun.

5-B: Deciding on the degree of leadership that will be shared within the group is a role/function of the leader(s) in the initial stage of the group process. Challenging resistance, identifying and processing feelings, and increasing risk taking are all key roles and functions of the leader(s) in the transition stage.

6-B: We know that this group has been meeting for several weeks, has developed a set of group norms and rules, and has decided on some mutual goals. This tells us that they have accomplished many of the key tasks of the initial stage of a group. Judging by the resistance that you have been witnessing and the anxieties that you have heard expressed by group members, the best estimate of the stage at which this group is functioning would be the transition stage.

7-A: This vignette gets at the definition of "family." According to the definition under which CRCs operate, a same-sex couple would be considered a family, and their son would be a part of this family. Therefore, if one's training is in family dynamics, then one would most likely feel prepared to work with this particular family unit and would know that the fact that they are a same-sex couple does not exclude them from being eligible to receive family therapy.

8-C: One should have noted in this vignette several key points that hint at the stage of group development in which the group is currently operating:

- *Group beginning to exhibit signs of trust, cohesion, and a sense of inclusion*—In the initial stage of group development, members are unfamiliar with each other and therefore these signs are not yet present. It is during the working stage that we begin to see these group elements.
- *Members have begun to take on more of a leadership role*—During the initial stages of group development, the leaders take on most of the leadership responsibility as the members acclimate to the group environment and to each other. It is during the working stage where members begin to feel secure enough in the group that they take on more leadership responsibility.

Based on these signs, one should deduce that this group is operating in the working stage of group development.

9-C: One should have noted in this vignette several key points that hint at the roles which the leader(s) should be occupying at this point in time within the group's development:

- Group is exhibiting a great deal of resistance in discussing and dealing with common issues
- There has been a lot of conflict between group members
- Group exhibiting a lack of trust

Based on these observations, the leader(s) should key into the fact that the group needs a more active leadership role from group leader(s) at this time to assist with resolving the current conflicts occurring within the group and to help group members to build trust in one another. Therefore, reducing an active leadership role would not be helpful at this time. Recognizing and dealing with unfinished business is a leader's role during the final stage of group development, which the group is not currently in considering that they have not developed a sense of trust and are continuing to resist dealing with common issues. The best functions that the leader can perform for the group at this time would be those of processing the feelings, thoughts, and behaviors surrounding the within-group conflict to assist the group to move forward, developing trust and working on common issues.

10-D: Decreasing formal leadership and structure would be the best option at this point in time. By increasing control, the leader(s) would be stifling the group's progress and inhibiting further development. Compared with a democratic leadership style, the laissez-faire leadership style would be the only leadership style which is less structured and exerts less control.

◾ REFERENCES

Association for Specialists in Group Work. (2000). *ASGW professional standards for group counseling.* Alexandria, VA: Author.

Association for Specialists in Group Work. (2008). ASGW Best Practice Guidelines 2007 revisions. *Journal for Specialists in Group Work, 33*(20), 111–117.

Bowen, M. (1978). *Family therapy in clinical practice.* New York, NY: Aronson.

Bowers, W. A. (1988). Beck's cognitive therapy: An overview for rehabilitation counselors. *Journal of Applied Rehabilitation Counseling, 19,* 43–46.

Commission on Rehabilitation Counselor Certification. (2010). *Code of professional ethics for rehabilitation counselors*. Schaumburg, IL: Author. Retrieved from https://www.crccertification.com/filebin/pdf/CRCC_COE_1-1-10_Rev12-09.pdf

Corey, M. S., & Corey, G. (2006). *Groups: Process and practices* (7th ed.). Pacific Grove, CA: Brooks/Cole.

Hill (1958). Generic features of families under stress. *Social Casework, 49,* 139–150.

Huebner, R. A. (2004). Group procedures. In F. Chan, N. L. Berven, & K. R. Thomas (Eds.), *Counseling theories and techniques for rehabilitation health professionals* (pp. 244–280). New York, NY: Springer Publishing.

Kosciulek, J. F. (2004). Family counseling. In F. Chan, N. L. Berven, & K. R. Thomas (Eds.), *Counseling theories and techniques for rehabilitation health professionals* (pp. 264–281). New York, NY: Springer Publishing.

Marsha, L. E., & Seligman, M. (1993). *Counseling for persons with physical disabilities.* Austin, TX: Pro-Ed.

Minuchin, S., & Fishman, H. C. (1981). *Family therapy techniques.* Cambridge, MA: Harvard University Press.

Mpofu, E., Beck, R., & Weinrach, S. (2004). Multicultural rehabilitation counseling: Challenges and strategies. In F. Chan, N. Berven, & K. Thomas (Eds.), *Counseling theories and techniques for rehabilitation health professionals* (pp. 386–404). New York, NY: Springer Publishing.

Napier A. Y., & Whitaker, C. A. (1978). *The family crucible.* New York, NY: Harper & Row.

Nichols, M. P., & Schwartz, R. C. (2001). *Family therapy: Concepts and methods* (5th ed.). Boston, MA: Allyn & Bacon.

Patterson, J. B., McKenzie, B., & Jenkins, J. (1995). Creating accessible groups for individuals with disabilities. *Journal for Specialists in Group Work, 20,* 76–82.

Power, P. W. (1995). Family. In A. E. Dell Orto & R. P. Marinelli (Eds.), *Encyclopedia of disability and rehabilitation* (pp. 312–326). New York, NY: MacMillan.

Roessler, R. T., Chung, W., & Rubin, S. E. (1998). Family-centered rehabilitation case management. In R. T. Roessler & S. E., Rubin (Eds.), *Case management and rehabilitation counseling: Procedure and techniques* (3rd ed., pp. 231–254). Austin, TX: Pro-Ed.

Sampson, E. E., & Marthas, M. S. (1981). *Group process for the health professions* (2nd ed.). New York, NY: Wiley.

Talmon, T. (1993). *Single session solutions: A guide to practical, effective, and affordable therapy.* Reading, MA: Addison-Welsey.

U.S. Census Bureau (May, 2010). *Current population survey: Definitions and explanations.* U.S. Census Bureau, Housing and Household Economic Statistics Division, Fertility & Family Statistics Branch. Retrieved from http://www.census.gov/population/www/cps/cpsdef.html

Worden, J. W. (2003) *Grief counselling and grief therapy: A handbook for the mental health practitioner* (3rd ed). New York, NY: Springer Publishing.

Assessment

7

Eun-Jeong Lee and Nicole Ditchman

A ssessment is an important aspect of rehabilitation across settings. Formal assessment approaches are often used to determine eligibility for services, provide diagnostic information, assist individuals with reaching career goals, evaluate the effectiveness of intervention strategies, and ultimately recommend a course of action (Rubin & Roessler, 2008). In this chapter, we review the role and purpose of assessment in rehabilitation, psychometric concepts related to assessment, assessment tools and approaches, and ethical considerations. Specific topics include the following:

- Role of assessment in rehabilitation
- Assessment procedures
- Basic measurement concepts and principles
- Consumer involvement in assessment planning
- Selecting and administering appropriate measures and approaches
- Ethical, legal, and cultural implications in assessment

ROLE OF ASSESSMENT AND ASSESSMENT PROCEDURES IN REHABILITATION

Overview

The focus of assessment in rehabilitation is to gather relevant data to assist in making useful recommendations for service planning (Rubin & Roessler, 2008). Comprehensive assessment approaches generally evaluate personality, intelligence, educational achievement, work experience and adjustment, personal and social adjustment, employment opportunities, environmental characteristics, and other relevant factors helpful in determining the nature and scope of rehabilitation services needed to achieve successful vocational and independent living outcomes. In this section, we define assessment broadly and discuss the role of assessment in rehabilitation.

LEARNING OBJECTIVES

By the end of this unit you should be able to:

1. Define assessment and related concepts.
2. Understand the role of assessment in rehabilitation.
3. Identify recommended steps and procedures in rehabilitation assessment.

KEY CONCEPTS

Assessment is defined broadly as "any systematic method of obtaining information from tests and other sources, used to draw inferences about people, objects, or programs" (American

Educational Research Association [AERA], APA, & National Council on Measurement in Education [NCME], 1999). Test is defined broadly as "an objective and standardized measure of a sample of behavior" (Anastasi & Urbina, 1997). Assessment is more complex than testing; it typically requires integrating information from multiple sources and clinical judgments that go beyond psychometric data. Measurement is defined as "the assignment of numbers to attributes of persons according to rules stated explicitly" (Bolton, 2001).

The purpose of assessment in rehabilitation is to integrate information from multiple sources to plan a course of action. In rehabilitation, assessment is usually vocationally related. Vocational assessment involves exploring a person's strengths, weaknesses, and preferences and discovering how the individual's potential for vocational adjustment can be enhanced. The scope of assessment is sufficiently broad to include the identification of specific and potential problems relevant to achieving career goals, the development of career goals, and the planning of strategies to resolve problems and attain established objectives (Berven, 1997). Assessment must be understood in a context of legislation, consumer empowerment, environmental factors, professional collaboration, ethnically diverse consumer populations, and assistive technology (Power, 2006; Rubin & Roessler, 2008). Assessment procedures can include interviews, standardized tests, inventories, observations, job tryouts, simulated tasks, and medical examinations.

Intake Interview

A comprehensive assessment begins with the information–collection process, called an intake or initial interview. The intake interview generates a social-vocational history, which is useful in formulating the rehabilitation plan and in determining whether subsequent evaluations are needed based on questions that the consumer can answer directly. According to Rubin and Roessler (2008), the focus of intake interviews should be (1) determining the person's reason for rehabilitation services, (2) providing the individual with necessary information about the role and function of the agency, (3) developing adequate rapport, (4) initiating the diagnostic process, and (5) informing the consumer of any medical, vocational, or psychological evaluations that must be completed and the purposes of such evaluations.

Medical Evaluation

The medical examination is required by all public state rehabilitation agencies when working with a consumer with a physical disability or chronic illness. This evaluation is used to (a) establish the presence and extent of the disability, (b) provide information on the physical functioning of the consumer, (c) determine the types of activities precluded by the disability, and (d) identify any additional medical evaluation necessary for achieving the first three purposes. The medical examination provides information (a) clarifying the consumer's general health at present; (b) describing of the extent, stability, and prognosis of the present disability as well as any recommended treatment; (c) assessing present and future implications of the disability and its potential effects on performance of essential job functions; and (d) reporting the presence of any residual medical conditions that could impact the individual during the rehabilitation process (Rubin & Roessler, 2008). When working with individuals with physical disabilities, the counselor should refer the consumer to a physician for the medical evaluation and inform the physician of any tentative vocational goals the consumer is considering.

Psychological Evaluation

Psychological assessments yield information regarding consumers' intelligence, aptitudes, achievement, personality, interests, and adjustment related to vocational functioning. Psychological assessment results help to determine (a) the appropriateness of long-term vocational training, (b) the need for adjustment services, and (c) the need to confront the consumer regarding unrealistic vocational choices (Rubin & Roessler, 2008). This evaluation can also be used to establish the presence of cognitive or psychiatric disability.

Vocational Evaluation

The purpose of vocational evaluation is to provide reliable and valid data to (a) generate information about the consumer's current vocationally relevant levels of social, educational, psychological, and physiological functioning; (b) estimate the consumer's potential for behavior change and skill acquisition; (c) determine the consumer's most effective learning style; (d) identify possible jobs the consumer can perform without additional vocational services; (e) identify education or special training programs that might increase the vocational potential; (f) identify potentially feasible jobs for the consumer with further vocational services; and (g) identify the community support services that might augment job retention following a successful consumer placement (Rubin & Roessler, 2008). This step consists of different techniques, focusing on assessing the relationship of the person's skills, abilities, personality characteristics, and physical tolerance to perform the required tasks associated with potential jobs.

BASIC MEASUREMENT CONCEPTS AND PRINCIPLES

Overview

When using standardized tests and work samples, rehabilitation professionals have to determine each measure's appropriateness for the individual consumer. Certain standards for evaluating these methods should be employed to choose the most appropriate and available measures. In this section, key terms and concepts in measurement and assessment will be introduced, salient features of standardized tests will be discussed, and basic types of standard scores will be described.

▓ LEARNING OBJECTIVES

By the end of this unit you should be able to:

1. Understand basic methodological and psychometric concepts related to assessment procedures.
2. Identify important considerations when interpreting test scores.

▓ KEY CONCEPTS

Scales of Measurement

The intent of psychological measurement is to convert characteristics of people to quantifiable data or numbers. An ongoing concern in assessment and score interpretation is the extent to which test scores are meaningful. These measurement issues can be addressed through scaling techniques. Four measurement scales are generally recognized:

1. *Nominal:* Classifies, assigns numerals but does not distinguish size, amount (e.g., any categorical variable, such as ethnicity or gender).
2. *Ordinal:* Indication of ordering, but no indication of distances between objects on the scale (e.g., placing first, second, and third).

3. Interval: Equal intervals on the scale (e.g., Celsius temperature scale).
4. Ratio: Possesses a nonarbitrary zero point (e.g., measures of weight).

Reliability and Validity

The concepts of validity and reliability are important when considering the appropriateness of a test for a particular use. Validity provides an estimate of how well a test measures what it purports to measure, and reliability refers to the dependability, consistency, and precision of an assessment procedure. A reliable procedure is one that produces similar results when repeated.

Reliability is a measure of consistency. (Is the test consistent, dependable, and precise?) There are several ways to estimate a test's reliability:

a. Test–retest reliability: A measure of consistency over time. Test–retest correlations indicate relationships between scores obtained by individuals within the same group on two administrations of the test.
b. Split-half reliability: A measure of internal consistency. Split-half correlations indicate consistency of scores obtained by individuals within the same group on two different parts of the test (e.g., odd vs. even items).
c. Parallel forms reliability: A parallel form correlation indicates the consistency of scores of individuals within the same group on two alternate but equivalent forms of the same test taken at the same time.
d. Cronbach's alpha: An internal consistency statistic calculated from the pairwise correlations between items.

Validity can be understood as the extent to which meaningful and appropriate inferences can be made from the instrument. (Does the test measure what it says it measures?) There are several types of validity evidence:

- *Face validity:* appraisal of test's content based on the "face" of the test (looking at the content).
- *Content validity:* evaluation by subject matter experts of test items' representativeness of the construct being measured.
- *Criterion or predictive validity:* comparison of the test with a related outcome measure.
- *Construct validity:* extent to which the measure actually measures the theoretical construct.

Types of Score Interpretations

Every test typically yields a score. It is essential to have information about the nature and number of items composing the test, the response format used, and the range of possible scores at least.

a. Self-referenced interpretation is when a score is compared with an internal frame of reference (e.g., changes in an individual's performance on a test over time).
b. Criterion-referenced interpretation is when a score is compared with an absolute standard, external frame of reference (e.g., meeting a proficiency standard).
c. Norm-referenced interpretation is when a score is compared with scores obtained by other individuals, external frame of reference (e.g., percentile comparison to norm group).

Raw score is performance on a test (e.g., percent of items correct). However, raw score is meaningless without additional knowledge concerning the instrument. There are three sources commonly used for comparative information.

Standard scores can be sometimes yielded as results and can be used to make norm-referenced interpretations. Standard scores are transformed scores with a specified mean (M) and standard deviation (SD) in relation to the comparison group (e.g., z-scores: M = 0, SD = 1; T-scores: M = 50, SD = 10; intelligence quotient (IQ) scores: M = 100, SD = 15).

Percentiles are rank order scores indicating the percentage of persons in the comparison group who attained a lower score. Percentiles should not be confused with percentage correct, which is the raw score.

CONSUMER PARTICIPATION AND PREPARATION IN ASSESSMENT

Overview

Consumers should be active participants and decision makers throughout the assessment process. This section is an overview of the steps recommended by Power (2006) to promote consumer empowerment.

▒ LEARNING OBJECTIVES

By the end of this unit you should be able to:

1. Understand the role of the consumer in the assessment process.
2. Identify steps to promote consumer empowerment during the assessment process.

▒ KEY CONCEPTS

Promoting Consumer Empowerment

Power (2006) provided the following steps to promote consumer empowerment in the assessment process: (1) establish a working relationship; (2) understand the needs, expectations, values, and goals of the consumer; (3) encourage active consumer involvement; (4) allow the consumer to make informed choices and express self-determination when selecting evaluation approaches; and (5) finally, the professional should monitor the consumer to ascertain that she or he is still actively participating in the planned, identified tasks of assessment.

Preparing people for assessment involves two important steps. First, rehabilitation counselors should communicate to consumers the importance of their input throughout the assessment process. Second, once a mutual decision is made for the assessment process, the consumer must be carefully prepared for what to anticipate. The professional needs to explain the purpose of the assessment and the ways the results can assist the consumer with achieving realistic rehabilitation goals.

SELECTING APPROPRIATE MEASURES AND APPROACHES

Overview

A range of measurement tools are used in assessment in addition to interviews. In this section, we provide an overview of commonly used standardized tests, inventories, and work samples, and describe situational and ecological assessments.

■ LEARNING OBJECTIVES

By the end of this unit you should be able to

1. Identify commonly used tests, inventories, and assessment tools and their designated purposes.
2. Gain a general understanding of psychometric properties and considerations of specific measurement tools.

■ KEY CONCEPTS

Standardized Tests and Inventories

Standardized tests are frequently classified as falling into one of the following five areas: intelligence, aptitude, achievement, personality, and interests. A number of tests in each area will be briefly reviewed in this section. Rehabilitation counselors need to be familiar with these tests because the results and interpretations based on these tests commonly appear in vocational evaluation reports used by rehabilitation counselors and consumers in service planning. In this section, commonly used tests and inventories associated with each area of assessment are discussed. These and additional tests and inventories that rehabilitation counselors should be familiar with are listed in Table 7.1.

Assessment of Intelligence

Many definitions have been offered for the construct of intelligence, and there remains considerable disagreement as to the meaning of this term and the best way to measure it. It is generally conceptualized as the ability to solve problems and to learn and retain new information (Power, 2006).

Commonly Used Intelligence Tests in the Vocational Rehabilitation Process

Wechsler Adult Intelligence Scale–IV (WAIS-IV) is an IQ test to measure adult and adolescent intelligence. The original WAIS was published in 1955, and the fourth edition of the test was released in 2008 (Wechsler, 2008). Two broad scores are generated, which can be used to summarize general intellectual abilities: (a) Full-Scale Intelligent Quotient (FSIQ), based on the total combined performance of four indexes (described in the following); and (b) General Ability Index (GAI), based only on the six subtests that comprise the Verbal Comprehension Index (VCI) and Perceptual Reasoning Index (PRI). The GAI can be used as a measure of cognitive abilities that are less vulnerable to impairment. Scores on the WAIS-IV indexes and full scale are based on a mean of 100 and SD of 15.

The WAIS-IV consists of 10 subtests and 5 supplemental subtests and generates 4 indices:

1. VCI includes four subtests: similarities, vocabulary, information, and comprehension.
2. PRI comprises five subtests: block design, matrix reasoning, visual puzzles, picture completion, and figure weights.
3. Working Memory Index (WMI) is obtained from three subtests: digit span, arithmetic, and letter-number sequencing.
4. Processing Speed Index (PSI) includes three subtests: symbol search, coding, and cancellation.

TABLE 7.1 ■ **Summary Table of Commonly Used Tests and Inventories in Rehabilitation by Assessment Construct**

Title of Measurement	Abbreviation	Title of Measurement	Abbreviation
Intelligence		**Achievement**	
Wechsler Adult Intelligence Scale–IV	WAIS-IV	Wide Range Achievement Test–4	WRAT-4
Stanford-Binet-V		Adult Basic Learning Examination–2	ABLE-2
Slosson Intelligence Test–R		Peabody Individual Achievement Test	PIAT-R
Peabody Picture Vocabulary Test–3rd Ed.		California's Achievement Test	
Beta III		SRA Arithmetic Index and Reading Index	
Raven's Progressive Matrices		Woodcock Johnson Tests of Achievement	
Quick-Test	QT	Wechsler Individual Achievement Test	WIAT
Kaufman Brief Intelligence Test	KBIT		
Luria-Nebraska Neuropsychological Battery		**Personality**	MMPI-2
Halstaed-Reitan Neuropsychological Test Battery		Minnesota Multiphasic Personality Inventory–2	
Test of Nonverbal Intelligence	TONI	Myers-Briggs Type Indicator	MBTI
Culture Fair Intelligence Test		Sixteen Personality Factor Questionnaire	16 PF
Wonderlic Personnel Test		California Psychological Inventory	CPI
Haptic Intelligence Test for the Blind		Psychological Screening Inventory	PSI
Woodcock Johnson Test of Cognitive Abilities		Tennessee Self-Concept Scale	TSCS
		Adult Personality Inventory	API
Aptitude		Jackson Personality Inventory–R	
General Aptitude Test Battery	GATB	Hogan Personality Inventory	
Differential Aptitude Tests–5	DAT	NEO Personality Inventory	NEO-PI
Armed Services Vocational Aptitude Battery	ASVAB	*Projective Measures*	
Bennett Mechanical Comprehension Test	BMCT	Rorschach	
Minnesota Paper Form Board–R	MPFB-R	Thematic Apperceptions Test	TAT
Career Ability Placement Survey	CAPS		
Hand-Tool Dexterity Test		**Interests**	
Ability Explorer	AE	Geist Picture Interest Inventory–R	R-FVII-2
APTICOM		Reading-Free Vocational Interest Inventory–2	
Ball Aptitude Battery	BAB	Strong Interest Inventory	
Minnesota Paper Form Board–R		Kuder Occupational Interest Survey	SDS
Career Scope		Self-Directed Search	CAI
Career Planning Survey	CS	Career Assessment Inventory	OASIS-3
Occupational Aptitude Survey & Interest Schedule-3	CPS OASIS-3	Occupational Aptitude Survey and Interest Schedule–3	OVIS-II
PESCO 2001		Ohio Vocational Interest Survey–2	CDM-R
Detroit Tests of Learning Aptitude		Career Decision-Making System–R	CISS
Occupational Aptitude Survey		Campbell Interest and Skill Survey	
Minnesota Clerical Test			
		Work Samples	MDS
		McCarron-Dial Evaluation System	
		VALPAR	MECA
		Microcomputer Evaluation of Careers and Academics	VIEWS
		Vocational Information and Evaluation Work Samples	VITAS
		Vocational Interest, Temperament, & Aptitude System	WREST
		Wide Range Employment Sample Test	

Stanford-Binet 5 (SB5; Roid, 2003) consists of 10 subtests (5 verbal and 5 nonverbal subtests). Nonverbal subtests can be used for people with hearing impairments, communication disorders, and limited English-language background. The SB5 yields FSIQ, verbal IQ and nonverbal IQ scores, and five factor indexes (Fluid Reasoning, Knowledge, Quantitative Reasoning, Visual-Spatial Reasoning, and Working Memory).

Peabody Picture Vocabulary Test–3 (PPVT-III; Dunn & Dunn, 1997) is an untimed, easily administered, oral test of intelligence. It can be administered in about 11 to 12 minutes. Reading is not required for this test and item responses are made by pointing. It can be applicable for people with intellectual disabilities.

Slosson Intelligence Test–Revised 3 (SIT-3; Slosson, Nicholson, & Hibpshman, 1990) is an easily administered, individual, oral test of verbal intelligence. It can be administered in about 15 to 20 minutes. It is designed as a quick screening test of intelligence and can be used for individuals with visual impairments, reading difficulty, and physical disabilities.

Assessment of Aptitude

Aptitudes are regarded as relatively stable abilities that are innate and developed over a long period of time (Power, 2006; Rubin & Roessler, 2008). Aptitude tests are used to (a) assess individuals' skills and abilities, (b) measure more specific or focused areas that predict the likelihood to learn and master knowledge or skills needed for success in a specific vocation, and (c) predict how successful an individual will likely be at learning different aspects of a formal training program.

Commonly Used Aptitude Tests in the Vocational Rehabilitation Process

General Aptitude Test Battery (GATB; U.S. Department of Labor, 1970) was developed by the U.S. Department of Labor in 1947. The GATB measures 8 aptitudes via 12 timed tests (Droege, 1987; Gregory, 1996). The GATB takes approximately 2 hours to administer and is considered a relatively lengthy test. The GATB yields three composite scores: cognitive, perceptual, and psychomotor scores. Nine aptitude factor scores are based on the 12 subtests, with standard scores based on a mean of 100 and a SD of 20 (Gregory, 1996). The nine aptitude factor scores are as follows:

G: General Learning Ability	S: Spatial Aptitude	K: Motor Coordination
V: Verbal Aptitude	P: Form Perception	F: Finger Dexterity
N: Numeric Aptitude	Q: Clerical Perception	M: Manual Dexterity

Armed Services Vocational Aptitude Battery (ASVAB) is the most widely administered multiple aptitude battery to classify and select potential military recruits (Parker, 2001). The ASVAB consists of 10 subtests:

GS: General Science	AR: Arithmetic Reasoning
WK: Work Knowledge	MK: Mathematics Knowledge
PC: Paragraph Comprehension	MC: Mechanical Comprehension
EI: Electronics Information	AS: Auto and Shop Information
CS: Code Speed	NO: Numerical Operations

Differential Aptitude Tests–Fifth Edition, Form C (DAT; Bennett, Seasher, & Wesman, 1990) is used for vocational and education counseling guidance. It features two levels. Level 1 is used for students in grades 7 to 9, and Level 2 is used for students in grades 10 to 12; both levels can also be used with adults. The total testing time is about 156 minutes. The DAT consists of eight subtests including verbal reasoning, numerical reasoning, abstract reasoning, perceptual speed and accuracy, mechanical reasoning, space relations, spelling, and language usage.

Assessment of Achievement

Achievement testing is used to provide an evaluation of the specific information that individuals have learned throughout their education and life experience to date. In this area, rehabilitation counselors are generally interested in assessment of the verbal and numerical skills of the consumer because these skills are important areas related to job efficiency.

Commonly Used Achievement Tests in the Vocational Rehabilitation Process

Wide Range Achievement Test–4 (WRAT-4; Wilkinson & Robertson, 2006) is a brief measure of fundamental academic skills. It is helpful in assessing academic achievement when the consumer has not had recent educational experience, and the rehabilitation professional wants to determine basic reading and arithmetic capabilities for possible training. The WRAT-4 has two equivalent forms (blue and green) and consists of four subtests: sentence comprehension, word reading, spelling, and math computation. It yields raw scores, grade equivalents, standard scores, and percentile ranks. It is brief to administer, approximately 35 to 45 minutes.

Peabody Individual Achievement Test–R (PIAT-R; Markwardt, 1998) is a wide range screening measure of achievement in the areas of mathematics, reading, spelling, and general information. The test yields six final scores: Mathematics, Reading Recognition, Reading Comprehension, Spelling, General Information, and a Total Score. It is administered individually, and the total testing time required is approximately 30 to 40 minutes.

Adult Basic Learning Examination–2 (ABLE-2; Karlsen & Gardner, 1986) is an achievement test used to determine the general educational level of adults who have not completed a formal eighth-grade education, to diagnose individual strengths, and to assist in the development of educational planning. It yields scores on five areas including vocabulary, reading, spelling, computation, and problem solving. This test contains three levels: Level I (grades 1 through 4), Level II (grades 5 through 8), and Level III (grades 9 through 12). Total testing time is about 2.5 hours for Level I and Level II and 3 hours for Level III.

Assessment of Personality

Personality is broadly defined as the system whereby individuals characteristically organize and process biophysical and environmental inputs to produce behavior in interactions with the larger surrounding systems (Sundberg, 1977). Personality tests are designed to measure an individual's emotional, interpersonal, motivational, and attitudinal characteristics (Anastasi & Urbina, 1997). The purpose of personality testing in rehabilitation is to identify personality strengths and weaknesses that might impact job acquisition and retention (Power, 2006).

Commonly Used Personality Tests in the Vocational Rehabilitation Process

Minnesota Multiphasic Personality Inventory–2 (MMPI-2; Hathaway, McKinley, & Butcher, 1990) is the most widely used personality inventory in general. The MMPI-2 consists of 567 statements to assess major psychological characteristics and is designed for adults aged 16 years and older. The test provides T-scores (M = 50; SD = 10) on 4 validity scales (L, F, and K) and on these 10 clinical scales:

1. Hypochondriasis (Hs)
2. Depression (D)
3. Conversion Hysteria (Hy)
4. Psychopathic deviate (Pd)
5. Masculinity-Femininity (MF)
6. Paranoia (Pa)
7. Psychasthenia (Pt)
8. Schizophrenia (Sc)
9. Hypomania (Ma)
10. Social introversion (O or Si)

Myers–Briggs Type Indicator (MBTI; Myer & Briggs, 1988) is based on Jung's concepts of perception and judgment. The MBTI is scored on eight scales yielding four bipolar dimensions:

1. Extroversion (E) versus Introversion (I)
2. Sensing (S) versus Intuition (N)
3. Thinking (T) versus Feeling (F)
4. Judgment (J) versus Perception (P)

The MBTI personality type is summarized in four letters; this combination indicates the direction of the person's preference on each of the four dimensions. All possible combinations of the four paired scales result in 16 different potential personality types. Each type combination has its own strengths. It is often used along with interest inventories and other psychological test results.

Sixteen Personality Factor–Form E (16 PF) was designed to provide information about an individual's primary personality factors (Cattell, 1986). The 16 PF has 128 items and requires a third- to sixth-grade reading level. Final scores are given on 16 primary factors:

A: Warmth	G: Rule-Consciousness	Q1: Openness to change
B: Reasoning	H: Social boldness	Q2: Self-reliance
C: Emotional stability	I: Sensitivity	Q3: Perfectionism
E: Dominance	N: Privateness	Q4: Tension
F: Liveliness	Q: Apprehension	

Assessment of Vocational Interests

Vocational interest inventories help consumers identify jobs in which the consumer is likely to experience greater job satisfaction. Knowledge of the match between the consumer's aptitudes and abilities and the skill demands of a job will enhance the prediction of the likelihood of a consumer's satisfaction with a given job. However, it is also important to consider the match between the consumer's interests and the extrinsic and intrinsic rewards that can be acquired from the job (Rubin & Roessler, 2008).

Commonly Used Interest Tests in the Vocational Rehabilitation Process

Self-Directed Search (Form R) (SDS; Holland, 1994) is based on Holland's theory. It is a self-administered, self-recorded, and self-interpreted vocational counseling tool. It has two forms (forms R and E). Form R requires at least seventh- to eighth-grade reading level and form E requires at least a fourth-grade reading level. It consists of an assessment booklet and an occupations finder. The booklet has five sections: Occupational Daydreams, Activities, Competencies, Occupations, and Self-Estimates. The SDS yields a total score for each of the six personality types (Holland's theory: Realistic, Investigative, Artistic, Social, Enterprising, and Conventional). The highest three summary scores determine a three-digit personality type (e.g., a person with high Investigative, Social, and Enterprising interests would be coded ISE).

Strong Interest Inventory (SII; Strong, Hansen, & Campbell, 1994) is one of the oldest and most scientifically developed interest surveys. It was developed to (a) give individuals information about themselves and their preferences that will help them make sound career decisions, (b) provide information to professionals, and (c) help in studying groups of individuals. It yields scores and scales based on the Holland R-I-A-S-E-C typology. The profile is divided into four major sections: (a) six general occupational themes, (b) 30 basic interest scales, (c) 244 occupational scales, and (d) five personal style scales. The test is easy to administer, requires at least sixth-grade reading level, and takes about 30 minutes to complete.

Reading-Free Vocational Interest Inventory–Second Edition (R-FVII-2; Becker, 2000) was developed to provide information about vocational preferences for people with cognitive and learning disabilities through the use of illustrations of individuals engaged in various occupational tasks. The R-FVII-2 can be used with people aged 13 years and older with intellectual disabilities. It consists of illustrated depictions of occupations in a forced choice format presented in 55 triads throughout the booklet. The R-FVII-2 provides scores in 11 interest areas for men and women.

Work Samples Assessment

Work samples are an assessment approach whereby the consumer is observed performing a simulated or actual work activity, usually in a rehabilitation center or vocational evaluation unit. Work samples are designed to see whether the individual follows the procedures and uses the tools and materials involved in actual jobs appropriately (Robin & Roessler, 2008). Work samples are used to measure a variety of constructs including vocational aptitudes, worker temperaments, vocational interests, hand dexterity, tolerance for standing or sitting, work habits and behaviors, learning styles, and understanding of written and oral instructions (Gice, 1985).

There are a number of commercially available systems:

McCarron-Dial Evaluation System (MDS; McCarron & Spires, 1991) was developed to predict an individual's ability for community-based employment. A battery of tests consists of eight separate instruments that assess five factors (verbal-cognitive, sensory, motor, emotional, and integration). The basic battery takes about 3 hours to administer and the comprehensive battery takes 5 days to complete.

VALPAR (Botterbusch, 1987) is a provider of vocational evaluation services that uses a criterion-referenced approach in accordance with the U.S. Department of Labor's job standards. VALPAR analyzes most of its work samples using Methods-Time-Measurement (MTM) standards, which is an approach to analyze tasks to determine how long it would take an experienced employee to repeatedly perform the exercise over an 8-hour workday.

Situational Assessments

Situational assessments offer a work assessment approach where a consumer's job performance and work behaviors are systemically observed in a realistic and controlled working environment, such as in a rehabilitation facility or sheltered workshop (Bolton & Parker, 2008). The terms situational assessment, community-based situational assessment, job tryouts, on-the-job evaluation (OJE), and supported employment evaluation are often used interchangeably. Situational assessments can provide valuable insights regarding the consumer's general employability behaviors. It focuses on assessing the consumer's work potential in regard to factors such as ability to (a) accept supervision, (b) get along with coworkers, (c) stay on task, (d) sustain productivity for 8 hours, and (e) tolerate frustration (Rubin & Roessler, 2008).

Ecological Assessments

Ecological assessment occurs in the natural setting, such as actual worksites where the individual could potentially be a long-term employee. The goal is to evaluate the individual's capacity to meet the productivity demands of that setting at present or in the near future through the provision of training or on-the-job supports. Examples of ecological assessment include supported employment placements and OJEs (Rubin & Roessler, 2008).

Supported Employment

Vocational evaluation in supported employment can occur *after* the person has assumed a particular job. This assessment is to predict what a person can do in a specific job setting with the necessary social and vocational support system in place (Robin & Roessler, 2008). This assessment focuses on (a) the need for work site accommodations and supports, (b) the level of the person's independent living skills, and (c) the types of continuing services the person will need (McAlees & Menz, 1992). The ecological assessment in supported employment allows the counselor and the consumer to engage in a closer working relationship at the job site to identify job modifications, supports, and training required to enhance the person-job match.

On-the-Job Evaluations

On-the-job evaluations (OJEs) assess the functioning of individuals with disabilities in actual work settings where they are involved in activities presumed to be compatible with their vocational interests and skills. OJEs can occur within work stations in institutions, rehabilitation facilities, or business and industries focusing on a variety of variables including personality, attitudes, aptitudes, work traits, work skills, and physical capacities (Robin & Roessler, 2008). The time period for an OJE can range from a single day to a month or longer. An OJE may be helpful for considering jobs that may be more appropriate to fit the skills and preferences of the consumer and may better fit with a job requiring a lower level of the specific vocational aptitudes in question. OJEs are also helpful in determining appropriate onsite supports or training needed to enable the consumer to perform the job successfully (Rogan & Hagner, 1990).

ETHICAL, LEGAL, AND CULTURAL IMPLICATIONS IN ASSESSMENT

Overview

This section draws on established guidelines for assisting rehabilitation counselors with decision-making strategies, such as the Commission on Rehabilitation Counselor Certification (CRCC) Code of Professional Ethics (https://www.crccertification.com/filebin/pdf/CRCC_COE_1-1-10_Rev12-09.pdf). Legal and ethical considerations are outlined and considerations related to the selection, administration, and interpretation of measures for individuals with disabilities are discussed.

LEARNING OBJECTIVES

By the end of this unit you should be able to:

1. Identify the key legal and ethical issues in assessment.
2. Understand the relationship of disability effects on the selection, administration, and interpretation of assessment measures.

KEY CONCEPTS

Ethical and Legal Issues in Assessment

Test Development and Selection

Power (2006) offers several guidelines for addressing issues related to test selection and development: First, caution must be exercised when depending on test instruments to provide information about consumer needs and traits. The selection of assessment measures should be carefully planned and tailored to the needs of the consumer, so as to avoid overuse or indiscriminant use of testing. Second, vocational assessment may be used as a descriptive appraisal of current levels of a consumer functioning and as an indicator of potential. It is imperative that the rehabilitation professionals assess the appropriateness of a test or assessment measure with regard to reliability, validity, and normative populations. Third, rehabilitation professionals should be aware of assessment measures available to choose from and the proper use of testing, and each test used in an assessment should be defined according to what it measures and its use, and the process of test development should be clearly outlined. Finally, when selecting a test battery, adequate interpretive strategies should be available (Power, 2006).

Test Fairness

The vocational evaluator is ethically obliged when reporting outcomes to indicate potential reasons why a consumer may fail to perform at average or above levels and suggests ways for remediating the deficiency (Matkin, 1980). It is also important to carefully consider the consumer's needs and reaction to the assessment process (e.g., environmental influences and consumer traits). To promote test fairness, Power (2006) suggests that tests should be administered under the same conditions that were established in their standardization. When there is a need to modify tests to accommodate certain disability groups, attention should be given to ensure appropriate assessment methods so as to not compromise the validity and reliability of the test. Types of testing accommodations include testing medium, time limits, and test content. Test interpretation should incorporate all other relevant information about the consumer, such as educational history, motivation, and adjustment to disability (Bolton, 1982). Important decisions about consumers should not be based on the results of a single test or testing session.

Test-Taker Rights in Assessment

According to the CRCC Code of Professional Ethics, test takers have the right to (a) know in advance of testing why they are being tested, how the testing will benefit them, how the test data will be used, and how much time and money the testing will cost them; (b) participate in planning and scheduling the testing; (c) be free of unnecessary and outdated tests; (d) be tested in an atmosphere that is free from distractions and conducive to positive test performance; (e) be assessed via the most appropriate instruments and techniques available; (f) have a complete, comprehensive, clear, and honest explanation, analysis, and application of test results; (g) discuss their test results with people competent to interpret their test protocols, relate test data to other available data, and answer any questions; (h) have their confidentiality protected; and (i) further counseling or assessment, if indicated.

Test Privacy

The privacy of the consumer must be respected, and all information and materials obtained during the assessment process should be safeguarded. The confidentiality of test instruments and test data is of paramount importance in maintaining the integrity of the tests and the validity of test results.

Evaluator Competencies

Vocational evaluators should demonstrate competencies, not only in the understanding and interpretation of assessment results but also be competent in their knowledge of the world of work, familiarity with studies of human behavior, and an awareness of the limitations of test interpretation.

Multicultural Issues

Rehabilitation counselors must recognize potential issues of test bias, criteria for cultural competence, and the unique considerations regarding ethnic minority consumers during the assessment process.

Test Bias

Tests may be biased against a person or group of persons by containing items that favor one group over another, by using test results if the criteria used for selection and prediction varies greatly among different groups, and by not considering such test-related factors as motivation, anxiety, and the test sophistication of those taking the assessment tool.

Cultural Competence

Sensitivity and awareness of values, attitudes, and beliefs appear to be essential components of cultural competence. Training for cultural competence includes (a) determining the acculturation status of consumer prior to the standard assessment approaches, (b) applying methodology and research findings throughout the assessment process, (c) using or appropriately adapting standard assessment instruments, and (d) developing an awareness of attitudes, beliefs, knowledge, and skills in working with culturally diverse groups. Response style, performance motivation, language, and acculturation can affect assessment results and contribute to the lessened usefulness of test results.

Disability Considerations in Assessment

Because standardized test instruments may not necessarily be the best way to assess factors such as motivation, work tolerance, or interest, observations of the consumer in various settings or trial work experiences may prove better methods for understanding rehabilitation potential. It is important that the rehabilitation counselor be aware of the potential for disability effects to impact the vocational assessment process.

Test Selection

Disability-related considerations are important with regard to the assessment measure selection process. It is important to assess whether the nature of the disability could impact the intended use of the test. Individuals with serious emotional or cognitive problems may have low attention spans and shorter tasks may be more appropriate (Power, 2006).

Test Administration

Power (2006) suggests that to minimize consumer's anxiety and time commitment, performance-based tests should be administered first. For some individuals with disabilities, tests administered in small blocks of time are preferable. Particular attention should be given to consumers with visual or hearing impairments or issues related to fatigue.

Test Interpretation

It is important to communicate test results at the consumer's level of understanding. Rehabilitation practitioners should consider how the consumer's disability influences the test-taking process.

▧ INTERNET RESOURCES

Professional Organizations

American Psychological Association Division 5: Evaluation, Measurement and Statistics
http://www.apa.org/divisions/div5

Association for Assessment in Counseling and Education (division of the American Counseling Association)
http://www.theaaceonline.com

Commission on Rehabilitation Counselor Certification (CRCC)
http://www.crccertification.com

Standards for Educational and Psychological Testing (AERA, APA, NCME)
http://teststandards.org

Vocational Evaluation and Career Assessment Professionals (VECAP)
http://www.vecap.org

Vocational Evaluation and Work Adjustment Association (VEWAA; division of the National Rehabilitation Association)
http://www.vewaa.com

To Learn About Various Tests
http://cps.nova.edu/~cpphelp
http://www.unl.edu/buros

Work Sample Tests
http://www.valparint.com/index.htm
http://www.vri.org

Transition Assessment Toolkit
http://www.nsttac.org/products_and_resources/tag.aspx

Supported Employment
http://www.worksupport.com

▧ MULTIPLE CHOICE QUESTIONS

1. An interpretation of a test score, such as a percentile score, that is based on the individual's performance relative to scores obtained by a group of individuals, would be considered a
   A. self-referenced interpretation
   B. criterion-referenced interpretation
   C. norm-referenced interpretation
   D. not enough information provided

2. A scale that classifies variables based on categorical information without distinguishing size or amount would be classified as
   A. nominal
   B. ordinal
   C. interval
   D. ratio

3. All of the following are best classified as vocational interest inventories, EXCEPT
   A. Strong Interest Inventory
   B. Kuder Career Search
   C. Self-Directed Search
   D. General Aptitude Test Battery

4. All of the following are among the four index scores generated by the Wechsler Adult Intelligence Scale–IV (WAIS-IV), EXCEPT
   A. Clerical Perception Index

B. Working Memory Index
C. Perceptual Reasoning Index
D. Verbal Comprehension Index

5. The Self-Directed Search can best be described as:
   A. A labor market survey
   B. A self-administered interest inventory based on Holland's career theory
   C. A standardized test measuring career motivation
   D. A work sample

6. A type of nonstatistical validity evidence based on a subjective appraisal of a test's content is
   A. face validity
   B. predictive validity
   C. construct validity
   D. concurrent validity

7. In the General Aptitude Test Battery, "Q" is the abbreviation for
   A. Motor coordination
   B. Color discrimination
   C. Clerical perception
   D. Eye-hand-foot coordination

8. All of the following are validity types of evidence EXCEPT
   A. Consent
   B. Test-retest
   C. Criterion
   D. Construct

9. Test A has an internal consistency in the .70s to .90s. Test B has an internal consistency of .40s to .50s. Which of the following is a true statement based on these statements?
   A. Test A is more valid than Test B
   B. Test B is more valid than Test A
   C. Test A is more reliable than Test B
   D. Test B is more reliable than Test A

10. A standard score based on the normal distribution curve with a M equal to 0 and a SD equal to 1 is a
    A. *T*-score
    B. *z*-score
    C. percentile
    D. raw score

ANSWER KEY

1. C; 2. A; 3. D; 4. A; 5. B; 6. A; 7. C; 8. B; 9. C; 10. B

ADVANCED MULTIPLE CHOICE QUESTIONS

1. During the assessment process in rehabilitation, test-taker rights include all of the following, EXCEPT
   A. Knowledge in advance why they are being tested
   B. Assessment provided by a competent evaluator
   C. Protection of confidentiality and awareness of limits to confidentiality
   D. Immediate access to all testing materials and scoring manuals if requested

2. John is a consumer with a significant visual impairment who is referred for intelligence testing to determine his cognitive functioning. His rehabilitation counselor recommends that John take

the verbal comprehension subtests of the WAIS-IV but is not sure how to measure performance-based intelligence. Of the following tests, which would you recommend?
A. Raven's Progressive Matrices
B. Stanford-Binet V
C. Haptic Intelligence Scale
D. Processing Speed Index from the Wechsler Adult Intelligence Scale–IV

3. Your consumer scores in the 92th percentile on a reading comprehension exam, meaning
A. She answered 92 of 100 answers correctly
B. She received a score of 92% on the test, after the examination was curved
C. She scored higher than 91% of the other test takers
D. Both B and C

4. All of the following statements are true about assessment with individuals with disabilities, EXCEPT
A. It is important to consider how response style, performance motivation, disability effects, and language may affect test performance and consequently usefulness of test results
B. Only tests that have separate norms for individuals with disabilities are considered valid measures in vocational rehabilitation assessment approaches
C. Sensitivity and awareness of values, attitudes, and beliefs are considered the essential components of cultural competence in assessment
D. Test bias is an important consideration when selecting tests and interpreting results

5. Kelly is a 21-year-old consumer. She is administered the WAIS-IV. She receives a FSIQ score of 70. Her index scores are: 65 on the Working Memory Index, 60 on the Verbal Comprehension Index, 60 on the Processing Speed Index, and 80 on the Perceptual Reasoning Index. Assuming these scores are representative of her true performance and valid, what inferences could be made?
A. Kelly is considered to have a severe intellectual disability (or severe mental retardation)
B. Kelly's abstract verbal reasoning and verbal comprehension fall in the average range relative to her same age peers
C. Kelly's spatial reasoning and visual processing are relative strengths
D. Nothing can be concluded from these scores

6. All of the following are true statements regarding a true normal curve, EXCEPT:
A. Approximately 68% of the total cases fall within two standard deviations of the mean
B. Approximately 98% of the cases are within three SDs of the mean
C. The mean, median, and mode all have the same value
D. The limits of the curve are infinite

7. You are a rehabilitation counselor working with Teri. Teri is a 30-year-old female who would like to find employment. She left high school in the 10th grade to raise her child and has never worked. She is interested in obtaining a GED and would like to pursue a college degree in elementary education. You are interested in a brief measure to assess Teri's basic reading and arithmetic capabilities and would likely choose to administer the
A. Wide Range Achievement Test (WRAT-4)
B. Wechsler Adult Intelligence Scale (WAIS-IV)
C. Armed Services Vocational Aptitude Battery (ASVAB)
D. Beta-III

8. You are working with a new consumer who reports to you that she took a test several years ago in which her scores were elevated on the psychasthenia and schizophrenia scales. You believe she took the
A. Myers-Briggs Type Indicator
B. 16 Personality Factor (16 PF)
C. Minnesota Multiphasic Personality Inventory (MMPI)
D. Raven's Progressive Matrices

9. According to the CRCC Code of Ethics regarding evaluation, assessment, and interpretation:

A. Rehabilitation counselors are not responsible for preventing the misuse of obsolete or out-dated measures and assessment data by others
B. Rehabilitation counselors are able to reproduce or modify published assessments without acknowledgment and permission from the publisher under some circumstances
C. Prior to assessment, rehabilitation counselors are expected to explain the nature and purposes of assessment in the language and/or at the developmental level of the consumer, unless explicit exception has been agreed on in advance
D. As it may be necessary to accommodate consumers with disabilities, a test may not be administered under standard conditions. If this occurs, it is up to the rehabilitation counselor to decide whether or not to note this change in the interpretation of the test results

10. E-S-F-P (extroversion, sensing, feeling, perception) is a possible score summary of a personality type on this well-known personality test based on the works of Jung
A. Sixteen Personality Factor
B. Myers-Briggs Type Indicator
C. Minnesota Multiphasic Personality Inventory–2
D. NEO-PI

ANSWER KEY AND EXPLANATION OF ANSWERS

1-D: The CRCC Code of Ethics clearly protects the rights of test takers. It is the responsibility of the rehabilitation counselor to ensure that consumers are aware in advance as to why they are being tested, so that they can provide informed consent, that the assessment is provided by a competent evaluator, and that confidentiality is protected. Because it is important to maintain the integrity and security of tests and other assessment techniques, rehabilitation counselors must comply with legal and contractual obligations even if a test taker requests access. Rehabilitation counselors are not able to appropriate, modify, or reproduce published assessments without explicit permission from the publisher.

2-C: The Haptic Intelligence Scale was specifically designed to parallel the performance-based measures of the WAIS for individuals with visual impairments. On the other hand, Raven's Progressive Matrices, many of the subtests of the Stanford-Binet V, and the Processing Speed subtests of the WAIS-IV all require vision.

3-C: Percentiles are rank order scores that indicate the percentage of persons in the comparison group who the test taker has outperformed. It is important not to confuse percentile scores with raw scores (which usually represent the percentage correct). Although percentile ranks are reported frequently because of their ease of understanding, they exaggerate differences near the mean and collapse differences at the extremes. For example, the raw score difference between two individuals scoring at the 47th and 75th percentiles may only be a few points.

4-B: Disability, cultural background, language, test bias, and motivation can affect an individual's test performance and results and should be considered during test selection, administration, and interpretation. In some cases, it may be important to use comparison norms based on a specific disability population; however, this is not always the case. For example, if you are interested in assessing the clerical aptitude of an individual with a lower back injury, you would likely be interested in how this individual's performance compares with others successfully working in clerical occupations rather than a specific disability population.

5-C: Kelly scored an 80 on Perceptual Reasoning Index of the WAIS-IV. Although this score falls in the low average range compared with her same age peers, this score is notably higher than her own performance on the other scales and suggests that her spatial reasoning and visual processing are strengths relative to the other areas measured by the WAIS-IV. Kelly's full-scale score of 70 would be classified as borderline intellectual functioning range but not indicative of a *severe* intellectual disability. The Verbal Comprehension Index of the WAIS-IV provides an estimate of Kelly's abstract verbal reasoning and comprehension. Her score of 60 suggests that she falls in the extremely low range on this scale relative to the norm group, whereas a score of 90 to 109 would suggest average performance.

6-A: Approximately 68% of the total cases fall within one standard deviation of the mean on a true normal curve; 95% within SDs; and 98% within three SDs.

7-A: The Wide Range Achievement Test–Fourth Edition (WRAT-4) is a commonly used brief measure of achievement level. The Beta-III and the WAIS-IV are classified as intelligence tests and the ASVAB is an aptitude test. In addition to not measuring the construct of interest, these latter three tests are also more extensive and lengthier to administer relative to the WRAT-4.

8-C: *Sychasthenia* and *Schizophrenia* are among the 10 clinical scales on the Minnesota Multiphasic Personality Inventory (MMPI-2). Increased scores on the Clinical Scales reflect maladjustment and psychological dysfunction. The Myers-Briggs Type Indicator and the 16 Personality Factor are used to assess broad personality characteristics rather than psychopathology. Raven's Progressive Matrices measure nonverbal intelligence.

9-C: The CRCC Code of Ethics clearly specifies that rehabilitation counselors are expected to communicate the nature and purpose of assessment to the consumer. In addition, rehabilitation counselors (a) are responsible for preventing the misuse of assessment data by others, (b) should never reproduce or modify published assessments without permission from the publisher, and (c) are expected to note any changes made to standardized testing conditions in the interpretation of test results.

10-B: The Myers-Briggs Type Indicator (MBTI) was designed based on Jung's concepts of perception and judgment. The MBTI is scored on eight scales yielding four bipolar dimensions: Extroversion (E) versus Introversion (I); Sensing (S) versus Intuition (N); Thinking (T) versus Feeling (F); Judgment (J) versus Perception (P). An individual's personality type is then summarized in four letters based on the paired scales. On the other hand, scores on the 16 PF are given on 16 bipolar primary personality factors; scores on the MMPI-2 are based on the increases on specific Clinical Scales; and scores on the NEO-PI reflect the five-factor model of personality.

▨ REFERENCES

AERA, APA, & NCME. (1999). *Standards for educational and psychological testing.* Washington, DC: Author.

Anastasi, A., & Urbina, S. (1997). *Psychological testing* (7th ed.). Upper Saddle River, NJ: Prentice Hall.

Becker, R. (2000). *Reading-free vocational interest inventory-2.* Columbus, OH: Elbern.

Bennett, G. K., Seasher, H. G., & Wesman, A. G. (1990). *Differential aptitude tests-fifth edition.* New York, NY: Psychological Corp.

Berven, N. L. (1997). *Professional practice: Assessment.* In D. Maki & T. Riggar (Eds.), *Rehabilitation counseling* (pp. 151–169). New York, NY: Springer Publishing.

Bolton, B. (1982). *Vocational adjustment of disabled persons.* Austin, TX: PRO-ED.

Bolton, B. (2001). *Handbook of measurement and evaluation in rehabilitation.* Belmont, CA: Aspen.

Bolton, B., & Parker, R. (2008). *Handbook of measurement and evaluation in rehabilitation.* Austin, TA: PRO-ED.

Botterbusch, K. F. (1987). Commercial vocational evaluation systems. In B. Bolton (Ed.), *Vocational adjustment of disabled persons* (pp. 93–126). Baltimore, MA: University Park Press.

Cattell, R. B. (1986). *Sixteen personality factor questionnaire.* New York, NY: Psychological Corp.

Dunn, L. M., & Dunn, L. (1997). *Peabody picture vocabulary test-third edition.* Circle Pines, MN: American Guidance Service.

Gice, J. (1985). In search of… "The perfect vocational evaluation." *Vocational Evaluation and Work Adjustment Bulletin, 18*(1), 4–7.

Hathaway, S., McKinley, C., & Butcher, J. (1990). *Minnesota multiphasic personality inventory-second edition.* Minneapolis, MN: National Computer Systems.

Holland, J. (1994). *The self-directed search.* San Antonio, TX: Psychological Corp.

Karlsen, B., & Gardner, E. F. (1986). *Adult basic learning examination.* New York, NY: Psychological Corp.

Markwardt, F. C. (1998). *Peabody individual achievement test-revised.* Circle Pines, MN: American Guidance Service.

Matkin, B. (1980). Legal and ethical issues in vocational assessment. *Vocational Evaluation and Work Adjustment Bulletin, 13,* 57–60.

McAlees, D., & Menz, F. (1992). Consumerism and vocational evaluation. *Rehabilitation Education, 6,* 213–220.

McCarron, L. T., & Spires, H. P. (1991). *McCarron-Dial system vocational interest exploration instructor's manual.* Dallas, TX: McCarron-Dial Systems.

Myer, I. B., & Briggs, K. C. (1988). *Myers-Briggs type indicator.* Palo Alto, CA: CPP.

Parker, R. M. (2001). *Occupational aptitude survey and interest schedule-third edition.* Austin, TX: PRO-ED.

Power, P. W. (2006). *A guide to vocational assessment* (4th ed.). Austin, TX: PRO-ED.

Rogan, P., & Hagner, D. (1990). Vocational evaluation in supported employment. *Journal of Rehabilitation, 56,* 45–51.

Roid, G. (2003). *Stanford-Binet intelligence scale-fifth edition.* Itasca, IL: Riverside.

Rubin, S. E., & Roessler, R. T. (2008). *Foundations of the vocational rehabilitation process* (4th ed.). Austin, TX: PRO-ED.

Slosson, R. L., Nicholson, C. L., & Hibpshman, T. H. (1990). *Slosson intelligence test-revised.* East Aurora, NY: Slosson Educational Publications.

Strong, E. K., Hansen, J. C., & Campbell, D. P. (1994). *Strong interest inventory.* Palo Alto, CA: Consulting Psychologists Press.

Sundberg, N. D. (1977). *Assessment of persons.* Englewood Cliffs, NJ: Prentice Hall.

Wechsler, D. (2008). *Manual for the Wechsler Adult Intelligence Scale-fourth edition (WAIS-IV).* San Antonio, TX: Psychological Corp.

Wilkinson, G. S., & Robertson, G. J. (2006). *Wide range achievement test 4 professional manual.* Lutz, FL: Psychological Assessment Resources.

U.S. Department of Labor. (1970). *Manual for USES general aptitude test battery.* Washington, DC: U.S. Government Printing.

Research and Program Evaluation

8

CHUNG-YI CHIU, LINDSEY ROSE, ROBERT DRAKE,
AND GERALD CASENAVE

Knowledge in current research methods enables rehabilitation professionals to review research articles and perceptively apply the findings to enrich their own practice. It also empowers rehabilitation professionals to conduct their own research, whether it be for gaining insight into a particular problem or for program evaluation. This chapter reviews

- Research and program evaluation topics, such as basic statistics and psychometric concepts
- Research methods
- Effectiveness of rehabilitation counseling services
- Ethical, legal, and cultural issues related to research and program evaluation

BASIC STATISTICS AND PSYCHOMETRIC CONCEPTS

Overview

Knowing how to translate knowledge to utilize and apply research requires an understanding of basic research concepts, basic statistical knowledge, and psychometrics.

▓ LEARNING OBJECTIVE

By the end of this unit you should be able to:

1. Understand basic concepts of research methodology and statistics.

▓ KEY CONCEPTS

Variables and Relationships

The independent variable (IV) is believed to affect or cause changes in the dependent variable (DV) (Cozby, 2009). For example, exercise (IV) is thought to affect weight (DV). In an experiment, the IV is manipulated (e.g., subjects are randomly assigned to an exercise intervention and a no exercise program), and the DV is measured (e.g., subjects are weighed after completion of the exercise experiment). Variables can have a positive linear relationship (i.e., high values on one variable are associated with high values on the other and low values on one are associated with low values on the other), a negative linear relationship (i.e., high values on one variable are associated with low values on the other), a curvilinear relationship (i.e., a relationship that changes over the range of both variables), or no relationship at all (Cozby, 2009).

Measurement Scales

Nominal scales have no numerical properties and distinguish categories by labels. They are mutually exclusive, and the categories cannot be ordered in any meaningful way (e.g., genders, races). Ordinal scales also have named categories, but these categories can be put into an ordered sequence. Rating systems are usually good examples of ordinal scales (e.g., restaurant ratings). Interval scales have ordered categories, but unlike ordinal scales, the difference between each category choice is of an equal interval (e.g., temperature). Ratio scales also have ordered, equal intervals, but unlike interval scales, they have an absolute zero point that represents the absence of the variable being measured (e.g., height).

Reliability and Validity

Reliability is the estimate of the consistency or stability of a measure of behavior. Test–retest reliability is tested by measuring the same individuals at two different points in time. On the other hand, internal consistency reliability is assessed by using responses at only one point in time. Split-half reliability is a way to measure internal consistency by comparing an individual's score on one half of a measure to their score on the other half. Cronbach's alpha also measures internal consistency by correlating each item on a measure with every other item. Interrater reliability is the extent to which different raters agree on their observations of a behavior being measured. Validity is the degree to which an instrument measures what it is supposed to measure. Construct validity refers to how adequately the operational definition of a variable actually reflects the true meaning of the variable. One indicator of construct validity is face validity—the measure appears to measure what it is supposed to measure. Another indicator of construct validity is criterion-oriented validity—how well scores on a measure relate to a criterion (an indicator of the construct). Types of criterion-oriented validity include predictive validity (how well scores on the measure predict behavior at a time in the future), concurrent validity (how well scores are related to a criterion measured at the same time), convergent validity (how well scores on this measure are related to other measure of the same construct), and discriminant validity (the degree to which scores on this measure are not related to measurements of different constructs; or whether constructs believed to be unrelated are in fact unrelated).

Measures of Central Tendency

There are three measures of central tendency (Cozby, 2009). The mode is the most frequently occurring score in a data set. The median is the middlemost score when all scores are lined up in order from lowest to highest. If there is not a "middle" score because there is an even number of scores, the median is the average of the two middlemost scores. The *mean* is the average of scores in a data set (i.e., the sum of the scores divided by the number of scores). As an example, let us say a researcher gave an IQ test to seven people and they scored 87, 91, 96, 99, 100, 100, and 111. In this example, the mode is 100, the median is 99, and the mean is 98.

Measures of Variability

There are three ways to describe the variability of data (Cozby, 2009). The range of a set of scores is the highest score minus the lowest score. The variance describes the degree to which scores vary about the group mean. Mathematically, the variance is the average of the score's squared deviations. This is related mathematically to the standard deviation (SD), which is simply the square root of the variance. The SD expresses the variance of scores around the mean in units that are comparable with the mean. For this reason, the SD is frequently used in research literature to describe the average deviation of scores from the mean. Recall our set of IQ scores from the previous example: 87, 91, 96, 99, 100, 100, and 111. The range is 24, the variance is 58.57, and the SD is 7.65.

The Normal Curve and Standardized Scores

The normal curve (a symmetrical bell curve) is a mathematically defined curve in which the mean, median, and mode lie in the exact center (Cozby, 2009). The normal curve is divided into SDs and associated percentile ranks: about 68% of the scores fall between one SD above and one SD below the mean; about 95% of the scores fall between two SDs above and two SDs below the mean; and about 99% of the scores fall between three SDs above and three SDs below the mean. Common standardized scores are z-scores and T-scores. A z-score has a mean of zero and a SD of one. A T-score (used in behavioral, personality, and clinical research) has a mean of 50 and a SD of 10 (Cozby, 2009).

Statistical Hypothesis Testing

Researchers develop hypotheses that predict how variables will behave in a research study (Cozby, 2009). The null hypothesis is often the opposite of what the researcher predicts: that no difference exists. The alternative hypothesis is a statement of what will occur given the null hypothesis is rejected, meaning that differences do exist. Type I error occurs when the null hypothesis is wrongly rejected (i.e., the researcher determines that differences exist, but in actuality, there are no differences) (Cozby, 2009). Type II error (β) occurs when the null hypothesis is wrongly retained (i.e., the researcher determines that there are no differences, but in actuality, differences do exist) (Cozby, 2009). The level of significance, or alpha level (α), is the amount of Type I error the researcher is willing to allow in the study. Typical alpha (α) levels are set around .05 or .01, which allow for a 5% or 1% chance, respectively, that Type I error will occur. Statistical power is related to Type II error, and it is the likelihood of correctly finding that statistically differences exist when they truly do exist (Cozby, 2009).

Basic Statistical Tests

The t test is most commonly used to examine whether two groups are significantly different (Cozby, 2009). The chi-square (χ^2) test is used when dealing with frequencies (the number of subjects who fall into each of several categories) (Cozby, 2009). It is used with nominal data. For example, a χ^2 could be used to determine whether there is a significant relationship between geographical location and gender. The analysis of variance (ANOVA), or F test, is used to determine whether there is a significant difference between group means (Cozby, 2009). It is only used with interval or ratio scale data. For example, an F test could be used to see if different age groups had significantly differing scores on a measure of depression. The Pearson product–moment correlation coefficient (r) is used to find the strength of the relationship between two variables that were measured on interval or ratio scales. Correlations between about .10 and .20 are usually considered weak but may still be statistically significant depending on the sample size. Correlations of .50 or more are usually considered to be indicative of strong relationships between variables.

BASIC RESEARCH METHODS

Overview

This section reviews basic qualitative research designs and quantitative research designs.

▒ LEARNING OBJECTIVE

By the end of this unit you should be able to:

1. Understand common qualitative research designs and quantitative research designs to apply research literature in practice.

■ KEY CONCEPTS

Quantitative Research Design

In the experimental method, all extraneous variables are controlled, and confounding variables (uncontrolled variables that produce effects that are intertwined with the IV) are eliminated, so that clean cause–effect relationships can be determined (Cozby, 2009). The true basic experimental designs are a posttest-only design (e.g., participants are randomly assigned to either an experimental or control group and then measure the effect of the IV) or a pretest–posttest design. The pre-test step can help with selecting the participants. Once identified, the participants would be randomly assigned to groups. A pretest–posttest design can measure the extent of change in each individual and measure whether the mortality (a dropout factor in experiments) affects the final results.

A combination of the posttest-only and the pretest–posttest design is a Solomon four-group design, wherein half the participants receive only the posttest and the other half receive the pretest and the posttest. In independent groups design, the participants are randomly assigned to the various conditions. In repeated measures design, each participant is in all conditions. Repeated-measures design needs fewer participants than independent groups design. Repeated-measures design is sensitive to find the statistically significant differences between groups (Cozby, 2009). However, it is important to counterbalance the order of the conditions (Cozby, 2009). With complete counterbalancing, all possible orders of presentation are included. For example, for three conditions, there will be six orders of conditions. A technique to control-order effects without having all possible orders is a Latin square, in which a limited set of orders is constructed, so that each condition appears at each ordinal position and both precedes and follows every other conditions one time (Cozby, 2009). A matched-pairs design is another procedure less commonly used to assign participants that matches participants based on specific characteristics.

Quasi-experimental designs are similar to true experimental designs (e.g., one group posttest-only design, one-group pretest–post design, nonequivalent control group design, nonequivalent control group pretest–posttest design, interrupted time series design, control series design), but they do not use random assignment, thus limiting their ability to determine cause–effect relationships (Cozby, 2009). In addition, quasi-experimental designs are subject to a number of confounding effects, including history effects (any confounding effect that happens between the first and second measurements that is not part of the manipulation), maturation effects (any change that occurs systematically over time that is not part of the manipulation), testing effects (the effect of simply taking the pretest changes subjects' behavior), instrument decay (the basic characteristics of the instrument change over time), or regression toward the mean (when subjects' scores are extremely low or high on some variables, their scores will tend to change in the direction of the mean) (Cozby, 2009).

Single-case experimental designs examine the effects of a manipulated variable on a single case. The subject's behavior is measured at baseline, which is a control period of time before any manipulation is introduced. Later, a manipulation is introduced, and the subject's behavior is measured during this treatment period. To determine that it was the manipulation of the IV that caused any observed effects, a second baseline period can be introduced after the experimental treatment has been removed. That is the reversibility of the manipulation. A simple design is A (baseline period) → B (treatment period)—A (baseline period) design (ABA design, a.k.a. a reversal design). Several variations of this design (i.e. A–B–A–B or B–A–B) can be used depending on research needs. Another variation is a multiple baseline design in which several baseline behaviors are collected during the same time and then a researcher introduces the treatment at different times for each behavior.

Developmental research designs can be used to study human development or how people change over time. In the cross-sectional method, subjects of different ages are studied at one point in time. On the other hand, the longitudinal method studies the same group of people at different points in time as they grow older.

Qualitative Research Design

The primary purpose of qualitative research design is to increase our understanding of social phenomena as they occur naturally (Cozby, 2009). Interviews range from structured interviews (questions are planned in advance, and all participants are asked identical questions), to semistructured interviews (the interview is planned but may be modified while in progress), to unstructured interviews (questions are prompted by the flow of the conversation). Focus groups are a specific type of group interview wherein members provide insight into a specific topic or issue. Observation is a form of qualitative data in which the researcher watches participants in a natural setting and records what happens. Three common concerns that arise from observation are observer effect (the impact the observer has on participants), observer expectation (the observer has preconceived expectations that may not be true), and observer bias (the observer's attitudes or beliefs affect how they observe or interpret events) (Cozby, 2009). Archival data (e.g., statistical research, survey archives, written and mass communication records, content analysis of documents), which are data that were previously collected and stored away, can be reviewed to address a research question (Cozby, 2009).

EFFECTIVENESS OF REHABILITATION COUNSELING SERVICES

Overview

Rehabilitation counselors apply empirically supported interventions to clients, such as counseling/psychotherapy, working alliance, self-efficacy, motivational interviewing (MI), vocational rehabilitation services, and supportive employment, all of which have proved effective and beneficial to clients.

▓ LEARNING OBJECTIVE

By the end of this unit you should be able to:

1. Understand the meaning of program evaluation and be able to provide a rationale for the importance of research activities and the improvement of rehabilitation services.

▓ KEY CONCEPTS

Program Evaluation

Program evaluation is research on a program to evaluate the efficacy of the program. There are five phases of program evaluation research: needs assessment (to study whether there are problems that need to be addressed in program operations or participants), the assessment of program theory (to solve problems according to a theoretical assumption), formative or process evaluation (to monitor program), summative or outcome evaluation (to assess the program's impact on outcomes), and efficacy assessment (to examine whether the program is worthy) (Cozby, 2009).

Levels of Evidence

There are five levels of evidence in evaluating research (Holm, 2000): (1) Level 1 evidence is defined as strong evidence from at least one systematic review of multiple well-designed randomized-controlled trials; (2) Level 2 evidence is defined as strong evidence from at least one properly designed randomized-controlled trial of appropriate size; (3) Level 3 evidence is defined as evidence from well-designed trials without randomization, single-group pre–post, cohort, time series, or matched case-controlled studies; (4) Level 4 evidence is defined as evidence from well-designed nonexperimental studies from more than one center or research group; (5) Level 5 evidence is defined as opinions of respected authorities, based on clinical evidence, descriptive studies, or reports of expert committees.

Effectiveness of Vocational Rehabilitation

Many meta-analysis studies have shown that clients can benefit from the various kinds of counseling interventions and psychotherapy (Smith & Glass, 1977; Smith, Glass, & Miller, 1980; Wampold, 2001). From Smith et al.'s meta-analysis of 475 controlled outcome studies, they concluded that an average effect size is .85, which in their research translated to mean that clients receiving counseling were better off than 80% of those not receiving counseling. Likewise Wampold has concluded from several meta-analyses that the effect size related to absolute efficacy of counseling/psychotherapy falls within the range of .75 to .85. Furthermore, he suggested that a defensibly estimated efficacy of counseling/psychotherapy is .80, a large effect size in the behavioral and social science.

The working alliance has been found to be a common factor underlying active participation between clients and counselors in the rehabilitation process, counseling, and psychotherapy (Chan, Shaw, McMahon, Koch, & Strauser, 1997). Wampold (2001) found that at least 70% of psychotherapeutic effects are due to such common factors as working alliance, empathic listening, and goal setting. Among 2,732 vocational rehabilitation clients, employed clients have a stronger working alliance than those unemployed ($d = .73$, large effect), and the stronger the working alliance, the more positive the clients' perception of the future ($r = .51$, large effect) (Lustig, Strauser, Rice, & Rucke, 2002).

MI is a counseling intervention that has been broadly applied to rehabilitation practice, such as managing medical issues, adjusting either physical disability or cognitive impairment, improving psychosocial functioning, and returning to work (Wagner & McMahon, 2004). It has been shown to be a useful approach to promoting positive change and helping clients to move through ambivalence about making changes in their behavior. MI is based on a process of collaboration between counselor and client, inviting and allowing the individual to express their ideas, and promoting the client's autonomy in process and decision making.

In terms of the effectiveness of skill training for reducing symptoms of mental illness and increasing self-efficacy of social skill, coping skills, and job search and maintenance skills, a meta-analysis of skill training for clients in vocation rehabilitation programs found a weighted mean effect size across 15 studies of $d_+ = .82$ (large effect) and an estimated true population effect size of $d_+ = .93$ (large effect) (Bolton & Akridge, 1995). In other words, the average participant in the skills training programs exceeded 82% of nonparticipants. Dilk and Bond (1996) conducted a meta-analysis of 68 studies of skill training for people with mental illness. They found that for between-group studies, the overall effect size was $d = .40$ (small to medium effect), and at follow-up, the effect size was $d = .56$ (medium effect); whereas for within-group studies, the effect size was $d = .48$ (close to medium effect), and at follow-up $d = .30$ (small to medium effect).

A secondary data analysis of the Rehabilitation Services Administration case services report (RSA-911) data for fiscal year 2005 found that job placement and support services could improve the odds for obtaining competitive employment: job search assistance (odds ratio [OR] = 1.24; 95% CI [1.08, 1.43]), job placement assistance (OR = 1.89; 95% CI [1.66, 2.16]), and on-the-job support (OR = 2.20; 95% CI [1.90, 2.55]) (Dutta, Gervey, Chan, Chou, & Ditchman, 2008).

Bond (2004) found that the employment rate in supported employment program studies increased on average three times (from 12% to 38%). He also indicated that there is a 20% to 40% increase in the competitive employment rate when comparing supported employment and other vocational programs that applied randomized-controlled trial. In general, the average employment rate for consumers with mental illness in supported employment was 56% and 19% in traditional vocational programs. Mueser et al. (2004) conducted a randomized-controlled study to assign participants who were African Americans and Hispanic Americans to three vocational rehabilitation approaches, namely, the individual placement and support model of supported employment (IPS), a psychosocial rehabilitation program (PSR), and standard vocational services. They found that participants in IPS had better employment outcomes than those in PSR and standard services, for example, competitive work (73.9% vs. 18.2% vs. 27.5%, respectively); any paid work (73.9% vs. 34.8% vs. 53.6%, respectively).

ETHICAL, LEGAL, AND CULTURAL ISSUES RELATED TO RESEARCH AND PROGRAM EVALUATION

Overview

In order to apply knowledge of ethical, legal, and cultural issues in research and evaluation to the rehabilitation counseling practice, rehabilitation counselors need to know the principles of research ethics.

LEARNING OBJECTIVE

By the end of this unit you should be able to:

1. Understand research ethical principles and be able to apply ethical principles in research and practice.

KEY CONCEPTS

In 1979, the Belmont Report established three basic principles for ethical research on human research subjects—beneficence, respect for persons (autonomy), and justice. The principle of beneficence means that research should first do no harm, and it should be constructed to maximize the benefits of research (Sims, 2010). The Commission on Rehabilitation Counselor Certification (CRCC) Code of Ethics states that rehabilitation counselors must take care to avoid causing psychological, emotional, physical, or social harm throughout the research process (CRCC, 2010). If a study involves the potential to evoke psychological stress from study subjects, there must be safeguards in place to help the participants deal with the stress (e.g., debriefing sessions). Any physical risks must be evaluated in terms of whether the potential benefit of the research is sufficiently clear to outweigh the risk to the individuals involved (Cozby, 2009).

The principle of autonomy requires that researchers ensure that study subjects are provided the opportunity to make conscious and informed decisions about participating in research. Participants must be informed in clear and easily understood language about the purposes of a study, its risks and benefits, and their right to refuse to participate in the study or to terminate their participation in the study (Cozby, 2009).

The CRCC Code of Ethics requires that rehabilitation counselors inform research subjects if any of the procedures under study are experimental or relatively untried. Rehabilitation counselors also must disclose if there are any appropriate alternative procedures that may be advantageous for research subjects, must describe any limitations on confidentiality, and must provide participants with contact information for someone who can answer questions about the research (CRCC, 2010). The informed consent must be given freely and without coercion. The individual providing consent must be capable of providing that consent. For example, individuals with cognitive impairments and minor children are not presumed capable of providing informed consent (Cozby, 2009).

TABLE 8.1 ■ Summary of Key Concepts of Research and Program Evaluation

Key Concept	Interpretation
Positive linear relationship	As one variable value increases, the other increases too
Negative linear relationship	As one variable value increases, the other decreases however
Curvilinear relationship	As one variable value increases, the other increases and decreases
Nominal scales	Mutually exclusive categories
Ordinal scales	Ordered categories
Interval scales	Each unit has equal interval
Ratio scales	Each unit has equal interval but including an absolute zero point
Reliability	The estimate of the consistency or stability of a measure of behavior, such as test–retest reliability, split-half reliability, Cronbach's alpha, interrater reliability
Validity	The degree to which an instrument measures what it is supposed to measure, such as construct validity, face validity, criterion-oriented validity
Central tendency	Mode, median, mean
Variability	Range, variance, SD
Normal curve	68% of scores fall between one SD above and one SD below the mean; about 95% of scores fall between two SDs above and two SDs below the mean
z-score	A mean of zero and a SD of one
T-score	A mean of 50 and a SD of 10
Type I error (α) (.05, .01)	The null hypothesis is wrongly rejected
Type II error (β)	The null hypothesis is wrongly retained
t test, ANOVA, F test	Examine differences
Program evaluation research	There are five phases of program evaluation research: needs assessment, the assessment of program theory, process evaluation, outcome evaluation, and efficiency assessment
Five levels of evidence	From Level 1, at least one systematic review of multiple well-designed randomized-controlled trials, to Level 5—clinical evidence, descriptive studies, or reports of expert committees
Research ethics	Beneficence (do no harm), respect for persons (autonomy) (study subjects are provided the opportunity to make conscious and informed decisions), and justice (fairness and equity)

According to the CRCC Code of Ethics, participation in research by persons not presumed to be capable of providing informed consent may proceed if it is possible to obtain legally authorized informed consent on behalf of such individuals.

Finally, the CRCC Code of Ethics states that informed consent also involves notifying the research subjects of the potential target audiences to whom the research information will be disseminated (CRCC, 2010). When the methodology of the research requires that information be withheld from the participants, informed consent may be compromised. In general, it is considered ethically acceptable to withhold information if doing so would be unlikely to affect a subject's decision to participate.

In some research, it may not be possible or even necessary to obtain informed consent (e.g., observing behavior in a public setting). Another threat to autonomy involves the use of deception in research. The principle of autonomy does not necessarily preclude the use of deception in behavioral research (Cozby, 2009). The CRCC Code of Ethics permits deception in research only if the deception does not have the potential to cause physical or emotional harm to research participants (CRCC, 2010). One way to promote autonomy in such research is to provide a debriefing session to study participants. Debriefing provides the researchers an opportunity to be forthcoming to study participants about any deception used in the study and the reason(s) it was felt necessary (Cozby, 2009). If the methodology of the research requires deception or concealment, the CRCC Code of Ethics requires that the reasons for such actions be made known to the research participants as quickly as possible during debriefing (CRCC, 2010). In debriefing study participants, researchers may choose to explain the purpose of the study to its participants and to let them know what results the study had expected and how those results can benefit others (Cozby, 2009).

The principle of justice requires that researchers consider the issue of fairness and equity when selecting individuals for research. The Belmont Report identifies racial minorities, the economically disadvantaged, the very sick, and the institutionalized as disadvantaged populations who may unfairly be called on to assume potential risks involved with research (Harrison, 1993).

The ethical principles described previously have been formalized through federal regulations issued and updated by the U.S. Department of Health and Human Services. These regulations require every institution receiving federal funding to have an Institutional Review Board (IRB). An IRB is an agency that reviews all research conducted by an institution to ensure that it complies with federal law regarding the protection of human research subjects (Cozby, 2009). The CRCC Code of Ethics states that rehabilitation counselors must follow pertinent ethical principles, scientific standards, laws, and host institutional regulations. In addition to any IRB review, the CRCC Code of Ethics charges rehabilitation counselors to reflect cultural sensitivity and appropriateness in the planning, design, conduct, and reporting of research (CRCC, 2010) (Table 8.1).

▨ INTERNET RESOURCES

Commission Rehabilitation Counselor Certification. *CRC/CCRC Code ofsp Ethics*
http://www.crccertification.com/pages/crc_ccrc_code_of_ethics/10.php

Kiernan, Nancy E. *Program Evaluation*
http://extension.psu.edu/evaluation/Default.html

Prevention Research Centers. *Program Evaluation*
http://www.cdc.gov/prc/program-evaluation/index.htm

Trochim, William M. *The Research Methods Knowledge Base,* **2nd Edition**
http://www.socialresearchmethods.net/kb/

University of Minnesota Libraries. *Evidence-Based Practice*
http://hsl.lib.umn.edu/learn/ebp/mod01/index.html

▨ MULTIPLE CHOICE QUESTIONS

1. The condition that is being studied for its effect on another condition is the:
   A. IV
   B. DV
   C. Unknown variable
   D. Control variable

2. Temperature is an example of which scale?
   A. Nominal
   B. Ordinal
   C. Interval
   D. Ratio

3. Reliability means that a measure is
   A. correct
   B. consistent
   C. proven
   D. accepted

4. Predictive, concurrent, convergent, and discriminant validity are all types of what kind of validity?
   A. Construct
   B. Face
   C. Content
   D. Criterion oriented

5. *SD* is the average deviation from the
   A. Mode
   B. Median
   C. Variance
   D. Mean

6. A group of scores can have more than one
   A. mean
   B. mode
   C. median
   D. SD

7. With the normal curve, what percentage of scores fall within two SDs of the mean?
   A. 68
   B. 85
   C. 95
   D. 99

8. Which common standardized score has a mean of 50 and a SD of 10?
   A. Scaled score
   B. *T* score
   C. Standard score
   D. *z*-score

9. The statistical power of a research study is related to
   A. Type 1 error
   B. The level of significance
   C. The alpha level
   D. Type II error

10. Which of the following is a test of statistical significance?
    A. Correlation
    B. Effect size
    C. Mean differences
    D. χ^2

■ ANSWER KEY

1. A; **2.** C; **3.** B; **4.** D; **5.** D; **6.** B; **7.** C; **8.** B; **9.** D; **10.** D

ADVANCED MULTIPLE CHOICE QUESTIONS

1. In which research design are participants randomly assigned to groups?
   A. Single-case experimental
   B. Independent groups
   C. Repeated measures
   D. Matched pairs

2. Qualitative research collects data through
   A. Laboratory experiments
   B. Longitudinal studies
   C. Cross-sectional studies
   D. Interviews

3. In evidence-based practice, which level of evidence has evidence from randomized control trials?
   A. 2
   B. 3
   C. 4
   D. 5

4. Meta-analyses of studies of the effectiveness of counseling show what effect size?
   A. None
   B. Small
   C. Medium
   D. Large

5. What is the strength of correlation between interpersonal skills and job performance?
   A. None
   B. Small
   C. Small to moderate
   D. Moderate to strong

6. The process of seeking informed consent operationalizes the principle of
   A. Justice
   B. Autonomy
   C. Beneficence
   D. Nonmaleficence

7. The principle that promotes respect for persons is
   A. Justice
   B. Autonomy
   C. Beneficence
   D. Nonmaleficence

8. The principle that promotes fairness and equity is
   A. Justice
   B. Autonomy
   C. Beneficence
   D. Nonmaleficence

9. Which scale has an absolute zero point?
   A. Nominal
   B. Ordinal
   C. Interval
   D. Ratio

10. In a set of scores, the highest score minus the lowest score provides the
    A. Variance
    B. SD
    C. Mean
    D. Range

▨ ANSWER KEY AND EXPLANATION OF ANSWERS

1-B: In independent groups design, participants are randomly assigned to the various conditions, so that each participant is in only one group.

2-D: Qualitative research deals with narrative descriptions and interpretations; data are generally collected through interviews, observations, and archival data.

3-A: There are five levels of evidence. Level 2 evidence is defined as strong evidence from at least one properly designed randomized-controlled trials of appropriate size.

4-D: Meta-analyses of studies of the effectiveness of counseling show effect sizes ranging from .75 to .85, all of which are in the large range.

5-D: Meta-analyses of the correlation between interpersonal skills and job performance range between .39 and .93, that is, they are moderately to strongly correlated.

6-B: The principle of autonomy requires that researchers ensure that study subjects are provided the opportunity to make conscious and informed decisions about participating in research. Informed consent must be given freely and without coercion.

7-B: The basic principle of ethical research that promotes respect for persons is autonomy, which is also the right to free choice.

8-A: The basic principle of ethical research that promotes fairness and equity in the selection of individuals for research is justice.

9-D: Ratio scales have ordered, equal intervals as do interval scales, but in addition, they have an absolute zero point that represents the absence of the variable being measured.

10-D: The result of subtracting the lowest score from the highest score in a set of scores is the range of that set of scores. This is the simplest measure of their variability.

▨ REFERENCES

Bolton, B., & Akridge, R. L. (1995). A meta-analysis of skills training programs for rehabilitation clients. *Rehabilitation Counseling Bulletin, 38*, 262–273.

Bond, G. R. (2004). Supported employment: Evidence for an evidence-based practice. *Psychiatric Rehabilitation Journal, 27*, 345–359.

Chan, F., Shaw, L., McMahon, B. T., Koch, L., & Strauser, D. (1997). A model for enhancing consumer-counselor working relationships in rehabilitation. *Rehabilitation Counseling Bulletin, 41*, 122–137.

Commission on Rehabilitation Counselor Certification. (2010). *Code of professional ethics for rehabilitation counselors.* Schaumburg, IL: Author.

Cozby, P. C. (2009). *Methods in behavioral research* (10th ed.). Fullerton, CA: McGraw Hill.

Dilk, M. N., & Bond, G. R. (1996). Meta-analytic evaluation of skills training research for individuals with severe mental illness. *Journal of Consulting and Clinical Psychology,64*, 1337–1346.

Dutta, A., Gervey, R., Chan, F., Chou, C., & Ditchman, N. (2008). Vocational rehabilitation services and employment outcomes for people with disabilities: A United States study. *Journal of Occupational Rehabilitation, 18*(4), 326–334. doi:10.1007/s10926-008-9154-z

Harrison, L. (1993). Issues related to the protection of human research subjects. *Journal of Neuroscience Nursing, 25*(3), 187–193.

Holm, M. (2000). Our mandate for the new millennium: evidence-based practice—The 2000 Eleanor Clarke Slagle Lecture. *American Journal of Occupational Therapy, 54*(6), 575–585.

Lustig, D. C., Strauser, D. R., Rice, N. D., & Rucker, T. F. (2002). The relationship between working alliance and rehabilitation outcomes. *Rehabilitation Counseling Bulletin, 46*, 24–32.

Mueser, K. T., Clark, R. E., Haines, M., Drake, R. E., McHugo, G. J., Bond, G. R., &…Swain, K. (2004). The Hartford study of supported employment for persons with severe mental illness. *Journal of Consulting and Clinical Psychology, 72*(3), 479–490. doi:10.1037/0022-006X.72.3.479

Sims, J. M. (2010). A brief review of the Belmont Report. *Dimensions of Critical Care Nursing, 29*(4), 173–174.

Smith, M. L., & Glass, G. V. (1977). Meta-analysis of psychotherapy outcome studies. *American Psychologist, 32*(9), 752–760. doi:10.1037/0003-066X.32.9.752

Smith, M. L., Glass, G. V., & Miller, T. I. (1980). *The benefits of psychotherapy.* Baltimore, MD: Johns Hopkins University Press.

Wagner, C. C., & McMahon, B. T. (2004). Motivational interviewing and rehabilitation counseling practice. *Rehabilitation Counseling Bulletin, 47,* 152–161.

Wampold, B. E. (2001). *The great psychotherapy debate.* Mahwah, NJ: Lawrence Erlbaum Associates.

Medical, Functional, and Environmental Aspects of Disability

9

Chung-Yi Chiu, Robert Drake, Lindsey Rose,
and Gerald Casenave

It is critical to understand clients' physical and psychological conditions and how these conditions influence the way they cope, adapt, and adjust to their community and society in order to make proper and reasonable rehabilitation plans. This chapter reviews biopsychosocial aspects of disabilities, including functional and environmental perspectives. Topics include:

- The human body system
- Medical terminology and diagnosis
- Physical, psychiatric, cognitive, sensory, and developmental disabilities
- Assistive technology
- Environmental implications for disability
- Classification and evaluation of function

THE HUMAN BODY SYSTEM

Overview

This section lists the 13 human body systems with which rehabilitation counselors should be familiar.

■ LEARNING OBJECTIVE

By the end of this unit you should be able to:

1. Know basic human body systems and selected disabilities or chronic illnesses related to the system.

■ KEY CONCEPTS

The human body has 13 systems. The circulatory system pumps and channels blood, which is related to cardiovascular disease; the digestive system digests and processes food, which is related to gastrointestinal hemorrhaging and liver disease; the endocannabinoid system involves appetite, pain perception, mood, memory, and motor learning, and is related to multiple sclerosis (MS); the endocrine system regulates body functions, and is related to diabetes mellitus; the integumentary system protects the body, and can be related to burns; the immune system protects against disease, which can relate to human immunodeficiency virus infection and inflammatory arthritis; the lymphatic system circulates lymph, related to lymphoma; the musculoskeletal system provides support and movement, related to amputation; the nervous system processes information, related to traumatic brain injury (TBI); the reproductive system is for generation, related to sexually transmitted diseases; the respiratory system is for breathing, related to asthma; the urinary system balances body fluid, related to urinary tract infection; and the vestibular system controls balance and special orientation, related to vestibular balance disorders (Ahn, 1999).

MEDICAL TERMINOLOGY AND DIAGNOSIS

Overview

Familiarity with commonly used medical terminology is necessary to efficiently and accurately read medical records and communicate with medical professionals.

▓ LEARNING OBJECTIVE

By the end of this unit you should be able to:

1. Be aware of frequently used abbreviations associated with medical terms.

▓ KEY CONCEPT

The most common medical terminology abbreviations (Felton, 2002) are: ABP (arterial blood pressure), AEA (above elbow amputation), AFO (ankle-foot orthotic), amb. (ambulating), A/O (alert and oriented), aph (aphasia), c. (with), CAD (coronary artery disease), CHD (congenital/coronary heart disease), Chol (cholesterol), CNS (central nervous system), c/o (complains of), COPD (chronic obstructive pulmonary disease), CRD (chronic respiratory disease), CVA (cerebrovascular accident), DD (discharge diagnosis), DM (diabetes mellitus), Dx (diagnosis), e (without, or "o," "s"), EEG (electroencephalogram), FH (family history), F/U (follow-up), Fx (fracture), G.I. (gastrointestinal), HBP (high blood pressure), HIV (human immunodeficiency virus), ICF (intracellular fluid), ICU (intensive care unit), IUC (intrauterine catheter), IV (intravenous), LBP (lower back pain), L.E. (lower extremities), L.O.C. (loss/level of consciousness), MA (mental age), MH (marital history), MRI (magnetic resonance imaging), n. (nerve), NG (nasogastric tube), OBS (organic brain syndrome), OD (right eye), O/E (on examination), OHD (organic heart disease), OPD (outpatient department), OS(left eye), PNI (peripheral nerve injury), PVD (peripheral vascular disease), quad. (quadriplegic), RDS (respiratory distress syndrome), RO (R/O, rule out), ROM (range of motion), Rx (therapy, prescription), STD (sexually transmitted disease), Sx (symptoms), TENS (transient electric nerve stimulation), THR (total hip replacement), TMJ (temporomandibular joint), Tx (treatment), UCD (UCHD, usual childhood diseases), u/o (under observation for, or urine output), URI (upper respiratory infection), and UTI (urinary tract infection).

PHYSICAL, PSYCHIATRIC, COGNITIVE, SENSORY, AND DEVELOPMENTAL DISABILITIES

Overview

The following section reviews major physical, psychiatric, cognitive, sensory, and developmental disabilities, and commonly associated limitations and needed accommodations.

▓ LEARNING OBJECTIVE

By the end of this unit you should be able to:

1. Know the existence, onset, severity, progression, and expected duration of disabilities and understand functional limitation of disabilities.

▧ KEY CONCEPTS

Cardiovascular Diseases

Coronary artery disease (CAD) is the single leading cause of death in the United States. In CAD, plaque (atheroma) accumulates in the blood vessels and produces stenosis (hardening and narrowing of the blood vessels), ischemia (restriction of blood supply), and blood clots (thrombus). The major purpose of medication is to increase blood flow (Mola, Whiteson, & Rey, 2011). Congestive heart failure (CHF) occurs when the heart muscle is weakened or damaged over time and can no longer pump an adequate amount of blood to the rest of the body. The most common symptoms of CHF are dyspnea (difficulty breathing) and swelling (edema) in the extremities (Mola et al., 2011). When CHF is severe, patients will experience severe fatigue, physical weakness, anorexia, nausea, vomiting, and possible cognitive changes. Treatment of CHF generally involves the use of antihypertensives, diuretics, and medications to increase the heart's pumping action (e.g., digitalis) and heart transplantation (Falvo, 2009). Arrhythmias are abnormalities of heart rate or rhythm (Falvo, 2009). Treatment involves the use of medication to regulate heartbeat (e.g., beta-blockers, calcium-channel blockers, digitalis) and to prevent clot formation. Accommodations focus on fatigue/weakness (e.g., reducing physical exertion), respiratory difficulties (e.g., avoiding temperature extremes), and stress (e.g., providing counseling) (Job Accommodation Network [JAN], 2011).

Spinal Cord Injuries

Almost half of all spinal cord injuries (SCIs) occur as a result of motor vehicle accidents. More than 80% of all SCIs occur in men with the average age of injury of 40.2 years (National Spinal Cord Injury Center, 2010). The injury may be described as complete or incomplete. Damage at the cervical level will lead to impaired function in both the upper and lower extremities (tetraplegia, quadriplegia) (Crewe & Krause, 2002). Damage at or below the thoracic level will lead to paraplegia (function maintained in upper extremities, but some degree of impairment in lower extremities). Most individuals with injury at or above C3 will require a ventilator. Individuals with complete injury at the C4 level will require assistance with virtually all activities of daily living (ADL). Individuals with injuries that occur below the T12 level may be able to ambulate with crutches and braces. Sacral lesions may result in loss of voluntary control of bowel and bladder functions. Complications include spasticity (hypertonia), permanent joint contractures, pressure sores (decubitus ulcers), osteoporosis, bone fractures, repeated lung infections, sexual dysfunction, repeated urinary tract infections, and kidney and bladder damage (Crewe & Krause, 2002). Injuries about the T6 level may result in autonomic hyperreflexia (an episode of severe hypertension that can produce a severe headache, dizziness, sweating, and risk of stroke) (Crewe & Krause, 2002). Accommodations focus on ADL (e.g., a personal assistant at work to help with grooming, toileting, and eating), workstation access (e.g., alternative access for computers such as speech recognition), worksite access (e.g., accessible restrooms, lunchrooms, break rooms), and travel to and from work (e.g., accessible transportation) (Batiste & Loy, 2010).

Multiple Sclerosis

Multiple sclerosis (MS) is a chronic and unpredictable disease that attacks the central nervous system (Brandes & Willmott, 2002). Individuals with MS typically will experience one of four disease courses. About 85% of individuals are initially diagnosed with relapsing-remitting MS. In this course, individuals experience clearly defined attacks of worsening neurologic function (relapses) followed by partial or complete recovery periods (remissions). Secondary-progressive MS is a course in which the disease worsens more steadily, and exacerbations, relapses, and/or plateaus may not occur. Primary-progressive MS is slowly worsening neurologic functioning with no periods of remission. Progressive-relapsing MS is a state of steadily worsening disease along with periods of exacerbations, which may or may not be followed by periods of remissions (National Multiple Sclerosis Society, 2010). The most common symptoms are fatigue, numbness, walking/balance/coordination problems, bladder dysfunction, bowel dysfunction, vision problems, dizziness and vertigo, sexual dysfunction, pain, cognition dysfunction, emotional changes, depression, and spasticity. Treatment for MS includes immunomodulatory drugs used to alter the course of the disease by slowing progression and reducing relapse rate. Steroidal medications are used to reduce the severity and duration of exacerbations (Brandes & Willmott, 2002). Accommodations for symptoms of MS are related to weakness, fatigue (e.g., modified work schedules), motor dysfunction (e.g., automatic door openers), cognitive problems (e.g., written memos), sensory problems (e.g., use of large print), and heat insensitivity (e.g., an air-conditioned work environment) (Brandes & Willmott, 2002).

Diabetes

There are three general types of diabetes. Type 1 diabetes, which was formerly called juvenile or insulin-dependent diabetes, is typically first diagnosed in children, teenagers, or young adults. In this form of diabetes, the beta cells of the pancreas, a type of cell in areas called the islets of Langerhans, stop producing insulin because the body's immune system has destroyed them. Type 2 diabetes, or previously adult-onset diabetes, is the most prevalent form of diabetes. This type of diabetes typically begins with insulin resistance, which refers to a condition in which fat, muscle, and liver cells fail to use insulin properly and the pancreas, over time, loses the ability to secrete sufficient insulin in response to increased blood sugar levels. People who are overweight and inactive have an increased chance of developing type 2 diabetes.

Gestational diabetes occurs in some women during the late stages of pregnancy and typically resolves after the baby is born; however, a woman who has had gestational diabetes has a higher risk of developing type 2 diabetes later in life.

Type 1 diabetes has an acute onset and symptoms include polyuria (frequent urination), polydipsia (frequent drinking), polyphagia (frequent eating), and weight loss. If severe, a person can experience diabetic ketoacidosis causing coma and possible death. Type 2 diabetes has a slower, more insidious onset with symptoms such as loss of energy, nighttime urination (nocturia), and vision difficulties (Marrero, 2011). Long-term complications include damage to the eye (retinopathy), kidney (nephropathy, e.g., peripheral sensory neuropathy, end-stage renal disease), and nerve function. Additional complications include cardiovascular disease and peripheral vascular disease (e.g., foot ulcerations, gangrene, and amputations) (Marrero, 2011). Treatment of diabetes involves medication (insulin and oral hypoglycemic agents), nutrition therapy, exercise, and self-monitoring of blood glucose. People taking insulin or oral hypoglycemic agents need a work schedule and level of physical activity that remains as consistent as possible (Hornichter, 2002). Accommodations focus on hypo/hyperglycemia (e.g., allowing for storage of medications such as insulin), neuropathy (e.g., modifying job tasks requiring fine finger dexterity), fatigue or weakness (e.g., providing a rest area with a cot), and kidney disease (e.g., time off for dialysis) (JAN, 2011).

Hepatitis

Hepatitis is associated with liver inflammation and swelling (Falvo, 2009). Hepatitis can be caused by immune cells attacking the liver, infection from virus (e.g., hepatitis A, B, and C), liver damage from alcohol, and overdose of medication. Hepatitis may start and recover rapidly (acute hepatitis, hepatitis A), or cause long-term disease (chronic hepatitis, liver damage, liver failure, and liver cancer) (Falvo, 2009). Symptoms are abdominal pain or distention, breast development in men, dark urine and pale or clay-colored stools, fatigue, fever (usually low grade), general itching, jaundice (yellowing of the skin or eyes), loss of appetite, nausea and vomiting, and weight loss. People with hepatitis B or C do not have symptoms when they are first infected; however, they may develop liver failure later (Falvo, 2009). Major accommodation is for fatigue/weakness (e.g., flexible leave) (JAN, 2011).

Chronic Pain

Chronic pain is viewed as pain that persists for more than 6 months (Lindberg & Bluestein, 2002). Low back pain affects 60% to 80% of all individuals in the United States at some point in their lives. Ninety percent of low back pain will resolve spontaneously within one month of onset (Gharibo & Khan, 2011). Complex regional pain syndrome (CRPS) (reflex sympathetic dystrophy) is a neuropathic pain syndrome that develops when the peripheral and central nervous system becomes over-reactive after an initial localized injury. In CRPS, patients generally experience electrical shooting pain and burning pain, but additional complaints may include allodynia (pain from stimuli that is not usually painful), dyesthesia (unpleasant sensations), hyperalgesia (increased sensitivity to pain), tremors, swelling, hyperhidrosis (excessive sweating), edema, color and temperature changes of the skin, muscle atrophy that occurs when range of motion is limited by pain, contractures, and inability to use muscles because of pain.

Other common chronic pain diseases are migraine, myofascial pain syndrome (most commonly affects the temporomandibular region), and fibromyalgia syndrome (generalized aching, widespread muscle tenderness, muscle stiffness, fatigue, and poor sleep; much more common in women). Treatment for chronic pain syndromes involves a multidisciplinary approach, such as a comprehensive musculoskeletal examination, a neurologic approach (assessment of cranial nerves, motor function, sensory function, and reflexes), and a psychiatric approach (substance abuse, mood, anxiety, somatoform, factitious, and personality disorders). A psychological approach involves counseling (e.g., cognitive behavioral therapy) (Gharibo & Khan, 2011).

Accommodations for chronic pain focus on activities of daily living (ADL) (e.g., use of personal attendant at work), depression and anxiety (e.g., developing strategies to deal with work problems before they arise), fatigue and weakness (e.g., reducing or eliminating physical exertion and workplace stress), and muscle pain and stiffness (e.g., implementing ergonomic workstation design) (JAN, 2011).

Pulmonary Disorders

COPD is the most common pulmonary disorder that can cause disability. COPD encompasses two conditions: chronic obstructive bronchitis (disease of the airways) and emphysema (affects the airways and the alveoli). COPD is characterized by decreased airflow during expiration; a resistance to this passive process resulting from narrowed airways. Treatment involves antibiotics to treat infections, inhaled medication for bronchospasms, and corticosteroid drugs for inflammation (Bevelaqua & Garritan, 2011). Chest physical therapy along with breathing exercises, relaxation techniques, and exercise reconditioning is useful in decreasing dyspnea and fatigue (Bevelaqua & Garritan, 2011). Asthma is an inflammatory airway disease and can be allergic type (extrinsic) or nonallergic type (intrinsic). Therapy for asthma focuses on treating and preventing attacks by controlling inflammation in the lung (Bevelaqua & Garritan, 2011). Cystic fibrosis (CF) is a genetic disease in which thick, dehydrated mucus secretions lead to infection and destruction of obstructed lung passageways leading to progressive respiratory insufficiency.

Vocationally, the energy demands involved with travel to and from work is an extremely important consideration in COPD. Accommodations for COPD include allowing access to supplemental oxygen and avoiding placing patients with chronic cough in close proximity to others. Individuals with asthma should avoid any work environments containing pollutants to which they are sensitive (e.g., tobacco smoke, pollen, animal dander, and chemicals) (Falvo, 2009). In CF, patients may need time for airway clearance techniques or antibiotic therapy during the work day (Bevelaqua & Garritan, 2011).

Cancer

Cancer is the second most common form of death in the United States (Batra & Jajoo, 2011). Cancer is a general term used to describe a group of diseases characterized by the disorderly, uncontrollable growth and spread of abnormal cells (Orr & Orange, 2002). The most often used scale to categorize the patient's functional capacity is the Eastern Cooperative Oncology Group scale, rating from 0 (normal activity without physical limitation) to 4 (the patient is in bed 100% of the time). There are several modalities for treating cancer, including surgery, chemotherapy, radiation, and biologic therapy. The most common physical side effects of treatment include hair loss, weight loss or gain, appetite loss or increase, fatigue, disfigurement from surgery, lack of concentration, nausea, vomiting, changes in skin tone, sleep disruption, and sexual dysfunction. Severe fatigue lasting for months is the most prominent side effect, especially on work (Orr & Orange, 2002). Accommodations for cancer focus on fatigue (e.g., reducing physical exertion, scheduling rest breaks, allowing time off for medical treatment) (JAN, 2011).

Hematologic Disorders

The major hematologic diseases are lymphoma (a maturing and dividing lymphocyte undergoes a malignant change and begins to divide uncontrollably), leukemia (an abnormal proliferation of early stage leukocytes in the bone marrow, which results in a lack of normal bone marrow cells), hemophilia (a congenital illness in which there is a defect in the number or function of platelets), and sickle cell disease (problems with hemoglobin solubility cause red blood cells to assume a nonpliable sickle shape) (Raphael, 2011). Patients with lymphoma may present with nodal disease (swollen, growing lymph glands) or extranodal disease (tumors in other organs); some have symptoms, which include fever, drenching night sweats, itching, and loss of more than 10% of body weight. Patients with acute leukemia are generally critically ill with symptoms of low blood counts (weakness, shortness of breath, infection, fever, and bleeding). In addition to sleep disorders, depression, and concern about physical appearance, psychosocial adaptation varies with age. Chemotherapy in younger patients may create developmental disabilities. Older patients are concerned about financial issues and interpersonal relationships with spouses, children, and coworkers. Residual long-term problems may include fatigue, decreased energy level, depression, employment problems, marital problems, and negative body image. In patients with hemophilia, bleeding can occur anywhere, such as bleeding into joints (hemarthrosis), soft tissue, urine (hematuria), and the brain. Chronic bleeding into joints can lead to inflammation, scar tissue formation, and restriction of movement. Bleeding into the brain and spinal canal can lead to nerve damage with resulting functional and psychological disability (Raphael, 2011). Patients with sickle cell disease experience anemia and may experience an aplastic crisis (abrupt decrease in cell production), which is an extremely painful event requiring hospitalization. Accommodations for lymphoma and leukemia focus on fatigue (e.g., reducing physical exertion), and allowing time off for medical treatment. Jobs with a direct threat of physical injury should be avoided for individuals with hemophilia. In sickle cell disease, strenuous work or work environments with extreme temperature changes and low oxygen levels should be avoided (JAN, 2011).

HIV Infection

HIV gradually destroys the immune system (Falvo, 2009). Acquired immune deficiency syndrome is the final stage of HIV, and the sixth leading cause of death among 25 to 44 year olds in the United States (Pub Med Health, 2011). Symptoms are diarrhea, fatigue, fever, headache, frequent vaginal yeast infection, mouth sores, rash, and sore throat. HIV is spread through sexual contact, blood, and mother to child. Accommodations are about fatigue/weakness (e.g., an accessible ramp) and chronic diarrhea (e.g., a work site near a restroom) (JAN, 2011).

Psychiatric Disorders

Criteria for diagnosis of schizophrenia include positive symptoms such as delusions, hallucinations, disorganized speech, grossly disorganized or catatonic behavior, and negative symptoms such as lack of emotional expression (affective flattening), poverty of speech (alogia), or lack of motivation (avolition). Delusions are erroneous beliefs involving a misinterpretation of perceptions or experiences. Hallucinations are perceptual distortions that can occur in any sensory modality such as gustatory (taste), visual, olfactory (smell), and touch (tactile), but auditory hallucinations are the most common (APA, 2000). Disorganized symptoms of schizophrenia can appear in both behavioral domain (e.g., unpredictable agitation and difficulties performing ADL) and language domain (e.g., loose associations and the use of neologisms). Individuals with schizophrenia may experience impairments in verbal and nonverbal memory, working memory, attention, executive functioning, and processing speed. If an individual experiences symptoms of schizophrenia and a co-occurring affective disorder such as depression and/or mania, the individual is diagnosed with schizoaffective disorder. Schizophreniform disorder is diagnosed when an individual experiences sufficient symptoms to qualify for a diagnosis of schizophrenia, but the symptoms have not been present for at least 6 months (APA, 2000).

Approximately 10% to 25% of women and 5% to 12% of men will experience a major depressive disorder over a lifetime (APA, 2000). A dysthymic disorder has many features in common with major depressive disorder, but it typically has fewer vegetative symptoms (e.g., sleep problems, appetite problems, weight changes, and psychomotor symptoms) (APA, 2000). Symptoms of depression include negative, pessimistic beliefs, negative self-image, suicidal thoughts, difficulty concentrating, and physical symptoms (e.g., lethargy, insomnia, hypersomnia, loss of appetite, overeating, and loss of sexual interest) (APA, 2000).

Bipolar I disorder is a more severe form in which the individual experiences phases of depression along with episodes of severe mania (an episode of elevated, expansive, or irritable mood lasting from several days to several months). Bipolar II disorder is a less severe form in which the individual experiences periods of depression along with periods of hypomania (APA, 2000).

Anxiety disorders are the most prevalent of all psychiatric disorders affecting approximately 29% of individuals across a lifetime (Kukla & Bond, 2011). Panic disorder is characterized by sudden and unanticipated attacks involving a sense of imminent doom accompanied by symptoms such as increased heart rate, difficulty breathing, dizziness, and terror. Generalized anxiety disorder is characterized by constant worrying across many situations. Phobic disorders can involve simple phobias or may involve more pervasive and enduring fears such as social phobia. Obsessive-compulsive disorder involves obsessions (recurring, intrusive thoughts and impulses) and compulsions (ritualistic, repetitive behaviors) (APA, 2000). Posttraumatic stress disorder (PTSD) can develop in response to a traumatic event in which the individual witnessed, experienced, or was confronted with actual or threatened death or serious injury or a threat to the physical integrity of themselves or someone else. Symptoms of PTSD may include re-experiencing the event through nightmares, intrusive memories, physiological reactivity when exposed to internal or external cues surrounding the event, illusions, hallucinations, and dissociative flashbacks. An individual with PTSD may persistently avoid stimuli associated with the traumatic event and experience persistent symptoms of increased arousal (e.g., difficulty falling asleep/concentrating and exaggerated startle response) (APA, 2000).

Personality disorders are organized into three groups or clusters based on descriptive similarities (APA, 2000). Cluster A includes paranoid, schizoid, and schizotypal personality disorders, and individuals diagnosed with any of these would often appear to be odd or eccentric. Cluster B includes antisocial, borderline, histrionic, and narcissistic personality disorders, and individuals diagnosed with any of these would often appear as dramatic, emotional, or erratic. Cluster C includes avoidant, dependent, and obsessive-compulsive personality disorders, and individuals diagnosed with any of these would often appear as anxious or fearful (APA, 2000).

Pharmacologic treatment for schizophrenia primarily involves the use of antipsychotic medications, which have significant side effects with tardive dyskinesia (involuntary stereotyped movements of the mouth and face). Other side effects include hypotension, tremors of the arms, rigidity in extremities, listlessness (akinesia), internal listlessness (akathisia), dry mouth, blurred vision, sexual dysfunction, and weight gain (Kukla & Bond, 2011). Treatment for depression includes a wide range of antidepressant medication options (e.g., tricyclics and monoamine oxidase inhibitors, selective serotonin reuptake inhibitors [SSRIs]). Two additional classes of antidepressants are mixed reuptake inhibitors and dopamine and norepinephrine uptake inhibitors (Kukla & Bond, 2011).

Mood-stabilizing medications (e.g., anticonvulsants, Lithium), valproic acid, and the anticonvulsant lamotrigine are used for bipolar disorder treatment. Pharmacologic treatment for anxiety disorders involves the use of anxiolytics (antianxiety drugs), such as benzodiazepine and Valium. Benzodiazepines have the potential to lead to dependence. BuSpar (buspirone) is used to treat anxiety and seems to avoid issues of dependence. SSRIs can also be used to treat anxiety disorders and seem particularly effective in treating panic disorder, social phobia, and obsessive-compulsive disorder (Kukla & Bond, 2011).

Occasionally, people with psychiatric disorders may have difficulty relating to others, may be socially isolated, and may have limited social support. They may have limited tolerance to stress of any kind and tend to function poorly in emotionally charged or socially critical situations. Substance abuse is a common co-occurring disorder and is associated with increased relapses and hospitalizations, homelessness, violence, problems with physical health, treatment nonadherence, problems with the legal system, and occupational problems (Kukla & Bond, 2011). Accommodations include later starting time because of morning drowsiness as a result of medications and flexible leave for therapy (JAN, 2011).

Traumatic Brain Injury

The leading cause of traumatic brain injury (TBI) in young children and the elderly is falls. In adolescents and young adults, motor vehicle accidents are the leading cause followed by violence, assault, and suicide attempts (Schwartz, 2002). TBI may be described as open, closed, blunt, sharp, penetrating, or nonpenetrating. Brain contusions (bruises of the brain) are caused by coup (injury caused by the initial impact of the brain against the skull) and contrecoup injuries (injuries that occur as the side of the brain opposite the initial impact rebounds against the skull).

The Glasgow Coma Scale is used to determine the patient's level of responsiveness and yields a score from 3 (more severe injury) to 15 (least severe injury). Physical sequelae include balance problems, fatigue, pain, weakness on one side of the body (hemiparesis), uneven gait, movement coordination/gait problems (ataxia), motor planning problems (apraxia), decreased motor speed, seizure disorders, and sensory deficits. Cognitive sequelae include impairments in attention and concentration, memory, visual or auditory processing, verbal reasoning, critical thinking, language, and awareness. Psychosocial sequelae include personality changes, emotional lability, depression, flat affect, substance abuse, low frustration tolerance, impulsivity, disinhibition, and lack of initiative (Schwartz, 2002). Possible work accommodations for TBI include written instructions, assigning one task at a time, additional time to perform assigned tasks, and so forth (JAN, 2011).

Cerebral Palsy

Cerebral palsy (CP) is an umbrella term describing a group of nonprogressive, noncontagious motor conditions that appear in infancy or early childhood, that are caused by abnormalities in parts of the brain that control muscle movement and that affect muscle tone, movement, and motor skills. There are several types of CP, including spastic (muscle and joints are tight, abnormal walk), dyskinetic, ataxic, hypotonic, and mixed types (Falvo, 2009). Other types of symptoms are abnormal movements (twisting, jerking, or writhing) of the hands, feet, arms, or legs while awake, which gets worse during periods of stress, tremors, unsteady gait, loss of coordination, and floppy muscles. Some people with CP may have decreased intelligence quotient (IQ), speech problems, hearing/vision diseases, or seizures (Falvo, 2009). Accommodations are for ADL (e.g., accessibility in the restroom), fine motor control (e.g., writing aids), and gross motor control (e.g., unobstructed hallways) (JAN, 2011).

Epilepsy

Epilepsy is an umbrella diagnosis covering a wide range of etiologies and presentations, with the unifying factor being recurrent seizures. Epilepsy has the potential to significantly impact personal experience and functioning across the wide range of physical, psychological, and social domains of living. Partial seizures are seizures in which the initial activation of a system of neurons is limited to one part of a single cerebral hemisphere. A partial seizure is classified primarily according to whether or not consciousness is impaired. When consciousness is impaired, the seizure is classified as a complex partial seizure. If consciousness is not impaired, the seizure is classified as a simple partial seizure. Simple partial seizures may evolve into complex partial seizures, and a partial seizure may progress to a generalized seizure (involving both cerebral hemispheres).

Generalized seizures are those in which the seizures appear to begin simultaneously in both hemispheres. Consciousness is usually impaired, and this impairment may be the first manifestation. The most common generalized seizure is the generalized tonic-clonic—the body becomes rigid (tonic) for a period of seconds and then the individual begins to experience a series of rhythmic jerking (clonic) movements (Fraser, Miller, & Johnson, 2011). This type of seizure usually lasts between one and three minutes, but if it lasts more than 10 minutes or if the individual has several seizures in this time and does not regain consciousness, this is known as status epilepticus and is a true medical emergency. The other common type of generalized seizure is an absence seizure (petit mal seizure), which consists of a brief disruption of consciousness (usually less than 20 seconds) and autonomic symptoms such as dilated pupils and mild rhythmic movements of the eyelids, but sometimes may involve blank stares. Simple partial seizures may involve motor, sensory, autonomic, or a combination of symptoms without impaired consciousness. They usually last less than 30 seconds and do not necessarily represent a significant problem in regard to job performance.

Complex partial seizures are accompanied by impairment of consciousness and symptoms such as repetitive motor movements, fumbling with hands, lip smacking, or aimless wandering (Fraser et al., 2011). Many individuals with complex partial seizures experience a brief aura or warning before an oncoming seizure, leading them to take precautionary safety measures (Fraser et al., 2011).

Treatment for epilepsy usually involves the use of antiepileptic medications. Because persons with epilepsy are likely to have diverse patterns of cognitive impairment, a neuropsychological evaluation is essential when developing a rehabilitation plan. It is important to understand the degree to which the client is able to control his or her seizures and whether there are patterns to seizure activity (e.g., early mornings, when sleeping), and if there are specific triggers/warning (e.g., flickering lights, aura), what type of recovery, medication, and whether the client has other disabilities (Fraser et al., 2011). Accommodations may need to focus on workplace safety (e.g., keep aisles clear of clutter), memory (e.g., provide written or pictorial instructions), and so forth (JAN, 2011).

Burns

Burns are described by depth of damage. First-degree (partial thickness) burns involve damage to the upper layer of skin (epidermis). Second-degree (deep partial thickness) burns extend to the upper layers of the dermis, but sufficient dermal tissue remains, so spontaneous local healing can occur generally and heal over two to three weeks if treated appropriately, but these can result in severe scarring. Third-degree (full thickness) burns involve complete damage to all layers of the skin and involve loss of vascular and neural structures. Rehabilitation focuses on scar management, therapeutic exercise, pain management, psychological problems, and surgical resection of heterotopic ossification (Young, Dewey, & Wolf, 2011). Individuals with severe burns may require extensive reconstructive surgery and hospitalization over a one- to two-year period, which would represent a significant disruption to work activity. Burns can present cosmetic issues that may limit occupations involving contact with the public. Individuals with skin grafts may not be appropriate for work environments with extremes of temperature or outside work with sun exposure. Individuals with reduced lung function may need to avoid work environments filled with dust, smoke, or other air pollutants (Falvo, 2009).

Visual Impairment

In 1935 the Social Security Administration defined that legal blindness is based on visual acuity of less than 20/100 or if the central visual field is restricted to 20 degrees or less in the widest meridian of the better eye. Glaucoma or retinitis pigmentosa creates an overall peripheral field defect leaving only a small central field of vision intact. A cataract is a clouding that can occur in any and all parts of the lens and can result in decreased visual acuity, loss of contrast, and glare. Macular degeneration is one of the leading causes of visual impairments in older adults. Symptoms include object distortion, decreased visual acuity and color recognition, loss of contrast, or scotoma.

Individuals who lose vision later in life may find it more difficult to adapt and may experience grief and despair over the loss, become overly dependent on others, feel insecure in new situations, and avoid social interaction. Individuals with visual impairment may have difficulty with social interaction as much of communication involves visual, nonverbal cues (Falvo, 2009).

For individuals with no vision, accommodations such as auditory versions of printed documents, documents formatted in Braille, and document readers such as optical character recognition software may be useful. For individuals with low vision, using a closed circuit television system that magnifies text, providing information in large print, using magnifying devices, and providing frequent breaks to rest eyes can be helpful accommodations. For individuals with light sensitivity, lower wattage overhead lights, full spectrum lighting and/or filters, and flicker-free lighting can be helpful accommodations (JAN, 2011).

Hearing Impairment

There are four types of hearing loss: conductive (damage involving the outer or middle ear; for example, Treacher-Collins syndrome), sensorineural (damage involving the inner ear and/or auditory nerve), mixed (both conductive and sensorineural component), and central (damage along the auditory pathway or in the brain itself) (Eng & Lerner, 2011). Presbycusis describes progressive sensorineural hearing loss as a result of the aging process. Meniere's disease results from a cochlear lesion and is characterized by fluctuating sensorineural hearing and vestibular symptoms (e.g., vertigo, nausea, tinnitus, and fullness of the affected ear). Medical interventions are used in conductive or mixed hearing loss, but most sensorineural hearing loss does not respond to medical or surgical intervention.

American Sign Language may be the primary communication method used by individuals who are severely hearing impaired; however, speech reading (lip reading) is ineffective as a standalone tool as up to two thirds of English speech sounds are not visible. Telecommunication devices for the deaf (TDD) allow the individual with hearing impairment to send and receive typed messages to other TDD users via a telephone line (Eng & Lerner, 2011). In addition to daily life accommodations such as closed caption decoders for television, flashing smoke detectors, and vibrator alarm beds, workplace accommodations may include the use of qualified interpreters, signaling devices, amplified telephones, flashing lights and alarms, enhanced lighting, vibrating pagers, and modified acoustics (JAN, 2011).

Developmental Disorders

Intellectual disability (formerly mental retardation) is defined as significant limitations in both intellectual functioning and adaptive behavior (expressed in everyday social and practical skills) that appears before the age of 18 years (American Association of Intellectual and Developmental Disabilities, 2011; APA, 2000). The *DSM-IV-TR* classifies mental retardation according to IQ range: mild (50–55 to approximately 70), moderate (34–40 to 50–55), severe (20–25 to 35–40), and profound (below 20–25) (APA, 2000). Individuals with autism have impairments in reciprocal social interaction, verbal and nonverbal communication and imaginative activity, and restricted and stereotyped patterns of behavior, interests, and/or activities. Individuals with Asperger's disorder have impairments identical to autism with the exception of difficulties in communication. Rett's disorder is a progressive neurodevelopmental disorder that involves the development of clinical symptoms after apparently normal development during the first 6 to 18 months of life. Symptoms can include a slowing of growth in head circumference, microcephaly (smaller than normal head circumference), loss of muscle tone, loss of previously purposeful hand movements, stereotypical hand-wringing behaviors, and cognitive and functional regression (Morris & Morris, 2011).

Accommodations in the workplace for individuals with limited cognitive abilities include reading (e.g., providing pictures), writing (e.g., use of a scribe), memory (e.g., prompting with verbal cues), performing calculations (e.g., using talking calculators), organization (e.g., using color coding). Accommodations for individuals with limited motor abilities include using computers (e.g., using alternative input devices), using the telephone (e.g., use of a large-button phone), accessing the workplace (e.g., using motorized scooters), and handling/grasping objects (e.g., using grip aids). Accommodations for individuals with limitations in social abilities include emotional support (e.g., using coworkers as mentors) and interacting with coworkers (e.g., providing sensitivity training to coworkers) (JAN, 2011).

Learning Disorders

Learning disorders are a group of conditions that affect an individual's ability to acquire and/or use information through sources such as reading, writing, mathematical calculations, listening, speaking, or reasoning, but the individual does not have a global intellectual disability (Falvo, 2009). Examples of learning disability include dyslexia (impairment in the ability to interpret written language), dyscalculia (difficulty performing mathematical calculations), dysgraphia (inability to express oneself in writing), agnosia (inability to recognize and identify known objects through one or more senses), and dysphasia (impairments in language communication through speech).

Accommodations focus on difficulty reading text (e.g., read back written text), difficulty reading from a computer screen (e.g., screen reading software), spelling (e.g., electronic dictionaries), cognitive processes of writing (e.g., creating forms to prompt the employee for information), physical process of writing (e.g., type written responses), mathematics (e.g., talking calculators), and speaking and communicating (e.g., written responses) (JAN, 2011).

ASSISTIVE TECHNOLOGY

Overview

The following reviews the definition and categories of assistive technology (AT).

■ LEARNING OBJECTIVE

By the end of this unit you should be able to:

1. Understand the clients' needs in AT and evaluate those AT needs.

■ KEY CONCEPTS

Assistive technology is any item, piece of equipment, or product system, whether acquired commercially off the shelf, modified, or customized, that is used to increase, maintain, or improve the functional capabilities of individuals with disabilities (29 U.S.C. Sec 2202(2). "The device may be purchased commercially or modified to meet the individual's needs" (Resources for Rehabilitation, 1993, p. 57).

There are different categories of assistive technology (the 17th Institute on Rehabilitation Issues, 1990): (1) aids for daily living are self-help aids for self-care on a daily-life basis, such as a fork with a built-up handle, bath lift/seat, button/shoe aids and so on; (2) augmentative communication devices are used for expressive and receptive communication, such as a communication book/board, eye-controlled communicator and so on; (3) computer applications enable people with disabilities to use a computer, including input and output devices (e.g., cursor control accessories), alternate access aids (e.g., head sticks), modified keyboards, switches, and special software (e.g., computer access interfaces/instruction) and so on; (4) environmental control systems are mainly electronic systems that enable people with mobility limitations to control various appliances, electronic aids, and security systems, such as a house with a built-in automation and blinking locators and so on; (5) home/worksite modifications are structural adaptations or fabrications in the home, worksite, or other areas (ramps, lifts, and bathroom changes) for increasing accessibility, such as ramps, elevators, and stair lifts and so on; (6) prosthetics and orthotics are replacement, substitution, or augmentation of missing or malfunctioning body parts, such as a knee prosthesis, an ankle brace and so on; (7) seating and positioning are accommodations to a wheelchair or other seating system to increase stability, maintain posture, and reduce pressure on the skin surface, such as a cushion cover, trunk/pelvic supports and so on; (8) aids for vision/hearing impairment are magnifiers, Braille, large-prints, a telecommunications device for the deaf and so on; (9) wheelchairs/mobility aids include manual and electric wheelchairs, walkers, and mobility scooters, and so on; and (10) vehicle modifications are for personal transportation, such as adaptive driving aids, hand controls, modified vans, and an acoustic cue system. Although a rehabilitation counselor is in charge of introducing, evaluating, and selecting AT for a client, a client's involvement and support are important. It is critical to know a consumer's and his or her significant others' expectations in AT before the selection of AT. It is also important to consider to what extent the device fits a client's life style, preferences, and values (Brodwin, Star, & Cardoso, 2004; Falvo, 2009). A rehabilitation counselor works with a client to make sure a selected assistive technology is effective, reliable, easy, and comfortable to use (Brodwin et al., 2004).

ENVIRONMENTAL IMPLICATIONS OF DISABILITY

Overview

The following reviews the environmental factors that may influence disability.

█ LEARNING OBJECTIVE

By the end of this unit you should be able to:

1. Understand how environmental factors influence disability and be able to analyze environmental implications.

█ KEY CONCEPTS

Wright (1983) emphasized that person–environment interactions have a significant influence on an individual's integration into his or her community. The person–environment–occupations model (Crepeau, Cohn, & Schell, 2003) also describes the transactional relationship between the person and his or her environment, including occupations as a third force. Occupations are defined as self-care, productive, and leisurely activities. Occupational performance is the outcome of the transaction between the person, environment, and occupation—how well all these fit together.

The International Classification of Functioning, Disability, and Health (ICF) model conceptualizes health as the interaction between people with health conditions and the environments in which they live (WHO, 2001). The ICF environmental factors classification list includes products and technology (e.g., products for personal consumption or daily use), natural environment and human-made changes to environment (e.g., geography, climate), support and relationships (e.g., family), attitudes (e.g., societal norms), and services, systems, and policies (e.g., services for the production of social security). Universal design is an important concept for rehabilitation counselors to understand. Universal design is a comprehensive approach to the increase, maintenance, or improvement of the functional capabilities of individuals with disabilities. Universal design is the design of products and environments to be usable by all people, to the greatest extent possible, without the need for adaptation or specialized design.

CLASSIFICATION AND EVALUATION OF FUNCTION

Overview

The following section reviews assessment concepts of human daily function perspectives to communicate with health professionals regarding prognosis, prevention, and wellness strategies for individuals with a disability.

▓ LEARNING OBJECTIVE

By the end of this unit you should be able to:

1. Understand evaluations for functional performance.

▓ KEY CONCEPTS

Personal care activity assessments (e.g., the Barthel Index [Mahoney & Barthel, 1965]) involve assessing a person's ability to take care of himself or herself, including hygiene, dressing, eating, toileting, and caring for one's health in terms of physical well-being, diet, and fitness. This also includes the ability to transport oneself to the required places to perform self-care and transfer one's body from one location to another as needed. Body function assessments (e.g., range of motion) are evaluations of neuromuscular and movement-related functions, such as mobility of joints and bones, muscle tone, reflexes, and gait patterns. Assessments of activities of daily living (ADL) (e.g., Katz ADL scale [Katz, Down, Cash, & Grotz, 1970]) are commonly based on the clinical observation of clients when they are engaging in self-care activities in the environment in which they are usually performed. Interviews of clients and caregivers are often used in addition or in lieu of direct observation (Table 9.1).

TABLE 9.1 ▓ **Summary of Key Concepts of Research and Program Evaluation**

Dx	Key Information and Accommodation Needs
CAD	Reducing physical exertion, avoiding temperature extremes, stress management…
SCI	Injury at C3 needs ventilator, C4 assistance with virtually all ADLs, T12 able to ambulate with AT. Sacral lesions lose voluntary control of bowel and bladder functions ADLs, workstation access, worksite access, and travel to and from work…
MS	Modified work schedules, automatic door openers, use of large print, an air-conditioned work environment…
DM	Long-term complications: retinopathy, kidney (nephropathy, e.g., peripheral sensory neuropathy, end-stage renal disease), and nerve function Allowing for storage of medications such as insulin, modifying job tasks requiring fine finger dexterity, providing a rest area with a cot, time off for dialysis
Hepatitis	Flexible leave, modified schedule
Chronic pain	90% of low back pain will resolve spontaneously within one month of onset. Implementing ergonomic workstation design
COPD	Reducing physical exertion
HIV	AIDS is the final stage of HIV; HIV is spread through sexual contact, blood and mother to child. Accessible ramps, worksite near restroom

(continued)

TABLE 9.1 ■ Summary of Key Concepts of Research and Program Evaluation (*continued*)

Dx	Key Information and Accommodation Needs
Psychiatric disorders	Antidepressant medications (e.g., MAOIs, SSRIs); mood stabilizingmedications (e.g., anticonvulsants, Lithium) Later starting time because of morning drowsiness due to medications, and flexible leave for psychotherapy
TBI	Written instructions, assigning one task at a time, additional time to perform tasks
CP	Ataxia-movement coordination/gait problems; apraxia-motor planning problems Accessibility in the restroom, writing aids, unobstructed hallways
Epilepsy	Workplace safety
Burns	Individuals with skin grafts may not be appropriate for work environments with extremes of temperature or outside work with sun exposure Individuals with reduced lung function may need to avoid work environments filled with dust, smoke, or other air pollutants
Visual impairment	Legal blindness is based on visual acuity of less than 20/100 or if the central visual field is restricted to 20 degrees or less in the widest meridian of the better eye Auditory versions of printed documents, documents formatted in Braille, and document readers
Hearing impairment	Closed caption decoders, flashing smoke detectors, and amplified telephones
DD	Providing pictures, use of a scribe, prompting with verbal cues, using talking calculators
LD	Do not have a global intellectual disability Dyslexia (impairment in the ability to interpret written language), dyscalculia (difficulty performing mathematical calculations), dysgraphia (inability to express oneself in writing), agnosia (inability to recognize and identify known objects through one or more senses), and dysphasia (impairments in language communication through speech) Read back written text, screen reading software, type written responses, talking calculators

■ INTERNET RESOURCES

Disability.gov. *Connecting the Disability Community to Information and Opportunities*
https://www.disability.gov/

Edwards, Dorothy. Stroke *Scales and Clinical Assessment Tools,* **Internet Stroke Center at Washington University**
http://www.strokecenter.org/trials/scales/index.htm

MediLexicon International Ltd. *Medical Dictionaries, Drugs & Medical Searches*
http://www.medilexicon.com/

Rehabilitation Research center. *The Center for Outcome Measurement in Brain Injury.*
http://www.tbims.org/combi/list.html

The Assistive Technology Training Online Project (ATTO). School of Punlic Health and Health Professions, University of Buffalo
http://atto.buffalo.edu/

The Office of Disability Employment Policy, U.S. Department of Labor. *Job Accommodation Network*
http://askjan.org/index.html

▨ MULTIPLE CHOICE QUESTIONS WITH ANSWER KEY

1. What is the most common cause of disability in the United States?
    A. Spinal cord injury (SCI)
    B. Cardiovascular diseases (CVD)
    C. Traumatic brain injury (TBI)
    D. Diabetes

2. A slow heart rate is called:
    A. Bradycardia
    B. Arrhythmia
    C. Dysrhythmia
    D. Tachycardia

3. The most common cerebral vascular accidents (CVA) are:
    A. Thrombotic strokes
    B. Embolic strokes
    C. Hemorrhagic strokes
    D. Transient ischemic attacks (TIAs)

4. Loss of ability to use or understand language is:
    A. Aphasia
    B. Apraxia
    C. Dysphagia
    D. Agnosia

5. Damage at the cervical level of the spinal cord will result in
    A. Hemiplegia
    B. Paraplegia
    C. Paraparesis
    D. Tetraplegia

6. Most Spinal Cord Injuries (SCIs) result from
    A. Falls
    B. Motor vehicle crashes
    C. Gunshot wounds
    D. Sports accidents

7. Autonomic hyperreflexia which is a potentially life threatening problem for individuals with injuries about the T6 level is
    A. An epileptic episode
    B. An episode of extremely high blood pressure
    C. A severe muscle spasm
    D. A loss of consciousness

8. Chronic pain is best understood from which model?
    A. Medical
    B. Rehabilitation
    C. Biopsychosocial
    D. Educational

9. Complex regional pain syndrome develops
    A. When the nervous system becomes overreactive after an initial localized injury
    B. As a result of severe, incapacitating headaches
    C. From back pain that is not treated in the first six weeks
    D. From muscle tenderness and stiffness that generalizes over a large area

10. What percent of individuals who experience an episode of low back pain return to work in one month?
    A. 10
    B. 25

C. 50
D. 80

◼ ANSWER KEY

1. B; **2.** A; **3.** C; **4.** A; **5.** D; **6.** B; **7.** B; **8.** C; **9.** A; **10.** D

◼ ADVANCED MULTIPLE CHOICE QUESTIONS

1. Type 1 diabetes is
   A. Decreased insulin sensitivity
   B. An autoimmune disorder
   C. Decreased insulin secretion
   D. Gestational diabetes

2. Chronic obstructive pulmonary disease (COPD) occurs in two types, emphysema and:
   A. Asthma
   B. Cystic fibrosis
   C. Chronic bronchitis
   D. Tuberculosis

3. For many individuals with cancer the most prominent side effect of cancer treatment that can last for months is:
   A. Hair loss
   B. Nausea
   C. Weight loss
   D. Severe fatigue

4. Cancer survivors who return to work
   A. Raise employer's insurance rates
   B. Have poor attendance
   C. Impose more duties on fellow employees
   D. Have reduced opportunity for advancement

5. The most severe of all mental illnesses is
   A. Bipolar disorder
   B. Major depressive disorder
   C. Borderline personality disorder
   D. Schizophrenia

6. The most prevalent of all psychiatric disorders is
   A. Mood disorders
   B. Psychotic disorders
   C. Personality disorders
   D. Anxiety disorders

7. A major problem for individuals with a psychotic disability who return to work is
   A. Lack of skills to do the job
   B. Poor endurance and fatigue
   C. Inability to follow directions
   D. Difficulty relating to coworkers

8. Damage to the frontal lobes is likely to result in
   A. Balance problems
   B. Memory problems
   C. Impulse control problems
   D. Visual problems

9. The eye disease that leads to the most visual disability is
   A. Macular degeneration
   B. Diabetic retinopathy
   C. Retinitis pigmentosa
   D. Glaucoma

10. The creation of products and environments to be usable by all people, to the greatest extent possible, without the need for adaptation or specialized design defines:
   A. Total access
   B. Assistive technology
   C. Complete accommodation
   D. Universal design

ANSWER KEY AND EXPLANATION OF ANSWERS

1-B: Type 1 diabetes is seen as an autoimmune disorder. Type 2 diabetes is a problem of decreased insulin sensitivity and/or insulin secretion. Women who have never had diabetes but develop high blood sugar in pregnancy have gestational diabetes.

2-C: The two major types of chronic lung conditions that obstruct airflow, COPD, are chronic bronchitis, an airway disease, and emphysema, disease of the alveoli.

3-D: There are many potential complications and side-effects from cancer treatment. The most prominent side-effect for many individuals is severe fatigue that can last for months.

4-D: There are many employment related myths surrounding cancer survivors who return to work. Among the real problems they face is reduced opportunity for advancement.

5-D: While any psychiatric disorder is significant, schizophrenia is considered the most severe because of its profound effect on the person, family, and society.

6-D: The most prevalent of all psychiatric disorders are anxiety disorders. They affect about 29% of individuals across a lifetime. They include panic disorder, generalized anxiety disorder, phobic disorders, obsessive-compulsive disorder, and PTSD.

7-D: While individuals with psychiatric disability who return to work face many challenges, difficulty or inability to get along with others is a common factor associated with poor rehabilitation outcomes in this population.

8-C: The effects of a TBI are related to the severity and location of the injury. Damage to the frontal lobes is likely to result in problems with impulse control.

9-B: Diabetic retinopathy leads to more disability than any other eye disease. Almost all persons with type 1 diabetes and nearly 60% of persons with type 2 diabetes will develop this disease which can cause retinal scarring, hemorrhaging into the vitreous, and possible retinal detachment.

10-D: Universal design is the design of products and environments to be usable by all people, to the greatest extent possible without the need for adaptation or specialized design.

REFERENCES

Ahn, J. H. (1999). Body systems: An overview. In M. G. Eisenberg, R. L. Glueckauf, & H. H. Zaretsky (Eds.), *Medical aspects of disability: A handbook for the rehabilitation professional* (2nd ed., pp. 26–50). New York, NY: Springer Publishing Company.

American Association of Intellectual and Developmental Disabilities. (2011). *Definition of intellectual disability.* Retrieved from http://www.aaidd.org

American Psychiatric Association. (2000). *Diagnostic and statistical manual of mental disorders* (4th ed., Text Revision). Washington, D.C.: Author.

Batiste, L. C., & Loy, B. (2010). *Accommodation and compliance series: Employees who use wheelchairs.* Retrieved from http://askjan.org

Batra, R., & Jajoo, P. (2011). The role of rehabilitation in cancer patients. In S. R. Flanagan, H. Zarestsky, & A. Moroz (Eds.), *Medical aspects of disability* (4th ed., pp. 103–117). New York, NY: Springer Publishing.

Bevelaqua, F. A., & Garritan, S. (2011). Pulmonary disorders. In S. R. Flanagan, H. Zarestsky, & A. Moroz (Eds.), *Medical aspects of disability* (4th ed., pp. 223–236). New York, NY: Springer Publishing.

Brandes, D. W., & Willmott, L. J. (2002). Multiple sclerosis. In M. G. Brodwin, F. Tellez, & S. K. Brodwin (Eds.), *Medical, psychosocial, and vocational aspects of disability* (2nd ed., pp. 351–362). Athens, GA: Elliott & Fitzpatrick, Inc.

Brodwin, M. G., Star, T., & Cardoso, E. (2004). Computer assistive technology for people who have disabilities: Computer adaptations and modifications. *Journal of Rehabilitation, 70*, 28–33.

Crepeau, E. B., Cohn, E. S., & Schell, B. A. B (Eds.). (2003). *Willard & Spackman's Occupational Therapy* (10th ed.). Philadelphia, PA: Walters Kluwer/Lippincott, Williams & Wilkins.

Crewe, N. M., & Krause, J. S. (2002). Spinal cord injuries. In M. G. Brodwin, F. Tellez, & S. K. Brodwin (Eds.), *Medical, psychosocial, and vocational aspects of disability* (2nd ed., pp. 279–291). Athens, GA: Elliott & Fitzpatrick, Inc.

Eng, N., & Lerner, P. K. (2011). Speech, language, hearing, and swallowing disorders. In S. R. Flanagan, H. Zarestsky, & A. Moroz (Eds.), *Medical aspects of disability* (4th ed., pp. 195–222). New York, NY: Springer Publishing.

Falvo, D. R. (2009). *Medical and psychosocial aspects of chronic illness and disability* (4th ed.). Sudbury, MA: Jones and Bartlett.

Felton, J. S. (2002). Medical terminology. In M. G. Brodwin, F. Tellez, & A. Browin (Eds.), *Medical, psychosocial and vocational aspects of disability* (pp. 15–26). Athens, GA: Elliott & Fitzpatrick.

Fraser, R. T., Miller, J. W., & Johnson, E. K. (2011). Epilepsy. In S. R. Flanagan, H. Zarestsky, & A. Moroz (Eds.), *Medical aspects of disability* (4th ed., pp. 65–87). New York, NY: Springer Publishing.

Gharibo, C. G. & Khan, M. F. (2011). Chronic pain syndromes. In S. R. Flanagan, H. Zarestsky, & A. Moroz (Eds.), *Medical aspects of disability* (4th ed., pp. 147–158). New York, NY: Springer Publishing.

Hornichter, R. D. (2002). Diabetes mellitus. In M. G. Brodwin, F. Tellez, & S. K. Brodwin (Eds.), *Medical, psychosocial, and vocational aspects of disability* (2nd ed., pp. 213–223). Athens, GA: Elliott & Fitzpatrick, Inc.

Job Accommodation Network. (2011). *Accommodation and compliance series.* Retrieved from http://askjan.org

Katz, S., Down, T. D., Cash, H. R., & Grotz, R. C. (1970). Progress in the development of the index of ADL. *The Gerontologist, 10*(1), 20–30.

Kukla, M., & Bond, G. R. (2011). Psychiatric disabilities. In S. R. Flanagan, H. Zarestsky, & A. Moroz (Eds.), *Medical aspects of disability* (4th ed., pp. 441–466). New York, NY: Springer Publishing.

Lindberg, J. & Bluestein, B. W. (2002). Chronic pain management. In M. G. Brodwin, F. Tellez, & S. K. Brodwin (Eds.), *Medical, psychosocial, and vocational aspects of disability* (2nd ed., pp. 129–141). Athens, GA: Elliott & Fitzpatrick, Inc.

Mahoney, F., & Barthel, D. (1965). Functional evaluation: the Barthel Index. Maryland *Medical Journal, 14*, 61–65.

Marrero, D. G. (2011). Diabetes Mellitus. In S. R. Flanagan, H. Zarestsky, & A. Moroz (Eds.), *Medical aspects of disability* (4th ed., pp. 223–236). New York, NY: Springer Publishing.

Mola, A., Whiteson, J. H. & Rey, M. J. (2011). Cardiovascular disorders. In S. R. Flanagan, H. Zarestsky, & A. Moroz (Eds.), *Medical aspects of disability* (4th ed., pp. 569–589). New York, NY: Springer Publishing.

Morris, R. J., & Morris, Y. P. (2011). Developmental disabilities. In S. R. Flanagan, H. Zarestsky, & A. Moroz (Eds.), *Medical aspects of disability* (4th ed., pp. 237–264). New York, NY: Springer Publishing.

National Multiple Sclerosis Society. (2010). *What is multiple sclerosis?* Retrieved from http://www.nationalmssociety.org/index.aspx

National Spinal Cord Injury Center. (2010). *Spinal cord injuries facts and figures at a glance.* Retrieved from https://www.nscisc.uab.edu

Orr, II, L. E., & Orange, L. M. (2002). Cancer. In M. G. Brodwin, F. Tellez, & S. K. Brodwin (Eds.), *Medical, psychosocial, and vocational aspects of disability* (2nd ed., pp. 171–184). Athens, GA: Elliott & Fitzpatrick, Inc.

Raphael, B. G. (2011). Hematological disorders. In S. R. Flanagan, H. Zarestsky, & A. Moroz (Eds.), *Medical aspects of disability* (4th ed., pp. 223–236). New York, NY: Springer Publishing.

Resources for Rehabilitation. (1993). Meeting the needs of employees with disabilities (2nd ed.). Lexington, MA: Author.

Schwartz, S. H. (2002). Traumatic brain injury. In M. G. Brodwin, F. Tellez, & S. K. Brodwin (Eds.), *Medical, psychosocial, and vocational aspects of disability* (2nd ed., pp. 363–373). Athens, GA: Elliott & Fitzpatrick, Inc.

World Health Organization. (2001). *ICF: International Classification of Functioning, Disability and Health.* Geneva, Switzerland: WHO.

Wright, B. (1983). *Physical disability: A psychosocial approach* (2nd ed.). New York: Harper & Row.

Young, A. W., Dewey, W. S. & Wolf, S. E. (2011). Rehabilitation in burns. In S.R. Flanagan, H. Zarestsky, & A. Moroz (Eds.), *Medical aspects of disability* (4th ed., pp. 89–101). New York, NY: Springer Publishing.

Rehabilitation Services, Case Management, and Related Services

10

Malachy Bishop, Veronica I. Umeasiegbu, and Christina T. Espinosa

In this chapter, we review rehabilitation counseling legislation, case management, and a variety of services that rehabilitation counselors provide or arrange in the public sector (i.e., the state–federal vocational rehabilitation [VR] system and other public VR agencies), the private nonprofit sector, and the private for-profit sector. Topics covered include:

- Vocational rehabilitation
- Case and caseload management
- Independent living (IL)
- School-to-work transition services
- Disability management
- Forensic rehabilitation, vocational expert practices, and life care planning
- Substance abuse treatment and rehabilitation
- Wellness and illness prevention concepts
- Community resources and Community-Based Rehabilitation Programs
- Insurance programs and social security
- Assistive technology and rehabilitation counseling

VOCATIONAL REHABILITATION

Overview

In this section, we review the history and current status of the public VR program in America and identify important elements and outcomes of key VR legislation.

LEARNING OBJECTIVES

By the end of this unit you should be able to:

1. Describe the history, current status, and purpose of the state–federal VR program.
2. Identify key VR legislation, legislative mandates, and outcomes.

KEY CONCEPTS

The state–federal VR program is a federally funded program authorized under the Rehabilitation Act of 1973 and subsequent amendments. The Rehabilitation Services Administration is the federal agency that oversees the program. The program operates in each of the 50 states, Washington, DC, and several U.S. territories, and many states operate separate VR programs for individuals who are blind (Fabian & MacDonald-Wilson, 2005). The state–federal VR program provides employment-related services for individuals with disabilities, giving priority to those individuals who are most significantly disabled.

To be eligible for VR services, an applicant must have a disability (a physical or mental impairment) that constitutes or results in a substantial impediment to employment, be able to benefit from rehabilitation services, and be able to eventually achieve an employment outcome (Fabian & MacDonald-Wilson, 2005). Once eligibility has been determined, a plan for employment, called an Individualized Plan for Employment (IPE) is developed collaboratively by the VR counselor and client. This plan identifies the specific types and number of services that will be provided to help the individual achieve his or her employment goal (Fabian & MacDonald-Wilson, 2005). Services that may be provided under the plan include medical, psychological, vocational, and other diagnostic assessments and evaluation services; counseling and guidance; physical and mental therapy or treatments; occupational and vocational training and education; interpreter services; job-placement services; rehabilitation technology services; post-employment services; and other equipment or services necessary to achieve an employment outcome.

Historical Foundation of VR in America

Prior to the establishment of public VR in the United States, rehabilitation services were provided by private religious, philanthropic, and charitable organizations. A combination of factors during the end of the 19th century and the first two decades of the 20th century created the conditions for the establishment of the state–federal VR. These included (1) the Industrial Revolution led to a national shift from an agrarian or farm-based economy to an industry-based economy and a relocation of the population base to the cities; (2) a federal government policy shift characterized by economic, social, and political reform and an increased government role in creating opportunities for individuals to compete; (3) compulsory public education, in large part as a means of teaching vocational skills and creating productive workers in cities that had large populations of people seeking to become employed and needing to be appropriately educated for employment; and (4) the federal income tax, which resulted in moneys that could, in part, be used in the federal sponsorship of VR programs for soldiers, veterans, and civilians. The income tax also enabled tax write-offs for rehabilitation ventures and established the Economic Argument for VR (i.e., an investment of funds in VR will, by enabling persons with disabilities to become employed tax payers, result in a severalfold increase in federal income over time).

The public VR of Americans with disabilities emerged from federal legislation including the Soldiers Rehabilitation Act of 1918 and the Smith-Fess Act in 1920. These acts and the subsequent federal VR-related legislation through the Rehabilitation Act of 1973 are presented in Table 10.1.

The Rehabilitation Act of 1973

The 1973 Rehabilitation Act was significant for several mandates and outcomes. Among these, the Act (1) mandated that states serve individuals with the most-severe disabilities before serving persons with less-severe disabilities; (2) promoted and ensured client involvement in rehabilitation plan development through the joint (counselor and client) development of an Individualized Written Rehabilitation Program (IWRP) that identified vocational objective, sub-objectives, and related services as well as the criteria for evaluating client progress; (3) implemented a pilot program of Client Assistance Programs (CAPs) through which clients could receive assistance with application and advocacy services. CAPs became the required program for every state in 1984; (4) established demonstration projects in Independent Living (IL) Rehabilitation Services; (5) mandated program evaluation, such that states became accountable for collecting information on the percentage of the target population being served, the timeliness and adequacy of VR services, the suitability of placements and retention of clients in employment, and client satisfaction with services; (6) increased funding for rehabilitation and disability research, establishing the National Institute of Handicapped Research, which later became the National Institute

TABLE 10.1 ■ **Key VR-Related Legislation 1935–1973**

Legislation and Year	Key Mandate/Outcome
Smith-Hughes Act 1917 (also known as the Vocational Education Act	Made federal monies available on a matching basis to states that developed a vocational education program. The act created the Federal Board of Vocational Education, which would become the first administrative agency for the VR program.
Soldiers Rehabilitation Act 1918	The first U.S. program for VR of people with disabilities. The Federal Board of Vocational Education had responsibility for developing VR programs and training for military veterans with physical disabilities for whom employment was seen as a feasible result of services.
Smith-Fess Act of 1920	This act provided federal money at a 50–50 match with states that provided vocational guidance, vocational education, placement, and occupational adjustment to civilians with physical disabilities (defined as a physical defect or infirmary). Because of the 50–50 match, there was a strong incentive for states to develop such programs, and 18-months after the act was passed 34 states had developed VR programs. The law was temporary and had to be extended every few years until 1935 when the 1935 Social Security Act made the state–federal VR program a permanent program that could only be discontinued through congressional action.
Barden-LaFollette Act 1943	Expanded services to persons with mental retardation and mental illness and expanded physical restoration services that could be provided. Established federal support for agencies that served people who were blind.
Rehabilitation Act Amendments 1954	This act increased the federal share of the state–federal match to 66%; expanded services and funding to persons with mental retardation and chronic mental illness; established research and demonstration grants aimed at the discovery of new knowledge in VR; provided grants to colleges and universities to develop preservice training programs for rehabilitation counselors.
Social Security Act Amendments 1956	Authorized Social Security disability allowances for persons permanently disabled, aged 50 years or older, who were deemed incapable of returning to competitive employment.

on Disability and Rehabilitation Research (NIDRR); and (7) advanced the civil rights of people with disabilities through Title V. Title V included sections covering:

■ Section 501 mandated nondiscrimination and affirmative action in federal hiring
■ Section 502 established the Architectural and Transportation Barriers Compliance Board to oversee compliance to the Architectural Barriers Act of 1968
■ Section 503 prohibited discrimination in employment on the basis of disability, and required affirmative action plans among recipients of federal contracts and their subcontractors of amounts in excess of US $10,000, and a written affirmative action plan of employers/contractors receiving over US $50,000 or with 50 or more employees
■ Section 504 prohibited disability-based exclusion of otherwise qualified persons with disabilities from participation in any federal program or activity, or any program or activity that receives federal funding (including school districts, colleges and universities, hospitals, day care programs, public welfare agencies, or nursing homes)

Rehabilitation Act Amendments of 1992

Important mandates and outcomes of the 1992 Rehabilitation Act Amendments included the following: (1) increased client involvement at the individual level by ensuring increased client choice and participation in the development, implementation, and evaluation of the

Individualized Written Rehabilitation Program (IWRP); (2) increased client involvement at the agency level by requiring the establishment of Rehabilitation Advisory Councils to guide state VR policies and procedures, and mandating that the majority of members be persons with disabilities; (3) increased access to VR services by incorporating (a) the presumption of benefit (the presumption that the applicant with a disability applying for services can become employed, and will therefore benefit from services; (b) the use of existing data; and (c) requiring that eligibility decisions be made within 60 days of application. The 1992 Amendments also mandated policy to prepare more people from minority backgrounds as professional rehabilitation counselors and increased the federal share of the state–federal funding match to 78.7%.

The Workforce Investment Act of 1998, Including the Rehabilitation Act Amendments of 1998

The Workforce Investment Act (WIA) of 1998 linked the state–federal VR program to the state's Workforce Development System. WIA consolidated several employment and training programs into a unified statewide workforce investment system. The linkage does not affect the integrity of the state–federal VR program as an individual and separate entity. The purposes of the act were to streamline services by integrating multiple employment and training programs in one agency, where customers can easily access the employment information and services they require through a "one-stop" system. Every state has at least one one-stop center in each major population area. VR is a mandated partner and must provide services to some extent via the one-stop center. The degree of participation varies from state to state.

Key Elements of the 1998 Rehabilitation Act Amendments

The 1998 Rehabilitation Act Amendments streamlined the VR administrative procedures by establishing eligibility for people already receiving Supplemental Security Income (SSI) or Social Security Disability Insurance (SSDI) benefits. The IPE replaced the IWRP to emphasize the employment focus of the VR program. Consumers were given an expanded role in the development of the IPE and the opportunity to either develop their own plans or to develop a plan with the assistance of the rehabilitation counselor. The Amendments stressed the need to expand outreach to minorities and recognized that people from minority background experience higher rates of disability. The 1998 Amendments also improved due process provisions by requiring state VR agencies to establish policies and procedures relating to the mediation of disputes and provide hearings before impartial hearing officers. Increased opportunities to obtain employment were provided through an emphasis on telecommuting, self-employment, and small business operation as legitimate employment outcomes.

CASE AND CASELOAD MANAGEMENT

Overview

In this section we define case management and caseload management, two critical elements of the rehabilitation counseling job function, and discuss certification as a case manager.

▒ LEARNING OBJECTIVES

By the end of this unit you should be able to:

1. Define and distinguish between case management and caseload management.
2. Describe the case management knowledge domains underlying rehabilitation counseling case management practice.

▥ KEY CONCEPTS

Case management is the process of coordinating and integrating case services and involves such functions and processes as intake interviewing; assessment and evaluation; planning, evaluating, coordinating, and evaluating services; and recording and reporting of case information. Each of these functions is associated with a further specified set of knowledge, skills, and abilities (Leahy & Phillips, 2011; Roessler & Rubin, 2006). Intake interviewing requires counseling and time-management skills applied in the process of learning about the consumer and his or her rehabilitation goals and objectives through a comprehensive interview, and providing information about the agency, its policies, information necessary for informed consent and professional ethics, expectations, services, and limits of services. In the assessment function, relevant information for current status and planning is obtained. In the planning function, information obtained in the intake interview, assessment, and other available information about the consumer is used to develop a plan for service provision and goal achievement. In the services coordination function, the case manager establishes contacts with other professionals for services, including referrals for evaluations and assessments. The case manager arranges for and monitors the services and assessments with, for example, psychologists and psychiatrists, vocational evaluators, and medical and health-related professionals. The recording and reporting function entails maintaining records and files, progress reporting, and preparing summary reports (Roessler & Rubin, 2006).

Knowledge domains underlying rehabilitation counseling case management practice have been found to include the following five domains (with examples of content): (1) medical treatment and services (e.g., pharmaceutical and pharmacological management, assessing clinical information for use in developing treatment plans, and establishing treatment goals that meet the client's health care and safety needs); (2) community resources and services (e.g., community-based funding resources, eligibility for community-based care, crisis intervention); (3) professional judgment and problem solving (e.g., legal and ethical issues related to confidentiality, planning and goal development techniques, and applying problem-solving techniques); (4) cost containment (e.g., understanding cost analysis and methods to determine cost-effectiveness); (5) psychosocial aspects of disability (e.g., theories of personality, understanding the interaction of psychological and social factors as they pertain to wellness and independence; Leahy, Chan, Shaw, & Lui, 1997).

Caseload management refers to a system based on the systematic synthesis of client information from diverse sources to enhance counselor decision-making and ensure the effective and efficient delivery of appropriate services to accomplish successful consumer outcomes within agency and ethical guidelines (Wheaton & Berven, 1994). Caseload management refers to the management of the total caseload, as opposed to a single client. Caseload management is a systematic process using both counseling and managerial skills to ensure efficient and effective decision making, and coordination of services. Caseload management approaches and styles vary by agency; therefore, caseload management is generally learned on an organizational level and counselors adopt the style of caseload management that is practiced within their agency while following state and federal guidelines and ethical principles of the overseeing professional organizations. It is imperative for caseload management that all activities, professionals referred to, collaborative efforts, timing, and planning be specifically documented during the caseload procedure.

INDEPENDENT LIVING

Overview

In this section, we define and describe the history of the independent living (IL) movement, review its legislative basis, and describe the roles of Statewide IL Councils and Centers for IL.

■ LEARNING OBJECTIVES

By the end of this unit you should be able to:

1. Define IL and describe the history of the IL movement
2. Describe the legislative basis for IL services.
3. Define and describe Statewide IL Councils and Centers for IL.

■ KEY CONCEPTS

Definition and History of IL

IL can be defined as being in control of one's life, choosing one's own goals and activities, and ultimately deciding one's own support system, including the strategies, people, and animal supports necessary to accomplish any given objective in the entire environment in which the support system is needed (Litvak & Enders, 2001). The major precepts of the IL philosophy are that: (a) it is not disability that prevents people with disabilities from living independently but external barriers such as stigmatizing attitudes; interpretations of disabilities; and architectural, legal, and educational barriers; (b) people with disabilities have the right to self-determination and to learn from their experiences; (c) people with disabilities can be experts in their own self-care; (d) people with disabilities must set the agenda for research and political actions in disability policy; and (e) IL services are mostly managed and administered by consumers (Braddock & Parish, 2001; Fabian & MacDonald-Wilson, 2005; Pratt, Gill, Barrett, & Roberts, 2007). The first IL center in the United States was established in early 1970s in Berkeley, CA; it served as a model for the development of such centers across the country.

Legislative Basis

The 1973 Rehabilitation Act called for an investigation of the feasibility of providing services to individuals with the most-severe disabilities who, due to the severity of the disability and other factors, were not expected to be rehabilitated for employment but for whom such services may improve their ability to live independently or function within their family and community. In the 1978 Rehabilitation Act Amendments, funds were authorized for the provision of IL services and this funding has been maintained in subsequent amendments. Title VII of the 1998 Rehabilitation Act Amendments mandate the services and administrative systems through which IL services are provided, including Statewide IL Councils and Centers for IL. Key concepts associated with IL are presented in Table 10.2.

TABLE 10.2 ■ **Key Concepts Associated With Independent Living**

Key Concept	Summary
Independent living (IL)	A consumer-driven movement to achieve control over one's life, choosing one's own goals, activities, and support system, including the strategies, people, and animal supports necessary to accomplish objectives
IL philosophy	Barriers and stigma, and not the disability prevent community inclusion of people with disabilities; people have the right to self-determination; people with disabilities are experts in their own self-care
SILC	Statewide IL council; a consumer-controlled council authorized by Rehabilitation Act Amendments to establish state IL plans
CIL	Centers for IL are cross-disability, nonresidential, community-based nonprofit programs that provide information and referral, IL skills training, peer counselling, and individual and systems advocacy

SCHOOL-TO-WORK TRANSITION SERVICES

▓ LEARNING OBJECTIVES

By the end of this unit you should be able to:

1. Understand the history of school-to-work transition services in the United States.
2. Outline the roles and functions of disability management specialists.

▓ KEY CONCEPTS

In 1975, the Education for All Handicapped Children Act (PL94–142) called national attention to the public education of children and youth with disabilities. This legislation mandated (1) free and appropriate education for all students with disabilities through age 21 or graduation, (2) required states to identify, locate, and evaluate all children in the state who required special education and related services, (3) required that education be provided for students in the Least Restrictive Environment (LRE) and to the maximum extent possible, with students without disabilities, and (4) mandated nondiscrimination in testing and evaluation services for children with disabilities.

In the mid- to late-1980s, professional and political attention turned to post-secondary outcomes for students with disabilities as increasing research suggested that special education students were more likely to be drop out of school, were significantly less likely to be employed after finishing school and if employed earned lower wages, and were more likely to live at home with their parents and less likely to participate in further education, community integration, or IL. As a result of increased attention and awareness of these problems, there was an increased legislative response as described below.

Individuals With Disabilities Education Act

The Individuals with Disabilities Education Act (IDEA) of 1990 (subsequently reauthorized several times, most recently in 2004) increased the focus on post-school transition and firmly placed transition planning in the Individualized Education Plan (IEP). The IEP is a written plan that specifies the special education goals and services that the school must provide to meet the unique educational needs of a student with a disability. (Students with disabilities who do not have an IEP but have a disability and require reasonable accommodation while attending school may have a plan under Section 504 of the Rehabilitation Act of 1973, referred as a 504 plan.)

In the 2004 reauthorization of IDEA, transition is defined as a coordinated set of activities for a child with a disability that is designed to be within a results-oriented process, that is focused on improving the academic and functional achievement of the child with a disability to facilitate the movement from school to post-school activities, including: postsecondary education; vocational education; integrated employment (including supported employment); continuing and adult education; adult services; IL; and community participation. IDEA (2004) states that transition is based on the individual child's needs, taking into account the child's strengths, preferences and interests; and includes instruction, related services, community experiences, the development of employment and other post-school adult living objectives, and if appropriate, acquisition of daily living skills and functional vocational evaluation.

For each student, beginning at age 16 (or younger, if determined appropriate by the IEP team), the IEP includes a statement of the needed transition services for students including, when appropriate, a statement of the interagency responsibilities or linkages before the student leaves the school setting. IDEA identifies rehabilitation counselors as related service providers.

The Rehabilitation Act Amendments of 1998

The Rehabilitation Act Amendments of 1998 described the state rehabilitation agency's role in transition. Each state is required to develop a plan containing plans, policies, and procedures for coordination with education officials responsible for the provision of the public education of students with disabilities. The plan is designed to facilitate the transition of the students from receiving services in school to receiving VR services, and includes information on a formal interagency agreement between the state educational agency and the state rehabilitation agency that provides for (1) consultation and technical assistance to assist educational agencies in planning for transition from school to post-school activities, including VR services; (2) transition planning by state agency and educational agency personnel that facilitates the development and completion of the IEP; (3) the roles and responsibilities, including financial responsibilities, of each agency; and (4) procedures for outreach to and identification of students with disabilities who need transition services (Rehabilitation Act Amendments of 1998). Key concepts associated with School to Work Transition Services are presented in Table 10.3.

DISABILITY MANAGEMENT

▓ LEARNING OBJECTIVES

By the end of this unit you should be able to:

1. Understand the need for the emergent area of disability management.
2. Outline the roles and functions of disability management specialists.

TABLE 10.3 ▓ **Key Concepts Associated With School-to-Work Transition**

Education for All Handicapped Children Act (PL94–142) of 1975	Concerning the public education of children and youth with disabilities, mandated (1) free and appropriate education for all students with disabilities through age 21 or graduation, (2) required states to identify, locate, and evaluate children who required special education and related services, (3) required that education be provided in the least restrictive environment, and (4) mandated nondiscrimination in testing and evaluation services for children with disabilities.
Individuals with Disabilities Education Act (IDEA)	Amendment and subsequent reauthorizations of the above Act, IDEA ensures that children with disabilities have available a free appropriate public education that includes special education and related services to meet their needs and prepare them for employment and IL. Increased the focus on post-school transition mandates transition planning in the IEP.
Individualized Education Plan (IEP)	Written plan that specifies the special education goals and services to meet the unique educational needs of a student with a disability, including beginning at 16 (or younger) a statement of needed transition services and interagency responsibilities or linkages before the student leaves school.

▓ KEY CONCEPTS

Disability management (DM) is an emerging professional area in rehabilitation counseling. DM involves prevention and remediation strategies to prevent disability from occurring in the workplace, and early intervention following the onset of disability. DM may involve the use of both proactive and reactive techniques. Proactive techniques such as wellness programs, safety awareness, and illness/injury prevention are used to reduce occupational disabilities. Reactive programs include employee assistance programs, transitional work programs, outplacement and work hardening (Dunn, 2001; Sawisch, 1989). DM practitioners have competencies in comprehensive individual case analysis and disability case management, performance of work site/job analysis, vocational counseling, development of individualized return-to-work and work retention plans, coordinating services and collaboration with other services providers and employers to provide needed services for clients, development of prevention and workplace intervention plans, ergonomic evaluation, health and wellness program development, and the development of worksite modifications and job accommodations (Rosenthal, Hursh, Lui, Zimmermann, & Pruett, 2005; Certification of Disability Management Specialists Commission [CDMSC], 2009). Key concepts associated with DM are presented in Table 10.4.

FORENSIC REHABILITATION, VOCATIONAL EXPERT PRACTICES, AND LIFE CARE PLANNING

▓ LEARNING OBJECTIVES

By the end of this unit you should be able to:

1. Define forensic rehabilitation and vocational expert services
2. Describe key concepts in workers' compensation
3. Understand the purpose of the emerging professional area of life care planning.

▓ KEY CONCEPTS

Forensic rehabilitation refers to a variety of rehabilitation counseling services provided in legal or quasi-legal settings or pertaining to legal proceedings (Shaw & Betters, 2004). These services may include testifying as a vocational expert in workers compensation or

TABLE 10.4 ▓ **Key Concepts Associated With Disability Management**

Key Concept	Summary
Disability management	A workplace prevention and remediation strategy involving the development and implementation of integrated services that promote the recovery and return to work of an injured worker, prevent injury or exacerbation of injury or disability, and control costs associated with the injury.
CDMSC	CDMSC; an independent body that protects the public by monitoring the competency of disability management specialists.
Work Interruption Case Management	A knowledge domain of disability management that includes comprehensive individual case analysis/disability case management, etc.
Disability prevention and workplace intervention plan	A knowledge domain of disability management that involves risk mitigation, ergonomic evaluation and recommendations, health and wellness initiation, development of worksite modifications, and job accommodations.

Social Security Administration (SSA) hearings, civil court proceedings, personal injury litigation, life care planning, marriage dissolution or family court hearings, employment discrimination, or medical malpractice cases (Brodwin, 2008; Shaw & Betters, 2004). Required qualifications for serving as a vocational expert witness include completion of a graduate degree in rehabilitation counseling or the behavioral sciences and several years of experience in rehabilitation counseling practice, and knowledge and experience in the medical aspects of disabilities, functional limitations, rehabilitation and vocational potential, transferable skills analysis, marketability, and employability (Brodwin, 2008).

Workers' Compensation

Workers' compensation is an insurance-based program deigned to provide monetary compensation for workers who are injured on the job. Historically, before workers' compensation laws, an injured worker was forced to sue his or her employer to obtain payment for medical services and recover wages. However, the existence of three defenses made success in such lawsuits doubtful. These included (1) the assumption of risk, which held that injury was a normal and accepted danger associated with employment; (2) the fellow servant doctrine, which prevented recovery if the injury was caused by a fellow worker's negligence; and (3) contributory negligence, which prevented recovery if the worker's own negligence contributed to the accident or injury. Workers' compensation essentially guarantees compensation benefits for workers who forego most of their rights to sue their employer in the event of injury. Workers' compensation is described as a "no-fault" system. Benefits are paid regardless of who is at fault for the injury, as long as the injury or disease happened at work or was caused by work. Persons injured on the job receive money to replace lost wages at a fixed amount, medical expenses, and usually VR.

In the United States, workers' compensation is an employer-funded program, achieved either through the purchase of commercial insurance or by setting up a self-insurance account. Most states have exclusion criteria for small companies and for domestic and agricultural workers (Guyton, 1999). Claims by injured workers are generally handled by state-based compensation boards and statutes regulating eligibility, compliance, and the administrations of benefits and services are legislated at the state level. Certain basic standards for the provision of workers' compensation are set by the federal government. Federal employees, workers on interstate railroads, seamen, persons loading and unloading vessels, and some construction workers working around navigable waters are covered by federal laws. Federal workers' compensation programs include the Federal Employer's Compensation Act (FECA), Longshore and Harbor Workers' Compensation Act, and the Railroad Retirement and Unemployment Acts.

Workers' Compensation Laws

Wage loss benefits are calculated using an impairment rating, a wage loss system, or loss-of-earning capacity. The impairment rating system has five categories: (1) temporary total disability (TTD), (2) temporary partial disability (TPD), (3) permanent partial disability, (4) permanent total disability, and (5) survivor (death) benefits. With TTD, wages are usually paid to the claimant while he or she is off work due to a workers' compensation claim. If the injured worker can return to his or her former employment in some modified capacity, but at reduced function or earnings compared to the preinjury status, then the worker is classified into the TPD status. The worker receives income maintenance at a percentage of the difference between preinjury and postinjury earnings. TPD usually covers the medical bills and a wage differential if the claimant is able to work, but not in the same capacity while recovering from a work-related injury. Permanent total disability means the worker is unable to work in any capacity. Permanent partial disability means the worker is able to work, but has a permanent, residual deficit. TTD is the worker's status following an industrial injury or illness and a brief qualifying period of generally days or weeks. TTD usually involves the period a worker receives reimbursed medical services directed toward maximum medical improvement (MMI) or medical stability. During this period, the worker receives wage loss benefits based on preinjury earnings while regarded by the attending physician as unable to work. Wage loss benefits are often *two thirds* of the injured worker's average weekly wage at the time of injury.

Scheduled and Unscheduled Injuries In cases of permanent total or partial disability, at the point of MMI, the attending physician determines the degree of loss, disability, or impairment, if any, through guidelines established by The American Medical Association's *Guides to Evaluation of Permanent Impairment* (1990). The "impairment rating" is determined by medical guidelines as well as by individual state statues that classify the injury as either "scheduled" or "unscheduled." "Scheduled" injuries involve the extremities, eyes (vision) or ears (hearing). Schedules of impairment list the disability and the corresponding compensable payment for the loss. Industrial injuries not found in the statutorily defined schedule generally become "unscheduled" injuries (e.g., spinal cord injury, double amputation). The benefits for unscheduled injuries are calculated differently. At the date of MMI and release to return to work by the attending physician, the injured worker is entitled to compensation based on the: difference between preinjury and postinjury earnings. The benefit is paid over the life of the worker and periodic adjustments can be made if the earnings capacity of the individual worker changes.

Earning Capacity At the time permanent partial or total disability is determined, the individual's state workers' compensation regulatory body receives a petition from the insurer with evidence of the degree of loss and offering a specific compensation settlement or award. At this time, litigation becomes germane. The worker has the right to protest the award, and then may hire an attorney. This is an area where VR interventions may be effective. The vocational expert may play a vital role in the hearing process by presenting evidence on behalf of either the plaintiff (injured worker) or the defendant (insurer and employer).

The Purpose of Rehabilitation Services in Workers' Compensation

VR has been an important benefit in workers' compensation since the 1970s. The primary goal of VR services in workers' compensation is the early return to work and minimized loss of earnings capacity by the injured worker to help mitigate insurer and employer losses.

Knowledge and Skill Domains Related to Workers' Compensation

The major rehabilitation knowledge domains were identified by Matkin (1985) as including: (a) human disabilities, (b) case management, (c) job placement, (d) vocational assessment, (e) rehabilitation disability legislation, (f) rehabilitation resources, and (g) forensic issues. More recently, Leahy, Chan, Taylor, Wood, and Downey (1998) identified seven empirically derived knowledge factors as important for effective private rehabilitation practice. These knowledge factors include: (a) vocational assessment and planning, (b) case management and reporting, (c) expert witness testimony, (d) employment and disability-related legislation and regulations, (e) community resources, (f) psychosocial, and (g) functional aspects of disability, and job analysis and modification.

THE RETURN-TO-WORK HIERARCHY IN WORKERS' COMPENSATION A return-to-work hierarchy is described in workers' compensation VR that describes the preferred order of service goals and seeks to capitalize on existing capacities and relationships with the injured worker's employer. These are

1. Return to work in the same job, with the same employer
2. Return to work in the same but modified job with the same employer
3. Return to work in a different job (capitalizing on transferable skills), with the same employer
4. Return to work in the same job, with a different employer
5. Return to work in the same but modified job, with a different employer
6. Return to work in a different job (capitalizing on transferable skills) with a different employer
7. Return to work in a different job with re-training, with the same or a different employer
8. Return to work in self-employment

Life Care Planning Services

Life care planning services are a form of medical and catastrophic case management involving the design of a plan of comprehensive and long-term rehabilitation and related services for an individual who has experienced a catastrophic injury or has significant chronic health care needs (Brodwin, 2008; McCollom, 2002). Life care plans are designed to identify and communicate the details of care that will be necessary from the point of evaluation through the projected end of the individual's life. Among the areas that may be addressed in a life care plan are projected needs for evaluations and therapies, diagnostic testing, educational assessments, vocational and educational planning, equipment needs and aids for independent functioning, medication and medical supply needs, care setting considerations and the need for architectural renovation, transportation, health maintenance and services, and leisure and recreational services (Brodwin, 2008). Professionals who may be involved in the development of the life care plan include physicians and medical specialists, physical and occupational therapists, rehabilitation professionals, lawyers, and economists, as well as family and friends of the individual and the individual himself or herself.

SUBSTANCE ABUSE TREATMENT AND REHABILITATION

▧ LEARNING OBJECTIVES

By the end of this unit you will be able to

1. Define the key terms used in substance abuse counseling and rehabilitation
2. Discuss the relationships between substance abuse and disability
3. Describe major models of substance abuse and counseling theories related to substance abuse treatment and rehabilitation

▧ KEY CONCEPTS

Substance Abuse and Substance Dependence

The *Diagnostic and Statistical Manual of Mental Disorders, fourth edition, Text Revision* (*DSM-IV-TR*; American Psychiatric Association, 2000) defines substance abuse (SA) as a maladaptive pattern of substance use that leads to clinically significant impairment or distress as manifested in one of the following areas within a 12-month period: recurrent substance use that results in failure to fulfill major role obligations at work, school, or home; recurrent use in situations in which it is physically hazardous; the experience of use-related legal problems; or continued use despite persistent or recurrent social or interpersonal problems caused or exacerbated by the effects of the substance. The related term, *substance dependence*, also refers to a maladaptive pattern of substance use resulting in clinically significant impairment or distress, but is defined as being manifested in three (or more) of the following in the same 12-month period: tolerance (a need for markedly increased amounts of the substance to achieve intoxication or the desired effect; withdrawal, or use to avoid or relieve withdrawal symptoms; taking the substance in larger amounts or over a longer period than intended; a persistent desire or unsuccessful attempts at cutting down or controlling use; spending a great deal of time in activities necessary to obtain or use the substance, or recover from the substance's effects; giving up important social, occupational, or recreational activities because of substance use; or continuing to use the substance despite knowledge of having a persistent or recurrent physical or psychological problem likely to have been caused or exacerbated by the substance (American Psychiatric Association, 2000).

SA, Disability, and Rehabilitation

The prevalence of SA disorders is almost twice as high among adults with disabilities compared with the general population, and more than 20% of persons eligible for VR services experience SA or dependence (Krahn, Deck, Gabriel, & Farrell, 2007). People with disabilities as well as SA disorders have the lowest successful closure rates in VR agencies (Hollar, McAweeney, & Moore, 2008). The presence of a disability significantly increases the risk for SA, alcohol and illicit drug use, and prescription abuse (Brucker, 2007). Among people with disabilities, younger adults are more likely to use illicit drugs and older adults are more likely to abuse prescription medication. SA disorders are the most frequently occurring comorbid disability in persons with a mental health diagnosis (Bachman, Drainoni, & Tobias, 2004). Access to, and completion of, SA treatment for persons with disabilities may be affected by physical, attitudinal, or communication barriers and failure of physicians to identity and refer such individuals for treatment (West, Graham, & Cifu, 2009; West et al., 2009).

Models of SA and Addiction

The Moral Model

The moral model explains the etiology of substance addiction based on beliefs about right and wrong or acceptable and unacceptable behavior. SA is seen as a personal choice, and individuals as capable of making alternate choices, and this model is still prevalent in public policies and attitudes (Capuzzi & Stauffer, 2012).

The Disease Model

Addiction is seen in terms of a medical orientation as resulting from genetic predisposition, pathological metabolism, or as an acquired disease resulting from repeated exposure. SA is seen as a primary disease with progressive and irreversible stages and as chronic and incurable, thus the term "recovering" rather than "recovered" addicts is used by adherents of this perspective, and abstinence, rather than cure is seen as the goal of treatment (Capuzzi & Stauffer, 2012; Janikowski, Cardoso, & Lee, 2005).

Genetic, Biological, and Neurobiological Models

Biological and genetic models of SA suggest that the individual's biological and genetic constitution can predispose the individual to substance dependency. Research on addiction suggests that SA and alcohol dependency is associated with genetic factors; however, it is difficult to distinguish between social and environmental factors that are also likely to contribute to the development of addiction or dependence. The neurobiological model suggests that the actions of neurotransmitters (chemical messengers) cause chemical changes in the limbic system of the brain that may lead to addiction.

Psychological Models

Several psychological models of SA and addiction exist, including: (a) Cognitive-behavioral models, which state that people perceive or derive certain satisfactions and reinforcement from substance use. Addiction results from an inability to regulate or control the reward system. (b) Learning models suggest that substance use is a result of faulty learning, and that use is reinforcing and leads to repeating the behavior, which may lead to addiction, and that social or environmental conditions may be associated with or trigger the behavior. The aversive effects and tension associated with withdrawal may motivate the continued SA; (c) Psychodynamic models view SA as a symptom of other basic psychopathology, and problems with regulation of affect and link SA to inadequate parenting, ego deficiencies, attachment disorders, masturbation, homosexuality, and other issues; (d) Personality theory models assume that certain personality traits (e.g., dependency, immaturity, and inability to express anger) lead to addiction.

Treatment and Rehabilitation

A wide range of treatment and rehabilitation models and approaches are used, based on different models and theories of addiction, historical and emerging treatment theories and approaches, and the substance or addiction involved. These include residential models, including in-patient treatment programs (frequently based on the Alcoholics Anonymous [AA] 12-step orientation), and therapeutic communities (based on a social learning approach to prevention and skill development); intensive outpatient treatment programs; halfway houses; self-help groups (e.g., AA, Narcotics Anonymous, Rational Recovery) and family programs (e.g., Al-Anon, Alateen); and pharmacological therapies, which may be combined with the above treatment options (Janikowski et al., 2005).

WELLNESS AND ILLNESS PREVENTION CONCEPTS

▓ LEARNING OBJECTIVES

By the end of this unit you will be able to:

1. Define and distinguish between health and wellness.
2. Define and describe self-management, adherence, and major models of health promotion and health behavior.

▓ KEY CONCEPTS

For many people, the impact of disability on health and wellness is minimal, but for others, disability or chronic illness (CI) can limit participation in health-related activities and affect access to correlates of wellness, including social support, having basic financial needs met, optimism, and self-determination. Having a disability does not necessarily mean that one experiences poor health, but disability increases the risk for further CI and disability. Rehabilitation counselors are increasingly recognizing that promoting the health and wellness of consumers with disabilities is both a critical role and function of their work, and one that may increase the consumers' ability to achieve rehabilitation goals.

Health and Wellness

Health is increasingly defined as a multidimensional concept. For example, the World Health Organization (WHO) International Classification of Functioning, Disability, and Health (ICF, 2001) incorporates a multidimensional view of health, including both environmental and personal factors and including body, individual, and societal perspectives. The multidimensional and inter-related ICF approach to health incorporates (1) environmental factors external to the individual that may include the built environment and structural access, the physical environment, the social environment, including social support, societal attitudes, and cultural, legal, and political systems; (2) personal factors, including characteristics such as gender, race/ethnicity, socioeconomic status, and education, individual personal features and characteristics; (3) body structure and function, or the physiological and psychological functioning of body parts, systems, and the body structure; (4) activities or tasks the individual engages in; and (5) participation or the involvement and ability of the individual to participate in activities (ICF, 2001).

Wellness is a concept related to, but also distinct from health. Common to most definitions of wellness are that (1) wellness is a process, or a way of living, rather than an end state; and (2) wellness involves striving for or achieving and maintaining the optimal level of well-being and health of which one is capable. Health and wellness can be seen as existing on separate but parallel continuums, such that an individual could achieve or exist at different ends of each simultaneously, and thus having a disability or CI does not preclude being well or engaging in a wellness lifestyle (Sperry, Lewis, Carlson, & Englar-Carlson, 2005).

Rehabilitation counseling requires understanding of the concepts and effective methods practice in illness prevention and health promotion, including self-management, adherence, health assessment, health promotion models, and assisting clients to make informed personal decisions about health and wellness.

Self-Management

Self-management is defined as learning and practicing the skills necessary to carry on an active and emotionally satisfying life in the face of a chronic condition (Lorig, 1993). It includes such concepts as self-care, management of one's condition, including medication and treatment management, communicating with physicians, and caring for oneself through exercise and diet, maintaining, changing, and creating new meaningful behaviors and roles, engaging effectively in work and leisure activities, and maintaining social relationships, and coping emotionally with the feelings associated with living with illness, and realizing and developing a new sense of future (Corbin & Strauss, 2003). Self-management programs have been found to result in decreased pain, disability, anxiety, and health-care utilization, and increased psychological functioning, role functioning, adherence, and use of cognitive coping techniques. Lorig and Holman (2003) suggested that the following should be included in counseling to promote self-management: teaching and helping clients to develop problem-solving skills; helping consumers to become informed and aware of their illness or disability and its treatment; helping consumers to find and use health information and resources; helping consumers to form effective relationships with health care providers; and helping consumers to take actions that promote their health and manage their condition.

Models of Health Promotion and Health Behavior

Many models of health and wellness promotion have been suggested. Generally, these are based on models of health behavior and health behavior change. Among the more frequently discussed and researched of these models in rehabilitation counseling are the following.

The Health Beliefs Model

The basic tenets of the health belief model are that behavior depends on two variables: (1) the value placed by an individual on a particular goal and (2) the individual's estimate of the likelihood that a given action will result in achievement of that goal (Becker, Drachman, & Kirscht, 1974). The correlate in health behavior is that engaging in recommended health behavior depends on the following: (1) the value placed on avoiding illness (or maintain/achieve health) and (2) the belief that a health behavior will prevent illness (achieve/maintain health). Elements that moderate this relationship include perceived susceptibility (e.g., risk of threat of illness or poor health), perceived severity or seriousness of the risk, perceived benefits of engaging in the behavior, perceived barriers to taking action, and cues to action (availability of stimuli that trigger the decision-making process). More recently, self-efficacy has also been incorporated in this model.

The Theory of Reasoned Action

According to this theory, the intention to perform a behavior is the primary determinant of behavior (Fishbein & Ajzen, 1975; Ajzen & Fishbein, 1980). This intention is influenced by one's attitudes toward the behavior, including (1) the individual's belief that the action will lead to a certain outcome, (2) the value attached by the individual to the outcome, (3) subjective norms: the extent to which the person believes that other individuals or groups think that he or she should engage in the behavior, weighed by the individual's desire to comply with their wishes.

The Theory of Planned Behavior (Ajzen, 1991)

Similar to the theory of reasoned action, this theory posits that health behavior is driven by behavioral intentions. It is further delineated that behavioral intentions are a function of (1) the individual's attitude toward the behavior (i.e., the individual's positive or negative feelings about performing the behavior), (2) the subjective norms surrounding the performance of the behavior (i.e., the extent to which people who are important to the individual are perceived as thinking the behavior should be performed), and (3) behavioral control (i.e., the individual's perception of the ease with which the behavior can be performed).

Social Cognitive Theory (Bandura, 1989)

This model suggests that behavior change and maintenance are a function of expectations about whether the behavior will achieve certain outcomes, and efficacy beliefs (expectations about one's ability to execute the behavior).

The Transtheoretical Model (Prochaska & DiClemente, 1983)

The transtheoretical model can be seen as a model of health decision making and the stages of change, which are represented as categories along a continuum of readiness to change a behavior (precontemplation, contemplation, preparation, action, and maintenance). Transitions between the stages are modified by factors such as self-efficacy (confidence in the ability to change), and psychological, environmental, cultural, socioeconomic, and

TABLE 10.5 ■ Key Concepts in Wellness and Illness Prevention

Key Concept	Summary
Health	A multidimensional concept referring to physical, social, and emotional well-being, influenced by environmental, social, and personal factors.
Wellness	A lifestyle and process of striving for maintaining the optimal level of well-being and health of which one is capable.
Self-management	Learning and practicing the skills necessary to have an active and emotionally satisfying life with a chronic condition includes self-care, management of one's condition, maintaining, changing, and creating new meaningful behaviors and roles, and coping.
Adherence to treatment	The degree to which health-care recipients follow, or adhere to, treatment recommendations.

other variables or behaviors specific to the context of change. Key concepts in wellness and illness prevention concepts are presented in Table 10.5.

COMMUNITY RESOURCES AND COMMUNITY-BASED REHABILITATION PROGRAMS

■ LEARNING OBJECTIVES

By the end of this unit you should be able to:

1. Understand the importance of community resources for people with disabilities.
2. Identify existing community resources and how to provide access to people with disabilities.
3. Understand the need for collaborations with community service providers.

■ KEY CONCEPTS

To effectively refer, transfer, or coordinate rehabilitation counseling services, knowledge about the different services provided by agencies, facilities, and organizations is needed (Crimando & Riggar, 2005). Community resources may be unique to a community and counselors must become aware of organizations and services that deal with inclusive education, inpatient and outpatient rehabilitation programs, medical resources and facilities, IL services, assistive technology (AT) services, accessible public transportation, and advocacy organizations in the community (Patterson, DeLaGarza, & Schaller, 2005).

Community resources that rehabilitation counselors should be aware of include: (1) Health and Diagnostic Services, including (a) medical services, (b) home-based rehabilitation, and (c) mental and behavioral health care; (2) Rehabilitation and Vocational Services, including VR and supported employment, AT services, forensic rehabilitation, educational, and human services; (3) Career and Technical Education including adult education, special education, centers for IL, and public/specialized transportation; (4) Community Living Resources, including (a) public housing assistance, (b) supported housing for persons with disabilities, and (c) other state or local housing and rental assistance programs; and (5) Legal and Social Services, including those offered to low-income citizens.

Community-Based Rehabilitation Programs

Community-Based Rehabilitation Programs (CRPs) are community-based nonprofit organizations that provide a range of employment and rehabilitation services. Frequently these services are provided through contracts with the state VR agencies. Other sources of income include developmental disability, mental health, and other public and private agency sources. The Rehabilitation Act defines CRPs as programs that directly provide or facilitate the provision of VR services to individuals with disabilities. Employment-related CRP services frequently include testing or assessment; job development, training, placement, and retention services; supported employment services and job coaching.

INSURANCE PROGRAMS AND SOCIAL SECURITY

■ LEARNING OBJECTIVES

By the end of this unit you should be able to:

1. Define and describe the SSA disability benefits: SSDI and SSI, including eligibility criteria.
2. Define and distinguish between Medicare and Medicaid.
3. Describe work incentives associated with SSI and SSDI.

■ KEY CONCEPTS

The SSA provides disability benefits through the SSDI program and the SSI program. The SSA defines disability as the inability to engage in any Substantial Gainful Activity (SGA) by reason of any medically determinable physical or mental impairment that can be expected to result in death or has lasted or can be expected to last for a continuous period of not less than 12 months.

Social Security Disability Insurance

SSDI was established in 1954. SSDI provides eligible people with disabilities with monthly income benefits and Medicare insurance. SSDI is an eligibility Program; a person must have worked and paid Social Security taxes, be permanently disabled, and earn less than SGA. Eligibility is based on contributions the worker (or in some cases the spouse or parents) made to FICA while employed.

Supplemental Security Income

SSI provides monthly benefits and Medicaid to adults and children with disabilities and has limited income and resources; people with low income who are aged 65 years or older, or people who are blind. The amount of benefit received is based on the individual's other sources of income and living situation. The federal government determines that base SSI benefit rate annually.

Medicaid and Medicare

Medicaid is a federal–state matching program available to certain low-income and eligible individuals and families. Medicaid is state administered and each state sets its own guidelines regarding eligibility and services. Medicaid does not provide payments to the individual but directly to the health-care provider. Depending on the state's rules, the individual may also be asked to pay a small co-payment for some services. Medicaid covers hospital and doctor visits, medication, and in some states, personal assistant services.

Medicare is a federal health insurance program for people aged 65 years or older and SSDI recipients. Medicare is financed by payroll taxes and monthly premiums deducted from Social Security checks. Medicare covers up to 80% of inpatient hospital care, skilled nursing, home health care, and hospice care under Part A. Part B provides medical insurance for doctors' services and other medical services and supplies not covered by hospital insurance, and it requires an insurance premium.

Work Incentives and Terms Associated With Social Security Benefits

Through work incentives established in recent decades, and most recently through the Ticket to Work and Work Incentives Improvement Act (1999), SSI/SSDI recipients are eligible for several employment incentives to promote work and reduce dependence on SSA benefits.

Trial Work Period

Allows SSDI recipients engage in a work trial for at least 9 months. During this period, the person continues to receive full Social Security benefits regardless of earnings. Medical coverage through Medicare is also continued for at least 93 months beyond the 9-month trial work period, beginning the month after the last month of the trial work period. Also, after this period, some people may purchase continued Medicare coverage.

Extended Period of Eligibility (EPE)

SSDI recipients who complete a trial work period can, for a 36-month period, still receive benefits for any month in which earnings are below SGA

Plan for Achieving Self-Support (PASS)

PASS plans allow SSI recipients to set aside income or resources, so that the income/resource will not be considered when calculating initial and continuing eligibility for SSI payments, this helps the person to establish and maintain SSI eligibility and increase SSI payment amounts.

Impairment-Related Work Expenses (IRWE)

In determining SGA, the cost of certain impairment-related items and services that are related to work are deducted from the individual's earnings. To qualify as IRWE, the item or service must be necessary for the individual to work, be related to the individual's disability, be paid for by the individual, and be paid by the individual in a month during which he or she worked.

Ticket to Work

SSDI and SSI recipients receive a ticket (or voucher) to obtain employment services, or other support services that enable self-support, from a state VR agency or other approved employment services provider. The program is voluntary and the services are paid directly to providers through the Ticket to Work program.

ASSISTIVE TECHNOLOGY AND REHABILITATION COUNSELING

LEARNING OBJECTIVES

By the end of this unit you should be able to:

1. Define assistive technology (AT) and related terms.
2. Describe categories of AT.
3. Describe the process and important components of AT assessment.

■ KEY CONCEPTS

AT is technology used by individuals with disabilities to perform functions that might otherwise be difficult or impossible. AT can include mobility devices, computer hardware or software, and devices that help people with disabilities to access computers or other information technologies (National Center on Accessible Information Technology in Education [NCAITE], 2011). Section 508 of the 1998 Rehabilitation Act Amendments defined rehabilitation technology as rehabilitation engineering and AT devices, and mandated rehabilitation technology as a primary benefit to be included in IPEs.

Categories of AT

AT applications can be applied and used in a wide variety of applications, including: aids for daily living, augmentative communication, computer applications, environmental control systems, home and worksite modifications, health promotion, prosthetics and orthotics, seating and positioning, mobility aids, aids for vision and hearing impairment, and vehicle modifications (Rubin & Roessler, 2008). AT may involve low-tech solutions (such as screen magnifiers) as well as more hi-tech devices.

AT Assessment and Rehabilitation Counseling

In working with an individual consumer to provide effective AT, it is critical that a careful assessment is conducted. Specifically, the following should be considered: The consumer's goals and the role of AT; the consumer's abilities and disabilities as related to job performance and functions and AT use; the environment in which AT will be used; completion of a job/task analysis; barriers to job/task performance; research and identify the most effective available options to meet the goals identified; the likelihood of continued use of the AT by the consumer and potential revisions/modifications; consumer training, and follow-up to explore whether the equipment meets the needs of the consumer, or whether intervention/modification is required. Finally, it is important to consider funding sources for initial and continued AT products and services, which may include AT loans, private funding, VR, schools, Medicare, or Medicaid.

■ INTERNET RESOURCES

Links related to vocational rehabilitation and related legislation

Disability-related laws and legislation from Disability.gov
www.disability.gov/technology/laws_%26_regulations

Guide to Disability Rights Laws (including several laws discussed in this chapter) provided by the U.S. Department of Justice, Civil Rights Division, *Disability Rights Section*
www.ada.gov/cguide.htm

National Institute on Disability and Rehabilitation Research
www.ed.gov/offices/OSERS/NIDRR

Rehabilitation Services Administration
www2.ed.gov/about/offices/list/osers/rsa

Text of the 1973 Rehabilitation Act
www.dotcr.ost.dot.gov/documents/ycr/REHABACT.HTM

Text of the Current Rehabilitation Act Amendments
www2.ed.gov/policy/speced/reg/narrative.html

Links related to independent living

Independent Living Research Utilization (Research and information on independent living, the Americans with Disabilities Act, home and community based services and health issues for people with disabilities.)
http://www.ilru.org

The National Council on Independent Living (NCIL)
http://ncil.org

Links related to case management, forensic rehabilitation, vocational expert practices, and life care planning

Certification of Disability Management Specialists Commission
www.cdms.org

Commission for Case Manager Certification
www.ccmcertification.org

International Association of Rehabilitation Professionals in the Private Sector
www.rehabpro.org

The Commission on Rehabilitation Counselor Certification (CRCC)
www.crccertification.com

Links related to assistive technology and rehabilitation counseling

AbleData (Information on Assistive Technology)
www.abledata.com

Job Accommodation Network (JAN)
http://askjan.org

Rehabilitation Engineering and Assistive Technology Society of North America (RESNA)
http://resna.org

Links related to insurance programs and social security

Centers for Medicare and Medicaid Services (US Department of Health and Human Services)
www.cms.gov/home/regsguidance.asp

U.S. Social Security Administration (with links to disability benefits information)
www.SSA.gov

Other helpful links

Family Village (information and resources on a range of disability topics).
www.familyvillage.wisc.edu/index.html

Information on Mental Health & Substance Abuse Disorders from Disability.gov
www.disability.gov/health/disabilities_%26_chronic_health_conditions/mental_health_%26_substance_abuse_disorders

National Council on Disability
www.ncd.gov

Stanford University Chronic Disease Self-Management Program
http://patienteducation.stanford.edu/programs/cdsmp.html

Text of the Individuals with Disabilities Education Act re-authorization
http://idea.ed.gov/download/statute.html

University of Michigan Center for Health Communications Research
http://chcr.umich.edu/how_we_do_it/health_theories/healththeories2/chcr_document_view

▒ MULTIPLE CHOICE QUESTIONS

1. The fundamental concepts in the philosophy of the independent living movement in the United States include all but which one of the following?
   A. External barriers, such as attitudes, architecture, and legal and educational barriers, and not disability, prevent people with disabilities from living independently
   B. People with disabilities have the right to self-determination and to learn from their experiences
   C. With the exception of self-care, people with disabilities can be experts in their own lives.
   D. People with disabilities should be responsible for setting the agenda for disability research and political action

2. Which of the following provides monthly income benefits and Medicare for eligible people with disabilities who have worked and paid Social Security taxes, are permanently disabled, and earn less than Substantial Gainful Activity?
   A. Medicaid
   B. Workers Compensation
   C. Social Security Disability Insurance (SSDI)
   D. Supplementary Security Income (SSI)

3. In the calculation of their substantial gainful activity, an individual with a disability may be eligible to deduct the cost of certain disability-related items or services if these are necessary for the individual to work and paid for by the individual. These deductions are referred as:
   A. Medicaid reimbursable items and services (MRSI)
   B. Personal assistant services or systems (PASS)
   C. Plans for achieving self-support (PASS)
   D. Impairment-related work expenses (IRWE)

4. Self-management is best defined as an approach to health promotion in which:
   A. clients are encouraged to manage their health services through private insurance
   B. patients or health-care recipients are encouraged to follow or comply with beneficial treatment recommendations
   C. clients are encouraged to develop the skills necessary to take responsibility for managing their self-care, health care, and to cope with role changes
   D. clients are encouraged to develop the skills necessary to decrease pain, anxiety, and depression through cognitive coping techniques

5. Which of the following is not accurate with regard to substance abuse?
   A. Substance abuse disorders are believed to be almost twice as high in the general population as compared with the population of adults with disabilities
   B. It is likely that as many as one in five persons eligible for VR services experience substance abuse or dependence
   C. Among people with disabilities, younger adults are more likely to use illicit drugs and older adults are more likely to abuse prescription medication
   D. Substance abuse disorders are the most frequently occurring comorbid disability in persons with a mental health diagnosis

6. All but which one of the following is an accurate statement based on the research on substance abuse and disability?
   A. Diagnosis with a disability significantly increases the risk for alcohol and illicit drug use.
   B. People with disabilities, because they are more likely to have interactions with medical professionals, generally have better access to, and completion of SA treatment.
   C. People with disabilities abuse substances for many of the same reasons as people without disabilities (e.g., social isolation, depression, employment, and financial problems), but are more likely to experience these problems.

D. Substance abuse disorders are the most frequently occurring comorbid disability in persons with a mental health diagnosis.

7. The 1973 Rehabilitation Act was significant for a number of important mandates and outcomes, including all but which of the following?
   A. The mandate that states serve individuals with the most severe disabilities before serving persons with less-severe disabilities
   B. The mandate that VR expand outreach to minorities and recognized that people from minority background experience higher rates of disability
   C. Promotion of client involvement in development of an Individualized Written Rehabilitation Program
   D. The mandate that VR conduct program evaluation

8. In which of the following models is addiction seen as resulting from genetic predisposition, pathological metabolism, or as acquired through repeated exposure?
   A. The moral model
   B. The cognitive–behavioral model
   C. The learning model
   D. The disease model

9. The development of a public VR program America occurred primarily:
   A. Out of the realization that a public program could provide services more effectively than private religious, philanthropic, and charitable organizations
   B. Due to a combination of social, economic, and demographic factors that occurred in the two decades prior to 1920
   C. The rising goodwill of the American people who lobbied congress for action during the Progressive economic period of the early 20th century
   D. The development of the state income tax

10. A major function of disability management is to:
   A. Ensure that VR consumers have their rights respected throughout the application and service provision process
   B. Ensure that students in transition from school to work or post-secondary education continue to experience services until graduation or age 21
   C. Minimize the effects of impairment resulting from occupational injuries on the worker's ability to continue working
   D. Ensure that all necessary services are included in the IPE.

▨ ANSWER KEY

1. C; 2. C; 3. D; 4. C; 5. A; 6. B; 7. B; 8. D; 9. B; 10. C

▨ ADVANCED MULTIPLE CHOICE QUESTIONS

1. The economic argument for VR is best described as being based on the idea that:
   A. VR will be a more effective program economically if services are provided to individuals with the most severe disabilities before serving persons with less-severe disabilities
   B. VR will be a more economical program if services are provided to individuals with the less-severe disabilities before serving persons with more severe disabilities; this concept was revised in 1973.
   C. Investment in VR enables persons with disabilities to become employed tax payers.
   D. A society will generally benefit economically from providing "a square deal" to all its citizens.

2. Which of the following is most accurate concerning the state–federal VR program and its services?
   A. Eligibility for VR services is based on a philosophy of entitlement (all US citizens are entitled to services).

    B. Eligibility for VR services is based on a requirement that the applicant have a disability

    C. To be eligible for VR services, one must have a disability that presents an impediment to working

    D. To be eligible for VR services, one must have a significant mental illness or cognitive disability, while people with physical disabilities are served by private VR services (e.g., Workers Compensation)

3. An Individualized Plan for Employment (IPE) is best described as:

    A. An individualized educational plan that identifies needed educational and transition services

    B. A cooperatively developed plan for medical and psychological services necessary to develop the Individualized Written Plan for Employment (IWRE)

    C. A plan for VR services that is developed by the VR counselor on behalf of the VR consumer.

    D. A cooperatively developed plan for achieving an employment goal indentifying the types and number of services that will be provided.

4. The Workforce Investment Act of 1998:

    A. effectively eliminated the state–federal VR program by consolidated it with other employment and training programs into a unified statewide workforce investment system

    B. created a revised and state-based VR program where all VR consumers participate in employment services through a "one-stop" system

    C. linked the state–federal VR program to the state's Workforce Development System but does not affect the integrity of the state–federal VR program

    D. mandated that every state have only one one-stop center for each major population area

5. The Rehabilitation Act Amendments of 1998 mandate that independent living services are to be provided through centers for independent living, which receive federal and state funding and are required to provide core services including:

    A. Educational and vocational peer mentoring

    B. Employment services, educational services, social services, and emergency housing

    C. Information and referral, independent living skills training, peer counseling and individual and systems advocacy

    D. The services provided are determined at the local and state level and vary according to the needs of the citizens of the state

6. The required qualifications for serving as a vocational expert witness include:

    A. Completion of a doctoral degree in rehabilitation counseling, law (jurisprudence), or a related field

    B. Certification by the Social Security Administration (SSA) as a vocational specialist

    C. Certification as a rehabilitation counselor, disability management provider, or case manager

    D. A graduate degree in rehabilitation counseling or the behavioral sciences and several years of experience in rehabilitation counseling practice

7. The stages of readiness for health behavior change, including precontemplation, contemplation, preparation, action, and maintenance, are most associated with which of the following models of health and wellness promotion?

    A. Transtheoretical model

    B. Health beliefs model

    C. Theory of reasoned action

    D. Theory of planned behavior

8. The provision of assistive technology to consumers who either do not subsequently use the device, or use it for a short period of time and then abandon that it is a significant problem that could be reduced through:

    A. Increased fees for AT services

    B. Policies at the state and federal level that reduce the cost of AT devices and services

    C. Careful assessment

    D. Consumer-based insurance systems that are established as part of the IPE

9. The distinction between health and wellness would best be described as follows:
   A. Health is multidimensional, while wellness is unidimensional
   B. Whereas health concerns physical function, wellness is primarily concerned with mental function and well-being
   C. There is no meaningful distinction between these concepts
   D. Wellness incorporates the idea of the pursuit of health, but health does not necessarily incorporate wellness

10. The 1992 Rehabilitation Act was significant for a number of important mandates and outcomes, including all but which of the following?
    A. The mandate that VR expand outreach to minorities and recognized that people from minority background experience higher rates of disability
    B. Increased client involvement, choice, and participation in the development, implementation, and evaluation of the rehabilitation plan
    C. The Individualized Plan for Employment (IPE) replaced the IWRP to emphasize the employment focus of the VR program
    D. Increased access to VR services by incorporating the presumption of benefit, the use of existing data, and requiring that eligibility decisions be made within 60 days of application

ANSWER KEY AND EXPLANATION OF ANSWERS

1-C: The development of the federal income tax resulted in moneys that could in part be used in the federal sponsorship of VR programs for soldiers, veterans, and civilians. The income tax also enabled tax write-offs for rehabilitation ventures. The income tax established the Economic Argument for VR, which states that an investment of funds in VR will, by enabling persons with disabilities to become employed tax payers, result in a severalfold increase in federal income over the working years of the individual who receives VR services.

2-C: Eligibility for VR services is based on the requirement that the individual have a disability (a physical or mental impairment) that constitutes or results in a substantial impediment to employment, be able to benefit from rehabilitation services, and be able to eventually achieve an employment outcome.

3-D: The Individualized Plan for Employment (IPE) is developed collaboratively by the VR counselor and client. The plan identifies the specific types and number of services that will be provided to help the individual achieve his or her employment goal. A number of services may be provided under the plan, including, for example, assessments, counseling, therapy or treatment, placement services, and other equipment or services necessary to achieve an employment outcome.

4-C: The Workforce Investment Act of 1998 linked the state–federal VR program to the state's Workforce Development System and consolidated several employment and training programs into a unified statewide workforce investment system, but the linkage does not affect the integrity of the state–federal VR program or its existence as a separate entity. The Act streamlined services by integrating multiple employment and training programs where customers can easily access the employment information and services they require through a "one-stop" system.

5-C: Title VII of the Rehabilitation Act Amendments of 1998 mandates that independent living services are to be provided through centers for independent living (CILs). CILs receive federal and state funding through the SILCs, and other government and private contributions and are required to provide core services including (1) information and referral, (2) independent living skills training, (3) peer counseling, and (4) individual and systems advocacy.

6-D: Required qualifications for serving as a vocational expert witness include: (1) completion of a graduate degree in rehabilitation counseling or the behavioral sciences, and several years of experience in rehabilitation counseling practice, (2) knowledge and experience in the medical aspects of disabilities, functional limitations, rehabilitation and vocational potential, transferable skills analysis, marketability, and employability.

7-A: The Transtheoretical Model is a model of health decision-making and stages of change, represented as categories along a continuum of readiness to change a behavior (including precontemplation, contemplation, preparation, action, and maintenance). Transitions between the stages are modified by factors such as self-efficacy, and psychological, environmental, cultural, socioeconomic, and other variables or behaviors specific to the context of change.

8-C: In working with an individual consumer to provide effective assistive technology, it is critical that a careful assessment is conducted and include the consumer's goals, the consumer's abilities, the environment in which AT will be used; and identifying the most effective available options to meet the goals identified, and the likelihood of continued use of the AT by the consumer.

9-D: Whereas health is generally described as a state of physical, mental, and social well-being, wellness is distinct in that it is seen as a process, or a way of living, rather than a state. Health and wellness can be seen as existing on separate but parallel continuums such that an individual could achieve or exist at different ends of each simultaneously. One could be described as healthy, but not engaged in a wellness lifestyle, and having a disability or chronic illness does not preclude being well or engaging in a wellness lifestyle.

10-C: The 1992 Rehabilitation Act Amendments were associated with mandates that increased client involvement, choice, and participation in many ways, including the development, implementation, and evaluation of the Individualized Written Rehabilitation Plan (IWRP), but the title used for this rehabilitation plan changed to the Individualized Plan for Employment with the 1998 Rehabilitation Act Amendments.

▧ REFERENCES

Ajzen, I. (1991). The theory of planned behavior. *Organizational Behavior and Human Decision Processes, 50*(2), 179–211.

Ajzen, I., & Fishbein, M. (1980). *Understanding attitudes and predicting social behavior.* Englewood Cliffs, NJ: Prentice-Hall.

American Psychiatric Association. (2000). *Diagnostic and statistical manual of mental disorders* (4th ed. Text Revision). Washington, DC: Author.

Bachman, S. S., Drainoni, M., & Tobias, C. (2004). Medicaid managed care, substance abuse treatment, and people with disabilities: Review of the literature. *Health and Social Work, 29,* 189–196.

Bandura, A. (1989). Social cognitive theory. In R. Vasta (Ed.), *Annals of child development. Vol. 6. Six theories of child development* (pp. 1–60). Greenwich, CT: JAI Press.

Becker, M.H., Drachman, R. H., & Kirscht, J. P. (1974). A new approach to explaining sick-role behavior in low-income populations. *American Journal of Public Health, 64,* 205–216.

Braddock, D. L., & Parish, S. L. (2001). An institutional history of disability. In G. L. Albrecht, K. D. Seelman, & M. Bury (Eds.), *Handbook of disability studies.* Thousand Oaks, CA: Sage Publications, Inc.

Brodwin, M. (2008). Rehabilitation in the private-for-profit sector: Opportunities and challenges. In S. E. Rubin & R. T. Roessler (Eds.), *Foundations of the vocational rehabilitation process* (6th ed., pp. 501–524). Austin, TX: Pro-Ed.

Brucker, D. (2007). Estimating the prevalence of substance use, abuse, and dependence among social security disability benefit recipients. *Journal of Disability Policy Studies, 18,* 148–159.

Capuzzi, D., & Stauffer, M. D. (2012). History and etiological models of addiction. In D. Capuzzi, & M. D. Stauffer (Eds.), *Foundations of addictions counseling* (2nd ed.). Boston: Pearson Education, Inc.

Certification of Disability Management Specialists Commission. (2009). *CDMSC guide for candidate certification.* Schaumburg, IL: Author.

Corbin, J., & Strauss, A. (1988). *Unending work and care: Managing chronic illness.* San Francisco, CA: Jossey-Bass.

Crimando, W. & Riggar, T.F. (2005) *Community resources.* Long Grove, IL: Waveland Press.

Dunn, P. L. (2001). Trends and issues in proprietary rehabilitation. In P. D. Rumrill, Jr., J. L. Bellini, & L. C. Koch (Eds.), *Emerging issues in rehabilitation counseling: Perspectives on the new millennium*. Springfield IL: Charles C. Thomas Publisher, Ltd.

Fabian, E. S., & MacDonald-Wilson, K. L. (2005). Professional practice in rehabilitation service delivery systems and related system resources. In R. M. Parker, E. M. Szymanski, & J. B. Patterson (Eds.), *Rehabilitation counseling basics and beyond* (4th ed.) Austin, TX: Pro-Ed.

Fishbein, M., & Ajzen, I. (1975). *Belief, attitude, intention, and behavior: An introduction to theory and research*. Reading, MA: Addison-Wesley.

Guyton, G. P. (1999). A brief history of Workers' Compensation. *Iowa Orthopedic Journal, 19*, 106–110.

Hollar, D., McAweeney, M., & Moore, D. (2008). The relationship between substance use disorders and unsuccessful case closures in vocational rehabilitation agencies. *Journal of Applied Rehabilitation Counseling, 39*, 48–52.

Individuals with Disabilities Education Act of 2004, P.L. 108–446. [34 CFR 300.43 (a)] [20 U.S.C. 1401 (34)].

Janikowski, T., Cardoso, E., & Lee, G. K. (2005). Substance abuse counseling in case management. In F. Chan, M. Leahy, & J. Saunders (Eds.), *Case management for rehabilitation health professionals* (pp. 247–274). Osage Beach, MO: Aspen Professional Services.

Krahn, G., Deck, D., Gabriel, R., & Farrell, N. (2007). A population-based study on substance abuse treatment for adults with disabilities: Access, utilization, and treatment outcomes. *The American Journal of Drug and Alcohol Abuse, 33*, 791–798.

Leahy, M., Chan, F., Shaw, L., & Lui, J. (1997). Preparation of rehabilitation counselors for case management practice in health care settings. *Journal of Rehabilitation, 63*(3), 53–59.

Leahy, M., Chang, F., Taylor, D., Wood, C., & Downey, W. (1998). Evolving knowledge and skill factors for practice in private sector. *NARPPS Journal, 6*(1), 34–43.

Leahy, M. J., & Phillips, B. (2011). Certification: Practitioner certification in the delivery of vocational rehabilitation services to individuals with disabilities in the United States. In: J. H. Stone, & M. Blouin (Eds.), *International Encyclopedia of Rehabilitation*. Retrieved from http://cirrie.buffalo.edu/encyclopedia/en/article/42

Litvak, S. & Enders, A. (2001). Support systems: The interface between individuals and environments. In G. L. Albrecht, K. D. Seelman, & M. Bury (Eds.), *Handbook of disability studies*. Thousand Oaks, CA: Sage Publications, Inc.

Lorig K. (1993). Self-management of chronic illness: a model for the future (self care and older adults). *Generations, 17*(3), 11–14.

Lorig, K. R., & Holman, H. R. (2003). Self-management education: History, definitions, outcomes, and mechanisms. *Annals of Behavioral Medicine, 26*(1), 1–7.

Matkin, R. E. (1985). *Insurance Rehabilitation: Service Applications in Disability Compensation Systems*. Austin, TX: Pro-Ed.

McCollom, P. (2002). Guiding the way: The evolution of life care plans. *Continuing Care, 21*(6), 26–28.

National Center on Accessible Information Technology in Education. (2011). *What is accessible electronic and information technology?* Retrieved from www.washington.edu/accessit/articles?110

Patterson, J. B., DeLaGarza, D., & Schaller, J. (2005). Rehabilitation counseling practice: Considerations and interventions. In R. M. Parker, E. M. Szymanski, & J. B. Patterson (Eds.), *Rehabilitation counseling: Basic and beyond*. Austin, TX: Pro-Ed.

Pratt, C. W., Gill, K. J., Barrett, N. M., & Roberts, M. M. (2007). *Psychiatric rehabilitation* (2nd ed.). San Diego, CA: Elsevier Academic Press.

Prochaska, J. O., & DiClemente, C. C. (1983). Stages and processes of self-change of smoking: Toward an integrative model of change. *Journal of Consulting and Clinical Psychology, 51*, 390–395.

Rehabilitation Act Amendments of 1998, 29 U.S.C. § 701 et seq.

Roessler, R. & Rubin, S. (2006). *Case management and rehabilitation counseling*. Austin, TX: Pro-Ed.

Rosenthal, D. A., Hursh, N. C., Lui, J., Zimmermann, W., & Pruett, S. R. (2005). Workplace disability management: Case management implications. In F. Chan, M. J. Leahy, & J. L. Saunders

(Eds.), *Case management for rehabilitation health professionals* (2nd ed., Vol. 1). Linn Creek, MO: Aspen Professional Services.

Rubin, S. E., & Roessler, R. T. (2008). *Foundations of the vocational rehabilitation process* (6th ed.). Austin, TX: Pro-Ed.

Sawisch, L. P. (1989). Workers compensation: Strategies for lowering cost and reducing worker suffering. In E. M. Walsh (Ed.), *Creating a context for disability management*. Fort Washington, PA: LRP Publications.

Shaw, L. R. & Betters, C. (2004). Rehabilitation counseling and consultation in the private sector. In T.F. Riggar & D.R. Maki (Eds.). *The handbook of rehabilitation counseling*. New York, NY: Springer Publishing Co., 236–251.

Sperry, L., Lewis, J., Carlson, J. D., & Englar-Carlson, M. (2005). *Health promotion and health counseling: Effective counseling and psychotherapeutic strategies* (2nd ed.). Boston, MA: Allyn & Bacon,

West, S. L., Graham, C. W., & Cifu, D. X. (2009). Rates of alcohol/other drug treatment denials to persons with physical disabilities: Accessibility concerns. *Alcoholism Treatment Quarterly, 27*, 305–316.

West, S. L., Luck, R. S., Capps, C. F., Cifu, D. X., Graham, C. W., & Hurley, J. E., (2009). Alcohol/other drug problems screening and intervention by rehabilitation physicians. *Alcoholism Treatment Quarterly, 27*, 280–293.

Wheaton, J. E. & Berven, N. L. (1994). Education, experience, and caseload management practices of counselors in a state vocational rehabilitation agency. *Rehabilitation Counseling Bulletin, 38*(1), 44–58.

Index

Note: Page references followed by "*f*" and "*t*" denote figures and tables, respectively.